Glorious
Summer

Glorious Summer

Happy and healthy ageing

Wendy Shillam

Say Tomato!
BOOKS

Published in 2024 by Say Tomato! BOOKS, Urbaneye, a social enterprise, London W1W 6ST

This book is made from certified sustainable paper

The author believes that independent bookshops enrich our lives, while multinational commerce diminishes us. This book is only available via bookstores, or by post from the publishers and from Bookshop.org.

A catalogue record of this book is available from The British Library
ISBN 978-1-9015607-1-8

Dedication

Margaret Rosa Shillam 1926-2022

Contents

Preface

As a child, sixty years ago, I remember many glorious summer days following my grandfather around his vegetable patch, learning how to plant seeds, to tend them and later to enjoy harvesting fresh new potatoes or ripe strawberries. I learned that plants will always thrive when the gardener works with nature, not against it, by paying attention to the soil, to where the winds blow and where the sun shines.

It has taken me twenty years of practice, and a lifetime of experience, to realise that the same is true in people. Every living thing on the planet is designed to live; given the right climate, even annuals become perennials. And just as a diligent gardener would tend to their plants, we must self-nurture to remain strong, healthy, and vital into our old age. Being kind to yourself isn't a platitude; it is what keeping healthy is all about.

Nature's purpose is life. If you visit one of Britain's ancient woodlands on a fine summer day, you are likely to come across a yew tree that may easily be a thousand years old and a dragonfly that will live for one spectacular day. Being in the presence of such grandeur and beauty is the moment to reflect that all life on earth has evolved from a few simple primordial cells. They are the common ancestors of the life you see around you, honed by evolution and selected simply by virtue of their ability to survive and reproduce. We are the apogee; the fittest heirs to 3.7 billion years of evolution.

We humans have amazing bodies and even more amazing minds. We can solve complex problems, adapt to changing circumstances and devise tools to help us, in ways that no other creature can match. In the last few thousand years evolution has taken advantage of our intelligence; moulding human brainpower to imagine, to anticipate, to care for others and to create beauty and utility in equal measure.

Rewarding human life is no longer simply focused on existence. We seek amusement, we are curious, we are loving and we thrive on self-expression and friendship. Fortunately, old age rarely dulls those capacities; in many cases it can burnish them. It is worth taking a little time to consider the future, nurturing that amazing body and making use of that extraordinary brain to ensure that you too can enjoy your own old age as a long, happy, *glorious summer.*

Wendy Shillam, August 2023

Jeanne Calment on the day she became the World's oldest living person

1

Happy and healthy

If you've ever contemplated old age with foreboding, the image opposite should give you a bit more confidence. It's a press agency shot of an elderly French woman called Jeanne Calment, taken on 17 October 1995.

The press swarmed around Madame Calment on that day, almost thirty years ago, because at the age of 120 she had just become the oldest person in history. They reported that she was happy, humorous and remarkably sprightly. Being old, even very, very old, doesn't need to be a nightmare.

Studies across the world consistently show that the majority of old people are happier than they were in middle-age[1]. The things you may fear, such as decline, loneliness or poverty can be avoided with a little planning, a little self-care and by taking advantage of the knowledge that is out there. How to grow old happily and healthily is not a secret – but it does require you to think about and plan for a future that will help you live a *good* old life. Jeanne Calment is an excellent subject to start with.

Every journalist who interviewed Jeanne on that day asked the same question. They all wanted to know her secret.

It is natural to think that there might be a silver bullet, the one thing we can do to live for that long. She had a few quips ready in response, for example, observing that she had enjoyed sports in her youth. She recalled spending her free time cycling, playing tennis, swimming and roller-skating – and we know that keeping active will protect us from frailty as we grow older. She is supposed to have taken up fencing at the youthful age of 85, thereby demonstrating her enduring mobility. But remaining active wasn't her only 'life hack'.

Calment alluded to a naturally strong constitution, saying that she had never been ill in her life. And she gave us all a little bit of hope by admitting that she still smoked a bit, drank wine and loved chocolate.

Of course, in reality, she didn't know why she was so lucky and the medics that examined her in later life could not find anything conclusive, except to comment that she was an incredible example. She wasn't super-wealthy, she didn't set herself an impossible regimen of diet and exercise, she didn't take vitamins, swear by a superfood, or indulge in quack treatments. And her life, while comfortable, wasn't perfect. She'd had her fair share of troubles and tragedies. She died a couple of years after this picture was taken, in 1997, at the age of 122 years and 164 days. To this day she remains the oldest person in the word. No-one since has surpassed her age, or even got close to it. We still can't say why she lived longer than anyone else.

Jeanne Calment was born in Arles in French Provence in 1875, almost a century and a half ago. History suggests that Arles might always have been a good place to grow old. In Roman times it became a popular retirement spot for veterans of the legions. By the end of the nineteenth century, it had become a small city of 25,000 people.

Nothing in Jeanne Calment's childhood, her early life, or even her middle age made her stand out in any way. When she was in her nineties, no one gave her a second thought; it was only when she started breaking longevity records that people started to look twice.

Calment grew up in a middle-class household with her brother François, ten years her senior. Her early life was no different to other young women of her day. She married at the age of 21 into a well-to-do family of drapers and had one daughter, Yvonne, when she was 23. During her marriage she lived the typical bourgeois life of a well-to-do French woman at the end of the nineteenth century. Two world wars must have affected her, but in looking back she made light of them; luckily for her that part of Provence was never the focus of sustained conflict.

Modern medicine might suggest that the diet has made the people of this part of France healthier than their cream-guzzling Normandy cousins. Arles is favoured with a pleasant, frost-free climate, proximity to the sea, the mountains, the rich soils of the *Bouche du Rhone* and the well-stocked lakes of the Camargue. Today, this region offers many gastronomic delights, including the famous Camargue rice (reportedly the healthiest rice in the world), olive oil, sausage and meats, crayfish, salt and fresh-water fish, water fowl, organic fruit and vegetables, honey and local cheeses, as well as Provençal wines, herbs, spices and the much-valued sea-salt, known as *sel de mer*. It is the Mediterranean diet *par excellence*.

Social scientists might certainly say that there was something in the air in Arles during Jeanne's youth. The town became a magnet for artists and writers. In 1888, when she was 13, the Dutch emigre artist van Gough set up his studio in a yellow house just by the station, very close to her own home.

The climate, the people and the culture transformed van Gough's work. He was finally able to discard the dull hues of his northern European palette for brilliant and joyous paintings of the town and its surrounding countryside. Through his paintings we see Provence picked out in new bright colours, illuminated by a sharp sunlight and decorated with flowers. Gaugin called his portrait of van Gough *The Artist who Paints Sunflowers*. They are still common in the fields of Provence today.

The milieu of Arles, not least its lively café society, influenced other artists including Picasso. That vivacity might have rubbed off, just a little, onto Jeanne Calment, without her being seduced by the bohemian lifestyle. She seems to have been happy enough learning to play the piano, going to concerts and making music with friends. A healthy cultural and social life is probably as fundamental to a good old age as diet and exercise.

Many people have suggested that our longevity is due to our genetic makeup. Vast amounts of research have gone into analysing the link between genetics and lifespan. Calment died before the sequencing of the human genome was complete, so we do not have her genetic signature, but it has been suggested that part of her resilience was due to innate genetic strengths. Certainly, her parents and her brother Françoise were all long-lived. She was female, in itself a genetic indicator of a slightly longer life. She was naturally petite and never succumbed to middle-aged spread, which perhaps strengthened her heart. Her GP was impressed by the fact that her blood tests remained within the normal ranges right into her final years, never revealing high cholesterol or glucose spikes.

We know that genetic benefits might help us survive childhood and save us from genetic diseases, such as Alzheimer's, or certain forms of cancer. But genetics alone have a much smaller impact on longevity. Anyone who lives even to the age of 40 or 50 has long since passed the stage where pure genetics makes a big difference. Life happens, turning even genetically identical twins into different individuals, with different health prognoses.

Even if Jeanne Calment started out with a perfect set of genes, we know that her life was sometimes difficult. Her only daughter died at the age of

36 from pleurisy, in spite of Jeanne's careful nursing and then, only six years later, her husband succumbed to a fatal bout of food poisoning. After being widowed, she lived with her son-in law and took charge of bringing up her grandson. Perhaps that gave her a new lease of life in old age, as fresh responsibilities often do. Perhaps those brushes with death changed the way she lived her own life.

The tragedy of living a long time is that you tend to outlive the rest of your family. By the 1960s, when she was in her nineties, she had no close relatives. Even her beloved grandson, who became a doctor, died in a car accident in 1965 at the age of 36. There is a poignant image of her many years later, showing a framed studio photo of him taking pride of place on her bedside table. But loneliness didn't seem to have been a problem for Calment – perhaps because she lived in the same town all her life and had made many friends.

Reports suggest that her pleasure in life was never dulled. Even in her last years at the old people's home, she settled happily into a routine that included listening to music before breakfast, making a daily circuit of the home to chat with others, enjoying her favourite chocolate and a glass of port after dinner, and praying before sleeping.

The health of the psyche is as significant as the health of the body. Mental and physical strength are inextricably linked. Jeanne Calment comes across as thoughtful and optimistic, but she is also remembered as being strong-willed. The carers in her home called her *The Comandante*, alluding to her assertiveness; she always wanted, and apparently got, her own way.

Even in her 80s she was mentally alert and astute. After her grandson died, Calment made a bargain with a local notary, André-François Raffray. She sold him her valuable property in the town centre, where she had lived all her married life, in exchange for a lifelong right of occupancy and a monthly pension of 2,500 Francs (€380). Raffray, who knew her well, clearly found nothing in her demeanour that might indicate super-longevity. In the end, she outlived her much younger friend, by which time Calment had received more than double the apartment's value from him. She managed to remain in her own home until the age of 110, moving into a local nursing home for the last twelve years of her life.

By living in Arles all her life, she undoubtedly benefitted from a stable, supportive community and the stimulating cultural life that Arles offered. Her environment would have been relatively healthy, as Arles is not an industrial centre. There would have been little air pollution, such as that which blighted the lives of people living in the centre of larger towns and cities before clean air acts were brought in. Many people are still drawn to the concept of living in a busy market town, in a nice climate, large enough to have all the facilities, but small enough to be friendly. Had she been born in a different city, or another country, Jeanne's environment might have given her a completely different life story. If she had moved out of Arles later in life, that might have had a negative effect.

You could argue that there was nothing innately special about Jeanne Calment, but that being in the right place at the right time might have helped her dodge life's slings and arrows. Her birth in 1875 coincided with the dawn of a modern, healthier, more caring world. Scientific progress, artistic endeavour and social improvements were making life better for many people. During her lifetime Jeanne undoubtedly benefitted from this. Antibiotics came into common use after the Second World War and the French health system developed into one of the best in the world, giving her the chance to boast that she was never ill, or perhaps never 'seriously' ill.

Furthermore, communications were improving. In America, Alexander Graham Bell was making his first telephone transmissions. Society looked at the world through kinder eyes. In 1875 in Europe, Bizet was setting to music a tragic tale about female workers in a tobacco factory which became the opera, *Carmen*. One hundred years before, few people would have cared about the emotions of female factory workers. In France, Saint-Sans first performed the modernist orchestral tone poem *Danse Macabre*, demonstrating society's newfound interest in the metaphysical, as well as the physical.

The street-cry *Liberté, Egalité, Fraternité* was first shouted during the French revolution, but it was only formally adopted as the motto of the Third Republic of France, established in 1870, five years before Jeanne Calment was born. Perhaps she lived at just the right moment.

Had Jeanne Calment been born thirty years later, she may not have been so lucky. People often say that we are living longer these days, but Jeanne Calment's unbeaten record disproves that statement. Had she been born later, her life might have been marred by modern processed foods and pollution, she might have been run down by a car as a child, or developed cancer from an unspecified source.

Older French people who lived after 1997 may have suffered more than their recent forebears. Since then, Provence has seen terrible heatwaves, triggered by global warming, which has killed thousands of elderly people – many before their time. Covid deprived millions of people across the world of their proper lifespan. Before that, austerity in the 2000s had damaged even France's exemplary health and social services and rendered everyone's health less robust.

I have always been intrigued by Jeanne Calment. On the surface, it seems completely counter-intuitive that she should have been the one person in the world who lived so long, and that she could have held the world record for so long after her death. She had some advantages, but she never seemed exceptional until old age revealed her undetected strengths.

However much we try to investigate her case, we come up against an insurmountable problem; there was no one aspect of her life, her genetics or her environment that can explain why she, aside from all the other healthy, relatively happy, strong-willed, female octogenarians that live in France today, haven't lived as long as she did. And by the time people recognised her as exceptional, it was too late to really scrutinise how she had spent her early life. If the key to longevity exists in our upbringing and middle age, then we have little data on Jeanne; but if, as I believe, one key to her extreme longevity can be found in how she approached her old age, she makes for an illuminating case study.

The French paradox

In spite of modern upheavals, French people still retain their healthfulness, in a way that citizens of countries like the UK do not. Until the start of the Covid pandemic, people in France, along with Spain and Italy, have been able to boast the highest longevity in Europe since the 1990s. French people are more resilient to the high levels of heart disease that have plagued other European countries[2], in spite of the fact that a French penchant for rich food and heart health don't often go hand in hand. This apparent contradiction is called *the French paradox.*

Nobody knows exactly why this happens, but there must the something in the French way of life that promotes health and longevity. Jeanne Calment is not a one-off; she is an example of a longevity trend in this part of France. The oldest woman in the world to survive Covid lived in Toulon, also located in southern France. The French must be doing something right, but as yet, medicine has been unable to find out exactly what that something is.

One challenge is that research on ageing is thin on the ground. Medical research is directed by a series of different funding streams, and none of them pay particular attention to ageing. The majority of high-profile research is undertaken by the pharmaceutical industry[3]. In the UK, in 2018, £37 billion was spent on research and development for new drugs or for seeking new uses for old drugs; yet the type of research that ageing requires is much more about prevention than treatments. Anti-ageing drugs are therefore not high on the list of pharmaceutical priorities. Few pharmacists would hold out much hope of a medicinal breakthrough.

In the UK, a second, far smaller tranche of money is spent by government and charities, often in collaboration. In 2018 that amounted to £4.8 billion[4] but it is the big medical charities, such as Cancer Research UK, Diabetes UK and the British Heart Foundation that set the agenda. They too would far rather find cures for ailments that reduce working lives. There is probably more money spent on researching anti-ageing cosmetics than medical treatments to extend old-age.

Jeanne Calment was examined several times by doctors during her last years. One reporter recorded that her GP had said that her blood tests were very good, right up until the end. But even if we'd had unlimited resources to investigate her and interrogate her life history, we would be unlikely to be able to say what made her especially healthy. Even if we examined thousands of old people, we may discover clues to ageing successfully, but we'd be unlikely to discover much more. Studying centenarians, super-centenarians (over 110), or even super-duper centenarians (those few who reach their 120th birthday), can only tell us so much.

Another way would be to go back in time, to investigate when and why human lifespans began to increase and whether our species, Homo sapiens, has always had the capacity to live to 100 years and beyond. Perhaps there have always been outliers like Jeanne Calment?

Where it all began

Anatomically modern humans began to emerge in Africa about 300,000 years ago. These people were members of the genus Homo sapiens, genetically almost indistinguishable to you and me, but with a lifestyle very different to ours. For millennia, pre-historic hunter-gatherers lived in a harsh world of scarce resources. These Homo sapiens had to struggle to find enough food and water even to survive. Palaeontologists don't always agree with the 17th Century philosopher Thomas Hobbes' assertions that such an environment would inevitably lead to tribal warfare, forcing small hunter-gather groups of thirty or so related individuals to cut themselves off from strangers, or alternatively to arm themselves to the teeth, with such a life 'outside society' being 'solitary, poor, nasty, brutish, and short'. Yet the fossil record does seem to supports this analysis, suggesting that Early and Middle Palaeolithic life expectancy would have been about 30 years.

Pre-history burial grounds are full of tiny children's skeletons, evidencing the dangers of childbirth and the early years, and the imperative to found large families in order to keep tribal societies going. In skeletons of all ages, we find people who have died from injury or disease that today would be easily treated. But among adolescents, young – mainly male – skeletons show signs of battle scars, torture and execution. It is not difficult to conclude that the scarcity of older people might have been partly due to a society driven by youthful hot-heads[5].

Just because we can't find the fossil evidence of really old skeletons, that does not prove that some very early Homo sapiens didn't or couldn't have lived to a ripe old age. Nevertheless, the fossil record suggests that it was not until the Upper or Later Palaeolithic period that people started to live longer lives. That increase in lifespan coincided with a series of improvements in diet, social structure and culture.

Whether you look at artistic endeavour, technology, trading or settlement patterns, you come to the conclusion that something profound happened about 10,000 years ago that allowed humans to expand in number, and to live longer, more fruitful lives.

It is difficult for a modern archaeologist to unravel whether the changes in life and society were cause or effect. We know that during this period humans abandoned small isolated tribes and started to live in larger settlements, where cooperation and collaboration allowed people to specialise and perfect different trades. This eventually led to a more stratified community as crafts and skills defined wealth and status. Isolated groups gave way to outward-looking settlements that found benefit in trading between territories and eventually across vast distances.

At the same time people began to settle into an agricultural lifestyle, driven by the domestication of plants and animals. Hunting and gathering probably continued, but perhaps became more ritualised as it became less essential. People had a better sense of security, more social interaction and above all – at least for the richest in society – a far more varied and healthier diet. The old solitary life which according to Hobbes was 'poor, nasty, brutish, and short' was transformed to become communal, rich, pleasant and more civilised with the result that people lived for longer. As more people survived into adulthood the population boomed.

At times of population growth, within any species, genetic adaptation speeds up. More people mean more mutations and greater opportunities for advantageous adaptations to sweep through the community. Our DNA changed during this period, faster than it has ever done before or since.

The ten thousand-year explosion

A book by Gregory Cochran and Henry Harpending, *The 10,000 Year Explosion*[6], describes how gene variants during this period made it more comfortable for humans to live further north. This was the end of the ice-age; most of western and central Europe and Eurasia was open steppe-tundra, while the Alps, Scandinavia and Britain were still cold enough to remain as ice fields and glaciers. People who had only recently migrated north found an inhospitable climate, with lower levels of sunshine and warmth. Genetic adaptation kicked in, selecting for lighter skin colour and allowing for the absorption of more Vitamin D, an essential vitamin involved in growth, strength and maintaining the immune system.

In the glacial fringes, where the landscape is devoid of edible vegetation, only inedible bushes, grasses and mosses grew well. If people were to survive, they needed something other than hunted meat or the wild herbs and fruits that were abundant further south. People desperately needed a 'super food' that would sustain them through the long harsh winters.

The super food they discovered was milk. There is evidence of hunter-gathering tribes making cheese using milk taken from undomesticated ruminants for millennia. The legend of Romulus and Remus, who survived by drinking the milk of a she-wolf, is echoed in lactic folk-tales and myths all over the world. These stories demonstrate how well our early ancestors understood the nutritional value of animal milk. It may well have been the need to capture and breed aurochs, bison, goats and deer that encouraged people to live in larger groups, to settle in order to tend their herds and eventually to rely more and more on dairying rather than solely on meat.

The lactose leap

The hunter-gatherers that started to drink milk did not have the lactose gene, the tiny genetic adaptation that today allows about 95% of northerners to drink gallons of milk. Milk is the richest and most nutritious product of a pastoral landscape and unlike meat, cheese will keep for months in a cool atmosphere. We can assume that at first, drinking too much milk might have made some people a little sick, yet they must have persevered, and prospered. Milk contains quality protein, vitamins and carbohydrate, along with a host of specialist ingredients that protects the young animal against infections and disease. These benefits are passed onto human milk-drinkers.

Then as now, milk is not poisonous if you are lactose intolerant and don't possess the necessary gene to fully digest milk. An ancient milk drinker might have felt a little queasy if he had drunk more than about 100ml in one go, but he surely still had a better chance of surviving the cold, famine and pestilence than if he hadn't tasted a drop. So successful was the change in diet that the lactose gene became ubiquitous in just a few thousand years – an astonishingly fast genetic transformation (in fact, the fastest changing aspect of the European genome in the last 10,000 years).[7] Today, pretty well all northern Europeans possess the lactose gene that allows our digestive system to break down the sweet-tasting liquid into an easily absorbed, high-energy nutrient.

In addition, settled communities were able to plan to grow crops, to store food for the winter and increase the diversity as well as the nutritional content of their diet. But was the better diet the single cause of this increased longevity?

In the Late Palaeolithic period we can see there was a change in lifestyle, improvements in community governance and a flourishing in art and technology that very quickly (in anthropological terms) triggered a flowering of civilisations that filtered across the world in areas of moderate climate and pastoral landscape. All these changes, societal and dietary, worked together to improve health-span and extend lifespan.

Older and wiser

Crucially, the older (and wiser) members of the community, who were not as actively involved in day-to-day tasks began living long enough to pass on skills, medicinal know-how and lessons from their own experience.[8] It may well be this lengthening of lifespan that allowed the development of a more stratified modern society, where people who had lived long enough to acquire skills, like midwives, doctors, herbalists, judges and philosophers, were all revered for their experience and the wisdom of old age received recognition.

Rachel Caspari, a professor of anthropology at Central Michigan University, has focused her work on the origin of modern humans and the evolution of longevity:

"The relation between adult survivorship and the emergence of sophisticated new cultural traditions, starting with those of the Upper Palaeolithic, was almost certainly a positive feedback process. Initially a by-product of some sort of cultural change, longevity became a prerequisite for the unique and complex behaviours that signal modernity. These innovations in turn promoted the importance and survivorship of older adults, which led to the population expansions that had such profound cultural and genetic effects on our predecessors. Older and wiser indeed." [9]

The Gainj tribe

Skeletal and fossil remains are one thing; studying living, breathing humans is quite another. Fortunately for us, back in the twentieth century some remote tribes still lived archaic lives. Until the 1970s, when clinics and maternity services were brought in, people living in the remote uplands of Papua New Guinea inhabited a world untouched by modernity. When discovered by anthropologists they were treated like the Holy Grail, as a perfectly-preserved fossil society. Their lifestyle, their traditions and their medical histories provided a living window into the world of the Upper or Late Palaeolithic period.

One man who has studied these people for many years is the anthropologist, James Wood. He didn't know this at the time when he did his most influential work, but his choice of upland tribes from Papua New Guinea was ground-breaking. Recent genetic analysis showed that the tribes he worked with were genetically, linguistically and culturally isolated from the rest of the world for more than fifty thousand years. Furthermore, until the late 1960s, these people lived a lifestyle that was very close to that of the original communities who, tens of thousands of years ago, swapped hunting and gathering for farming. They lived as the

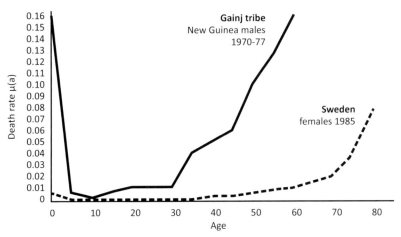

Age-specific mortality, in two human populations
with widely differing levels of mortality.

first farmers might have lived, untouched by the massive technological expansion that took place in many other parts of the world. There was no Bronze Age in Papua New Guinea, helping us understand the effects of changes from migratory hunting and gathering to a settled agricultural lifestyle, in its simplest form.

James Wood, now Professor Emeritus of Anthropology and Demography at Penn State in the US, worked for years to throw new light on the similarities modern people like us have with our ancestors. In order to make one comparison, Wood compared the lifespan data of a healthy developed-world population in Sweden (in 1985) with lifespan records of Gainj tribespeople of New Guinea in the 1970s, before modern medical interventions were available. As you might expect, the Swedish population tended to live longer; but the reason why was a revelation.

The main reason modern Swedish populations were living so much longer wasn't down to improvements in diagnosis and treatment of middle-aged diseases, or ways of caring for the elderly, though they probably had some impact. What stands out in the diagram above is the dramatic differences in infant mortality. The shape of the Gainj graph has become known as the 'bath curve', because it resembles the profile of an old-fashioned hip-bath. Among the Gainj there is a steep death rate at the beginning of life, and then a gradual curve as people start to die from other causes as they age.

The Swedish graph does not depict a shape that would hold water – there is no tap-end. The lack of a rapidly dropping early-years line demonstrates that, by 1985 in Sweden, thanks to modern maternity services, infant mortality had been almost eliminated. It is this reduction in infant mortality that distinguishes us from populations that lived right up to the nineteenth century. That is why in our modern world there are far more middle-aged people around and that is why more and more of them are able to live to a ripe old age. For Gainj people, the first year of life held a far higher risk than even old age.

Long life may not be new

We are gradually learning that ancient societies were not necessarily unhealthy. It is sobering to discover that some ancient individuals might actually have been as healthy as we are. One grave that was uncovered near Almeria in Spain, in an important 2nd Millennium BCE Bronze Age village, Cuevas de Almanzora, revealed the body of a man aged about 60. With him were buried the symbols of his status, including food, a bronze knife, a dagger and a solid gold bangle as thick as a thumb.

These treasures suggest that he was revered by his community. Perhaps he was a well-loved elder, perhaps even a leader? We don't know how he died; his body revealed no signs of disease, injury or arthritis. He had few rotten teeth, consistent with having eaten healthy fresh food all his life. He'd never experienced the toxicity of modern pollution, or the excess fats and sugars of an ultra-processed diet. He'd never become a couch potato, having doubtless been required to walk or ride everywhere. His diet, low in animal fats but high in lean proteins, fruits and vegetables, supplemented with fresh milk, cheese and wholegrain bread, would make a modern nutritionist proud. In many ways, he was eating the archetypal Mediterranean diet that we consider so healthful today.

To suggest that we are all living longer these days is disingenuous. The major difference between Swedish people and Gainj tribespeople is not the extent of life, but the waste of infant lives. These days, rather than implying that we are all living longer, it might be truer to say that people are not dying young any more.*

---

* Though sadly in the UK the threat of curable diseases like measles have recently come back to haunt childhood.

When we examine the ancient records, such as they are, we see that achieving our 'three score years and ten' is not a modern phenomenon. Indeed, the term's Biblical origin proves it. If you go back to the text, you will see that Moses thought the age of 70 was a bit too young to die. Given a fair wind, he expected to live into his 80s. Moses himself is said to have lived to the age of 120, and while we cannot verify exactly who wrote his words, there is no reason to believe that a man in that era could not have lived so long. The leaders of the tribe of Israel would have been the oldest and the wisest. Moses was said to be wiser than most – why not also older? In England, the provisional estimates showed that life expectancy in 2020 was 78.7 years for males and 82.7 years for females. That is to say, the twenty-first century, developed World life expectancy does not greatly exceed the reasonable hopes of a desert wanderer of the second millennium BCE.

Today the *Guinness Book of Records* requires verifiable data before they will enter you into their hallowed pages. Birth and death certificates are a modern invention; historically we had to wait for the invention of written texts to find any equivalent verification. Gravestones in classical Greece and Rome show people who were living into their eighties, nineties and beyond. Pliny wrote of Cicero's wife Terentia living to 103 and Clodia into her 115th year. And while some people simply forgot their age, this evidence is a good indicator of the sorts of ages that were considered exceptional – but not impossible. Today to live to 103 or even 115 would still be exceptional, worth mentioning, but would it be less exceptional today than in Roman times?

Modern studies of the very elderly do not show any appreciable pattern of increasing longevity. In the UK, what we perceive as increasing longevity is in fact a remarkable increase in the live birth rate, brought about by improvements in post-war healthcare.

Childhood illnesses have reduced a hundred-fold since the end of the nineteenth century. Breakthroughs in obstetrics and midwifery mean that babies have a much greater chance of growing up strong and healthy. Prosperity has helped parents to care for their children and governments have laid great emphasis on education and a sure start in life. Pretty well everyone living today in the developed world has been given a good start in life – and it is that start that gives the majority of us a very good chance of living long. One way or another, if we reach the age of five, we have already been given the gift of longevity. From then on, it is mostly up to us.

The facts of modern life

The graph below shows how average lifespan changed in England and Wales between 1851 and 2011. In recent years there have been far more

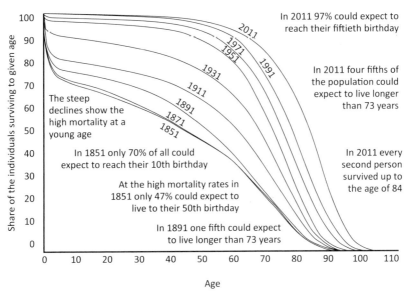

The survival curve for England and Wales from 1851 – 2011.
One World in Data from ONS figures.

elderly people, but not because we are all living longer. This diagram shows how the reduction of deaths in the first few years of life has created a corresponding extension in the number of people who are achieving their allotted lifespan. The difference by the age of 100 is less pronounced.

When a politician states that we're all living longer these days, the inference is that expensive care cannot be lavished on those people who should have died by now. At best, it is more than they deserve, and at worst, a drain on public finances. If you hear this myth being spouted, it's worth countering with the following:

- **Fact 1**

  Old people have always been around, and we can go way back into history and even pre-history to find evidence of this. Old age is a human right.*

- **Fact 2**

  Older people have always contributed to society, to our culture as well as directly to their families. The contribution of the wisdom and experience of older men and women may have been one of the principal triggers of the birth of what we know as 'civilisation'.

- **Fact 3**

  A child born in England or Wales in 1851 had only a 70 per cent chance of celebrating their 10th birthday. Today more than 97 per

---

* Article 2 of the Human Rights Act protects your right to life. This means that nobody, including the Government, can try to end your life. It also means the Government should take appropriate measures to safeguard life by making laws to protect you and, in some circumstances, by taking steps to protect you if your life is at risk. In addition, 'Public authorities should also consider your right to life when making decisions that might put you in danger or that affect your life expectancy.'

cent of children will grow up to celebrate their 50th birthday. It is this dramatic change in infant mortality and child health that has caused the increase in the proportion of older people. This trend increased significantly as the post-war baby boom met the newly born National Health Service.

Shocking to report, life expectancy in the UK has been flat-lining since 2009. The austerity years have impacted wealth, opportunity and education, which are inextricably linked to health. In addition, the last 10 years or so have seen an increase in long term illness. On average we in the UK are not only dying a bit younger, but living longer periods of our lives in the discomfort of ill-health. In order to be able to buck that trend, we have to understand how to look after ourselves and the world around us. For us, an untimely death is likely to be caused by what we eat (principally over-processed foods) or drink (alcohol, which can lead to overdoses and incidents like drunk driving), from suicide (often caused by alienation and depression) or from pollution and toxins (from cars, industrial products like petrochemicals and plastics, or from self-polluting cigarettes). Any one of these factors can destroy an otherwise healthy life.

Now there is another threat to a long and comfortable old age: climate change. The World Health Organisation warns us that temperatures in Europe have warmed significantly over the last fifty years, at an average rate of about 0.5°C per decade. According to the World Meteorological Organization (WMO), Europe, including the UK, is the fastest-warming region in the world. The climate emergency is killing us off, and unless we do something about it, will do so more and more as time goes by.[10] Extreme temperatures accounted for more than 148,000 lives lost in the European Region between 1961-2021. In 2021 alone, heatwaves, storms and floods directly affected over half a million people, many of them elderly. In 2022, across Europe 15,000 people lost their lives due to just one summer heatwave that lasted for 93 stifling days. In the UK 3,200 excess deaths were attributed to that summer's high temperatures.

Frightening images of natural disasters provide a glimpse of the potential impact on our lives, occasioned by what is already a 1°C rise in global average temperature compared to pre-industrial levels. The Intergovernmental Panel on Climate Change (IPCC) has stated that enduring average temperature rises above 1.5°C would constitute a global disaster. Some scientists believe that we have already reached a very serious tipping point.

The tribespeople of Papua New Guinea never had to take much notice of the outside world. For fifty thousand years they did their own thing, only having to concern themselves with the people 'over the hill' rather than any global issues. But we are now part of a world where we cannot simply concern ourselves with our own wellbeing. We must look outwards as well as inwards. We must do what all wise people and thoughtful communities do – we must help each other.

The difference between lifespan and life expectancy

Lifespan is normally described as the age 10% of any population can be expected to achieve. For example, the survival curves for England and Wales in 2011, on a preceding page, show that 10% of the population could expect to live beyond about 95 years. Life expectancy is an average, so the ages we see are far lower. By comparison a UK child born in 2011 can expect *on average* a life expectancy of 80.95 years[11].

By going back through historical records and by examining the remains of ancient settlements, we can be pretty sure that Homo sapiens have always been capable of long life. It is just as plausible that a man called

Moses reached the age of 120 over three thousand years ago as it is that Jeanne Calment reached the age of 122.* The maximum human life span may not have changed very much, but life expectancy has fluctuated throughout history as wars, plagues and natural disasters took their toll and were re-balanced by medical advances and the assent of what we might call 'civilisation'.

Scientists have scrutinised old people across the world, hoping to find the key to longevity. So far, they have only succeeded in establishing that we are not as a species, living demonstrably longer these days than before. There is no consistently upward pattern to life expectancy, either world-wide or nationally. Studies of exceptional people such as Jeanne Calment reveal a few pointers, but no persuasive data that can influence our own decisions. There may be a very clear statistical reason for this. These very old people are just too rare and too diverse to draw conclusions that might apply to all of us. The confounding factors are simply too great.

Luck or good judgement?

It's hard to believe that Jeanne Calment was simply lucky. I do think that her history reveals how much she took charge of her own future, in spite of the challenges life brought her. She played the hand she had been born with well, and that went some way to safeguard her in her old age. She became an accomplished survivor. She once said of the lawyer who'd bought her house in 1985, 'In life, one sometimes makes bad deals'.

That lawyer did make a bad bargain, gambling on the imminent death of a 90-year-old that just did not occur. But for every bad deal made, there

---

* Some scholars question the existence of a historical Moses, while there was a Russian article that claimed that Jeanne Calment was actually her daughter. To the disgust of the good people of Arles, who knew her well, it attempted to provide complex mathematical analysis to 'prove' that no one can live to the age of 122.

is a winner. Jeanne Calment probably made many good deals and many good decisions throughout her long life. She came from a trading family; her father was a shipwright, her mother a milliner and her husband a successful draper. She must have learned from a young age of the benefits that can stem from driving a hard bargain.

But you and I were not born in 1875. The world has moved on, and with modern changes come new challenges on a scale that has rarely been faced by humanity. However cleanly you may wish to live, however much you feel you can isolate yourself from the woes of the world, it is essential for us all to live in the world. Humans are social beings, and as Jeanne Calment demonstrated, companionship is essential, even in old age. To have any hope of a happy and healthy old age, each of us must use whatever skills we have to make sure that we are not alone in that endeavour.

Some things, such as England's arguably appalling care system, require fundamental changes far greater than one person can achieve. The solution seems to have evaded governments for decades. It is not just a matter of chance that in countries such as Finland, Japan, or Iceland life-expectancy, and quality of life indicators, are consistently higher than ours in the UK. And even the UK is streets ahead of the US, where life expectancy has plummeted in the last few years as social inequalities, together with distrust of the state, has left many people behind. The inability of such wealthy countries to improve life-expectancy figures proves that it is not simply a matter of money.

We should all be prepared to press for improvements and campaign for our rights. At the very least we should make sure we cast our vote. In the end, particularly when we are frail and vulnerable, we will all require strong and resilient national social systems to help us through. Lobbyists are portrayed as young and rebellious, though I am not sure this stereotype actually holds true. We surely need a combination of youth and experience, rebellion and wisdom to make the world better for all our futures.

Maintaining engagement with the world around us is, in my view, a vital part of healthy living, even though it is so often overlooked in a recipe for old age. Instead, old people are sometimes over-protected from the realities of life; yet the older generation has seen it all before. There is no need to shield us!

Ageism is perhaps the last prejudice to be confronted – and older people must do the confronting. We need to be able to live in a world that is not age-averse. The World Health Organisation (WHO) in their publication, *Healthy Ageing and the Sustainable Development Goals*, says:

"Creating environments that are truly age-friendly requires action in many sectors – health, long-term care, transport, housing, labour, social protection, information and communication – by many actors – government, service providers, civil society, older people and their organizations, families and friends." [12]

For me, having something to say, and do, and think about, and having causes and concerns outside of my own persona, provides the impetus to continue to keep my body and mind as resilient as possible. Of course, we need to maintain our personal fitness. Assertiveness can be important when medics, friends and family display the tendency to write us off before our time. Ageism, like the constant barrage of a wrecking ball, can demoralise us, can rob us of agency and even deny us life-saving treatment, but longevity, for its own sake, may be an empty ambition. Surely the prize is a long *and* healthy *and* fulfilling *and* active life?

I have no doubt that Calment was naturally strong, financially secure all her life, and in possession of 'good genes', as we say. These are the cards she was dealt. Being human means that we are not limited as other animals are. When faced with adversity, we have choices. We are far more capable of foreseeing challenges, seeking advice or help and making plans for the future. Jeanne Calment's example shows that playing the game of life is as important as being dealt a moderately good hand.

We know that a healthy lifestyle, including exercise and social interaction, will extend life span and healthspan. We'd be fools to ignore this. Ageing brings changes, but it is all too easy to forget that the spectacular in life can happen at any time, right to the end. Even if one day summer may be restricted to the view from an open window, that outlook may still be relished.

Surely the secret of longevity is to maintain the body as best we can, while nurturing a creative, thoughtful and actively sociable self? We should welcome maturity, for it is still the elders in any community who hold many of the answers to present-day challenges – and it is the elders who know that it is wise to savour every second of life's long and glorious summer, just as the child never wants to come in from the beach on a sunny afternoon. It is clear from her portrait that Jeanne Calment was just such a person.

Endnotes

1 DG Blanchflower, (2020) *Is happiness U-shaped everywhere? Age and subjective well-being in 145 countries,* Journal of Population Economics,34(2):575-624, 9 September 2020 DOI: 10.1007/s00148-020-00797-z

2 Source: Eurostat Database, ec.europa.eu/eurostat/data/database. NB: in order to compare countries some of the data were estimated, provisional, unavailable or broken in time series

3 E Haves, (2022) *Research and development spending: Pharmaceuticals, In Focus,* (London: House of Lords Library, 2022), at lordslibrary.parliament.uk/research-and-development-spending-pharmaceuticals

4 Health Research Classification System, UK Clinical Research Collaboration, *The UK Health Research Analysis 2018,* at hrcsonline.net/wp-content/uploads/2020/01/UK-Health-Research-Analysis-2018-for-web-v1-28Jan2020.pdf

5 Thomas Hobbes, (1651) *Leviathan,* Published Oxford: Routledge, 2006

6 Gregory Cochran & Henry Harpending, (2009) The *10,000 Year Explosion,* New York: Basic Books, 2009

7 Sabeti PC, et al. (2006) *Positive natural selection in the human lineage.* Science. June 16 2006, 312(5780):1614-20. DOI: 10.1126/science.1124309

8 A rather sexist interpretation suggests that older women were able to support their daughters with pregnancy and child-rearing, while the older men might have emerged as wiser tribal leaders

9 Caspari, Rachel (2011) *The Evolution of Grandparents; Senior citizens may have been the secret of our specie's success.* Scientific American Evolution, August 1, 2011

10 WHO (World Health Organisation) (2022) *Climate Change is Already Killing Us But Strong Action Now Can Prevent More Deaths,* Evidence to COP27 Statement, at who.int/europe/news/item/07-11-2022-statement

11 World Bank, (2011) *Life expectancy UK* Data Catalogue, Google Data 2011

12 WHO (World Health Organisation) (undated) *Ageing and life-course Healthy Ageing and the Sustainable Development Goals* Website who.int/ageing/sdgs/en/ [retrieved March 2021]

2

The average and the exceptional

It is difficult to decide whether Jeanne Calment led an average life but possessed some exceptional genetic traits, or whether she was medically unexceptional and simply followed a lifestyle that happened to give her a long life. How could she have seemed so average, for so long, when in fact she turned out to be extraordinary? We must be able to resolve this paradox if we are to make good life choices for ourselves. We need to know whether looking after ourselves will be worth it, or whether we should instead enjoy all of life's excesses in the hope that a naturally healthy body will accommodate most of the damage.

If your parents lived to a ripe old age, you may be excused for thinking that you have a good chance as well; that you possess a naturally healthy body, and that your genes make you exceptional. A few years ago, science would have agreed with you – but today we are realising that it isn't only the genes we inherit that make us strong. Environmental factors can switch our healthy genes on or off and our lifestyle can cause them to multiply, or atrophy.

Genetics

Genetics is certainly part of the story. At conception, a fertilised egg contains just one set of 23 chromosomes from the mother and one set from the father. These chromosomes consist of long strings of genetic code or DNA, *deoxyribonucleic acid*, which contain data a bit like a series of messages on a piece of ticker-tape. In every case one of the genes on the particular string, packed into either the mother's or the father's chromosomes, will be dominant. That dominance will dictate your gender, your eye colour, as well as many other characteristics that you were born with. Your genetic inheritance might also strongly influence your looks, your height, your temperament and your tastes.

Studies of identical twins who have been raised apart reveal astonishing similarities; they will look alike and often sound alike, but will sometimes also display similar character traits, and possess similar tastes in clothes or foods.

At first sight, it seems there is enough genetic material to preordain everything about us. It is certainly true that each active gene (there are about thirty thousand in the human genome) provides the blueprint for making a specific body protein; tissue, such as muscles or skin, as well as thousands of other bio-chemical bits and pieces like enzymes, hormones and metabolites. These genes are called protein-coding genes – we know which bits of the body they make and how they are likely to affect our health and happiness as we get older.

Throughout life the genetic code undergoes change and mutation. Under the circumstances of similar environments, we grow more alike. Studies show that upbringing, up to about the age of 18, can have a strong effect on characteristics such as body weight and smoking, regardless of genetic similarities.[1] We are influenced by our genes, but also by our family. Because our genes and our family are generally one and the same, the two influences can be difficult to separate.

In part the genetic mutations and changes are due to the sheer quantity of cells in the human body – approximately 30 trillion at the last count. Every single cell that carries a nucleus possesses the same chromosome set.[2] They carry the blueprint for heart and lung tissue, bones and brain, even if such information will never be required by that particular cell. After conception, foetus cells gradually lose the pluripotency of the egg (germline cells), meaning that they lose the ability to transform themselves into any type of cell. Other cells retain some of their potency throughout life and those are the stem cells that we now use in gene therapy and editing.

Any cell will respond well to good conditions, such as a generous supply of energy, nutrients (the raw materials), water and oxygen. Cell division, which is essential for growth, bodily repair and change, requires the entire genetic code within the mother nucleus to be unwound and re-packed into two new daughter cell nuclei. Sometimes division will fail, especially if conditions are unfavourable.

Even though the process is remarkably efficient, the sheer quantity of cellular turnover inevitably leads to errors. For example, some cells, such as brain cells, last a lifetime; other cells, like the surface of your gastric tract, may only exist for a few days. But just for the sake of doing the maths, let's assume that all 30 trillion cells in your body replicate once every seven years. That means that 30,000 individual bits of genetic code in our chromosomes are required to replicate 300 trillion times by the time we reach the age of seventy. Written out that means:

9,000,000,000,000,000,000

9x10^{18} complete genetic replications in a lifetime.

Any errors that occur are, more often than not, directly linked to environment. Cells won't replicate if there aren't enough nutrients, if they are damaged by toxins or if they don't possess enough energy or water. And because everything is connected to everything else inside our bodies, the failure of cells to replicate in one area often causes a ripple effect throughout the body.

DNA can self-repair and does a good job in keeping things on track, but over time, as we age, cell replication becomes more and more imperfect. What we see as ageing is really progressive imperfection. Grey hair, for example, is caused by a tiny fault within the hair follicle that stops new hair cells from being infused with melanin (hair colour). It's a simple flaw of cell replication and once started, it tends to continue. Going grey is often an inherited trait.

Until recently, we thought that ageing was also a genetically pre-ordained characteristic. Geneticists started to become suspicious about the pre-eminence of our 46 chromosomes, when genetic decoding in animals revealed that humans don't have many more protein-coding genes compared to tiny animals like fruit flies and worms. But while a typical bacteria harbours protein-coding genes in approximately 90% of its genome, only 5% of the human genome codes for proteins.

In humans, the vast majority of the DNA string, about 80% of it, remained undefined until very recently. We would expect the human genome to have a more complete set of genes than bacteria, while instead humans have all these genes which seem to be white noise. It doesn't seem logical. In between the protein-coding genes on the human DNA strand, there exists long strings of data that while at first glance have no function, on closer examination do a lot of work. We used to call non-protein coding genes 'junk genes', but now we know they are intrinsic to a process called epigenetics.

The Human Genome project, which was tasked with unravelling the human genetic code, was ostensibly completed in 2003, but as recently as 2022 another two million letters[3] were discovered. This work is gradually informing epigenomics, by explaining gene expression, genome regulation, and genome stability, ie. how genes are modified, maintained and switched on and off. The 'junk genes' turn out to have a significant impact on these processes, acting as gate-keepers, repair teams and linesmen.

Sometimes the environment that a cell inhabits will result in a new flowering of proteins. This is called up-regulation. It is this dynamic that can influence development, eventually resulting in more of a particular tissue being created, or different enzymes and hormones being produced. We think this is one reason why siblings often develop the same tastes for food, or even for smoking. Their proclivities are influenced by their genetic make-up and their environment. They represent the responses of the human genome to the stresses and strains of life. They are genetic *as well as* environmental. Up-regulation of a particular set of genes can result in changes in weight, different levels of muscle growth, new immunities or new characteristics.

It turns out that the non-protein coding genes actually fulfil some really important functions, and may well be the genes that separate higher order animals from the simpler species.[4] Perhaps a better term for junk DNA is 'dark matter'. We know it exists, we can sometimes see its effect, but we have in no way unravelled all its secrets. It may very well be that the dark matter genes are actually the sophisticated part of our genome, separating us from worms and fruit-flies, in a way that our protein-coding genes do not.

On closer analysis, the dark matter contains thousands of repeats of incomplete snippets of code, so they are difficult to understand: imagine decoding a message where some of the sentences are in foreign languages and some of the letters are missing as well. These repeated snippets of DNA code do contain recognisable forms, but never an entire gene, so they cannot make new proteins without something else happening to replace the missing links. But if by chance epigenetics, a snippet of code gets mixed up with one of our protein-coding genes, wonderful things can happen. Damaged genes can be repaired and dangerous mutant genes can be blocked. The dark matter seems to have a role in fine-tuning the development of complex systems in our body, especially where the accuracy of the cellular structure is vitally important, such as during the development of the brain.

In about 8% of the human genome, amongst all this dark matter, geneticists can see vestiges of ancient retroviruses. These vestiges are present in all mammals, and in particular in primates. This suggests they are important. The human versions of these are called HERVs (human endogenous retroviruses). A retrovirus uses the symmetry of our own DNA double helix to reverse-engineer new snippets of genetic code that fit in perfectly. The term 'endogenous' implies that it is found in our inherited genome.*

Most HERVs are vestiges of very ancient viruses which seem to have long since lost their potency. Under normal circumstances many of these retroviruses lie dormant because they are mere scraps of the original viral machinery. But under certain conditions they can be switched on and when this happens, they can produce an immune reaction, triggering thousands of new cells to grow that can fight disease or repair damage.

---

* By contrast an exogenous retrovirus is an external infection that will never-the-less insert itself into one of our protein-coding genes and damage them. HIV is the classic example. The alien virus triggers new code which the cell manufactures into novel and sometimes damaging proteins.

For example, HERVs are implicated in reducing the effects of ageing by modifying our immune system.

Recently, researchers at the Francis Crick Institute in London have been looking at $HERV_K$, which is just one example of the huge family of so-called junk genes that we find in the human genome. They discovered that the up-regulation (or switching on) of specific sections of $HERV_K$ could stimulate immune cells that have the power to attack and kill lung cancer tumours.[5] As if that were not enough, the researchers observed that once triggered the $HERV_K$ junk genes would also, just as a free extra protective measure, increase the patient's immunity to winter flu.

Unlike our inherited protein-coding genes (only 23 from our mothers and 23 from our fathers), some of the HERVs are now so numerous within our genetic material that almost everybody possesses them. For example, $HERV_K$ is also instrumental in helping the fertilised egg attach to the wall of the womb. The retrovirus burrows into the womb wall, locally modifying and multiplying specialist cells that securely attach the placenta. Without $HERV_K$ a foetus would simply not be viable.

The prospect of our own genetic material being up-regulated in order keep us younger and healthier is exciting. We have identified about 300,000 of these snippets of genetic material available for use in the human genome. As far as we know, these repeated snippets of code are available to almost all of us. It is not our parental inheritance that dictates them, but our evolutionary inheritance. They are what mark us out as 'higher order' animals, possibly distinguishing us from worms and fruit flies far more fundamentally than the handful of chromosomes we inherit from our parents.

We now know that this dark matter helps to regulate all our protein-coding genes and that every single cellular division – or even the tiniest scrap of protein production – relies on a healthy gene, a healthy environment to replicate (supported by the junk genes), ample resources and the strength of our immune system. It is fortunate indeed to inherit 'good genes', but unless they exist in favourable conditions, they can't do a thing.

While we may be able to benefit from inherited genetic strengths as well as learned habits, tenets of wisdom and inherited money or social positions, we cannot rely too heavily upon seeing ourselves as replicas of our parents. It doesn't necessarily follow that we will inherit parental weaknesses or strengths; it is far more likely that our personal strength and health will depend on how our bodies deal with the set of genes we have inherited, and how the lives we lead affect our bodies. If we wish to maintain our healthy genes, then we have to nurture them, and that means leading a healthy lifestyle that will give the body the best chance of replicating healthy cells and making use of the good genes we all possess, rather than punishing our systems too much.

Perhaps these junk genes represent another form of balance – a re-calibration back to the norm. It is informative to look at the exceptional people in our families, to learn from their strengths and to hope we have inherited some of them; but it is also important to realise that whatever our particular genetic make-up, there are no guarantees. We cannot predict that a son with exceptional parents will himself prove to be exceptional. Ageing may well be as much related to the junk genes that everybody shares as it is to exceptional inherited traits.

The Average

That which is normal or average is of exceptional interest to the world of medical research. For example, when we look at any treatment or therapy, we need to know whether it makes things better 'on average' and by exactly how much.

Medical trials have to undergo rigorous scrutiny. To prove the case, complex safeguards must be included, patients must be screened to ensure they represent an average cohort and each one must give informed consent. They must know what is happening, but that knowledge can't influence their reaction. In the case of testing medicines, the prescription must be blind. Half the cohort will be given an inactive placebo. In some cases, the trial is conducted double-blind, neither the subject, nor the physician knows who will get the active ingredient. However, when boiled down to the basics, a typical medical trial will give a group of people a treatment, such as extra exercise, and compare them with a similar set of people who go on as normal. By comparing the results, we can tell whether the new treatment leads to any improvement.

But what if the numbers are small? Say three people follow the new exercise regimen and three do not. Might it not just be pure chance that the three on the new treatment did better?

That is where statistics come in, and where we must find out how to identify the average so as to be confident that what we are seeing as the 'normal' response or result is in fact statistically significant. In layman's terms, we need to understand how to evaluate medical risk.

Adolphe Quetelet

Before we go any further, we need to know a bit about statistics in order to understand how to evaluate medical risk and to understand how to recognise an effective treatment. The best place to start is with a remarkable man called Adolphe Quetelet who devised the arithmetic back in the nineteenth century. Quetelet* was arguably one of the most enlightened of mathematicians. He cared deeply about ordinary people

---

* 1796 – 1874

The exceptional Adolphe Quetelet, from a lithograph by Madou

and their everyday lives. He was an exceptional man who decided to devote his life to investigating the average. Yet he was far from average. He was that rarest of birds – a famous Belgian. He devised the mathematical models that we still use today to explain the word 'normal' when it is used in its strict statistical sense.

Quetelet was a polymath; an intelligent, cultivated and lucid man. He pursued many different passions, all with equal skill. As well as studying mathematics, he wrote plays and an opera, became an accomplished – some say the first – social scientist, and made vast contributions to the science of demography and epidemiology.

He discovered that by assessing a small sample of individuals he could spot trends within the whole population and thus help doctors make smarter health predictions and politicians make better policies. You might say he was an early advocate of the 'nanny state'. He knew that wise public policies can influence our individual lives. He pressurised the Belgian government to recognise their powers and set about arming them with the information they needed to make ordinary people's lives that bit easier.

At the heart of this analysis of populations is the pursuit of the normal or average. If, for example, an administration can increase the average number of people who take exercise, chances are that public health expenses will go down. But what is enough exercise? What is normal for you or for me? This is the type of question that obsessed Quetelet for most of his life.

In his book *A Treatise on Man and the Development of His Faculties,*[6] Quetelet presented his conception of the *homme moyen*, the 'average man'. He went into prisons and the poor house gathering sample measurements from the inmates such as age, height and weight. He was looking for averages that might indicate universals.

The simplicity and symmetry of the mathematical models portraying the statistics he discovered never cease to amaze. Whatever measurements Quetelet took – like height or weight – led to a very similar scatter of results. There is very definitely a universal average and it covers many aspects of life, with a roughly equal scatter of results above and below the average. Both smoothly distributed and more balanced that you might imagine, this norm and scatter, when plotted on a graph, gives the same shape again and again – whether you are plotting human weight against height, the mature height of oak trees, the number of peas in a pod or the birthweight of kittens. It turns out that almost anything you care to plot in nature will return a symmetrical curve. This is the famous bell curve.

What is perhaps even more astonishing is that this results pattern is not limited to the physical aspects of nature. The bell curve can be found in our behaviours and in the ways we think. This single-curved plot (as depicted below) may be highly-peaked or broad and shallow, but it almost always displays the same distinctive shape. The peak of the bell curve shows us where the majority lies and its spread indicates the extent of outliers. The bell curve is accompanied by mathematical calculations which help us determine how closely aligned any results happen to be. By using Quetelet's bell curve we can determine whether the results are pure chance, or more likely to be statistically significant. Sometimes the outcomes are so clear that we only need 40 or 50 results to establish significance. Sometimes we need thousands or even millions of results to prove the point.

The Bell Curve

The diagram below shows a typical bell curve plot. For example, this one could depict the number of peas in a pod at a particular harvest. There is

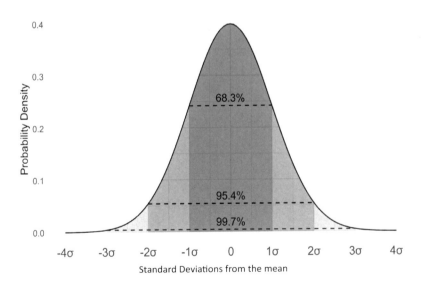

The bell-curve of *normal* distribution.

a peak representing the number of peas in most of the pods. The very tip of the peak is the average. As we go further from the average, looking at higher or lower numbers, we find fewer and fewer results. Once we know what the average is, we can assess whether there are benefits which relate to the average. In this case, a farmer might want to increase the yield by comparing different cultivars of pea, choosing the one with the highest average number of peas in each pod.*

Quetelet's work on average weight has endured like no other. The Quetelet Index, which he proposed in the mid-nineteenth century as one risk factor for health, is better known today as the body mass index, or BMI.[7] Countless studies since that time have shown, again and again, the relationship between average weight and being healthy. These days we have tables that plot weight and height, for males and females and more recently for different ethnic groups. These are still used every day by doctors all over the world to assess your chances of keeping healthy. There are nuances, which I will explain in later chapters, but for the time being if only one thing is taken away from this book, it's that a healthy weight is the norm.

---

* You will see that this example of the bell curve doesn't display numbers of peas in each pod, or number of pods. Instead, the vertical axis shows probability density. That is a mathematically more precise way of describing where the highest values sit. The horizontal axis shows standard deviation. This is also a mathematical way of describing how far from the average any result lies. Standard deviation is related to the total number of results, as well as spread of results. In this example, 95% (i.e. the overwhelming majority) of results are less than two standard deviations away from the average. A statistically significant result; in other words, a normal bell curve.

We are all far more average than we like to think. Whenever I have been prone to 'airs and graces', believing that I'm exceptional, something will come along to remind me that I am, in fact, like most other people. For example, during lockdown I started making sourdough. Where did that come from? Quetelet would say that we are all influenced by our environment. Perhaps the shortage of fresh bread, the scarcity of yeast and surplus of time influenced me, in the same way it did many others. I thought that it was my idea and that I was using freedom of expression by learning to make a different type of bread, but in fact I was simply swimming with the shoal.

Without wishing to undermine anyone's sense of individuality, I do recommend taking a little time to get to grips with the science of statistics. For example, the statistics on smoking are damning, it is the leading cause of premature, preventable death globally. Tobacco kills up to half of its users, this equates to 8 million deaths a year globally.[8] Yet some of us are lulled into thinking that it won't happen to us.

If we know what is normal, we can start to investigate the exceptions. We can all find examples of a smoker who lived to a ripe old age, or the unlucky person who contracted cancer even though they had led a healthy life. These types of people are the exceptions and they are worth studying. Anyone who is much over 80 years old is automatically an exception. They have already beaten the longevity odds. But they are all outliers, statistically unusual.

The genetics that influence our lives, particularly our old age, will always be subject to the 46 genes we have inherited; but the longer we live, all sorts of environmental influences and epigenetic modifications come into play. The way we grow and develop, our bodies, our ideas and which of our genes are switched on or off are affected by the lifestyle we lead and effect the body and mind we possess.

Risk of what?

Arguably, setting out to live to some randomly selected chronological age is not an adequate end in itself. Life should continue to be happy, engaging and vital for as long as we have it. A good old age is surely the prize, with all its complexities; the aim should not simply be the achievement of a certain number of birthdays.

The writer John Mortimer, in the guise of his endearing but unhealthy barrister Rumpole, once quipped:

> There's no pleasure on earth that's worth sacrificing for the sake of an extra five years in the geriatric ward of the Sunset Old People's Home, Weston-Super-Mare.[9]

With no disrespect to Weston-Super-Mare, Rumpole should also have considered the danger of his risky behaviour delivering him five years *earlier* to the rest home. Fear of the 'care home stage' should not push us into reaching the care home prematurely. Rumpole's overindulgence in eating, drinking, or making merry may have been considered by him to be a pleasure. But they may also have been palliatives, self-medication to answer some unmet need within him. These pleasures may pale into insignificance beside the active, engaged, commensal life that many of us would like to lead, all of the time.

We all aspire to live out our lives in the home we have made for ourselves, doing whatever we most enjoy, until the end comes. Making healthy lifestyle choices contributes to the chance that we shall do so, but that need not be seen as a denial of life's real enjoyment. Close to half a million people in the UK live in residential care homes or nursing homes, but a far greater number of old people live independently. The ones who do live contentedly at home are certainly to be envied. The good news is that in spite of what you may read, most old people do manage to live a happy and dignified old age, most staying in their own home until the very end.[10]

There are generally considered to be three key elements of living an enjoyable life (though it's worth adding your own priorities to this list):

- Maintaining physical capacity
- Keeping intellectually active and engaged
- Maintaining agency – controlling your own destiny

The overriding issue for anyone contemplating their chances of a healthy old age is not only escaping death, but escaping diseases and conditions that might limit physical or intellectual capacity. We all want to retain life's freedoms for as long as possible.

Staying alive

The fundamental of a happy life is the wish to prolong it. If you look at the diagram (overleaf), you will see the sorts of things that might catch up with us, and the relative risks they pose. Staying alive means avoiding accidents – keep that seat belt on! – but statistically speaking, the far bigger risks are from metabolic disease, heart disease and cancer. Cancer is the biggest killer in any age group and a major contributor to an early death. I hope that a mere glance at the graph below will convince you that doing anything to reduce your risk of getting cancer is a very good idea.

All these conditions are strongly correlated to diet, exercise, pollution, toxins like smoking and intoxication from alcohol and drugs. But do not dismiss the Covid 19 part of the graph; it is a stark reminder of how vulnerable we can also become to communicable diseases if we let our guard down.

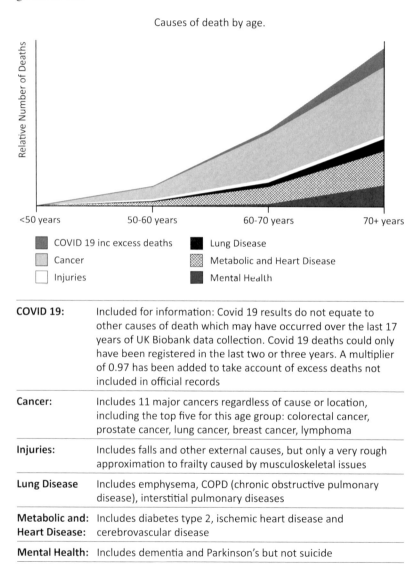

Causes of death by age.

■ COVID 19 inc excess deaths	■ Lung Disease
▢ Cancer	▨ Metabolic and Heart Disease
□ Injuries	■ Mental Health

COVID 19:	Included for information: Covid 19 results do not equate to other causes of death which may have occurred over the last 17 years of UK Biobank data collection. Covid 19 deaths could only have been registered in the last two or three years. A multiplier of 0.97 has been added to take account of excess deaths not included in official records
Cancer:	Includes 11 major cancers regardless of cause or location, including the top five for this age group: colorectal cancer, prostate cancer, lung cancer, breast cancer, lymphoma
Injuries:	Includes falls and other external causes, but only a very rough approximation to frailty caused by musculoskeletal issues
Lung Disease	Includes emphysema, COPD (chronic obstructive pulmonary disease), interstitial pulmonary diseases
Metabolic and: Heart Disease:	Includes diabetes type 2, ischemic heart disease and cerebrovascular disease
Mental Health:	Includes dementia and Parkinson's but not suicide

Staying alive *and* happy

Healthy life expectancy is the average number of years that a person can expect to live in *full health,* unhindered by disease or injury. Too often, long-term conditions can inhibit daily life but don't necessarily kill us. The global term for these conditions is long-term morbidities (from the Latin *morbus,* meaning disease). When someone has more than one condition these are called comorbidities. As we age, these limiting long-term illnesses can multiply. The big four chronic illnesses that may limit our enjoyment of old age are: hypertension (high blood pressure), diabetes, musculoskeletal problems and heart disease.

These conditions are grouped together under the title of non-communicable diseases or, in the medical jargon, NCDs. They often come in legion, because they have similar lifestyle causes, and one can trigger another. For example, if exercise is limited because of a weak heart, we may become more liable to developing conditions such as diabetes or osteoporosis.

Despite looking similar on the Scrabble board, morbidity has nothing to do with mortality. These conditions can be managed, but they are often challenging to cure. A morbidity does not imply a terminal or fatal illness, or even a particular level of seriousness. Pharmaceutical treatments are available for all of them but more often than not, they are best alleviated by the very lifestyle changes we might have put off in the first place.

The good news is that it is hardly ever too late. Even if our good health is reduced a bit, it need not destroy our quality of life or cramp our style. If you fear Alzheimer's, you may take comfort from the very thin and reducing baseline representing mental health in the diagram below. Of those over 65, only about one in 14 will experience any dementia in their lifetime, and 98% of us will never develop severe symptoms at all.[11] Overall mental health statistics reveal that we become happier as we get older and common middle-age conditions such as depression tend to resolve, especially with prompt treatment.

In 2009 the office of national statistics issued figures showing that more than half of those over-60 reported having one long-term health condition, while one quarter had two or more.[12] Shocking to read, these figures have continued to rise. Some of the conditions may be exacerbated by a genetic pre-disposition or simply bad luck – but most are a direct result of the lifestyle we have led, or have been forced to lead.

Prevalence of long-term illness in the UK.

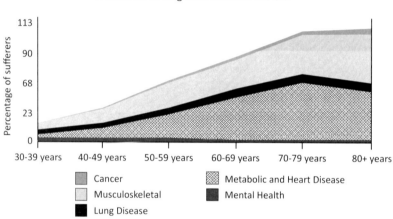

Vertical axis numbers refer to percentage of sufferers in each age group.

Limiting Long Term Conditions, definitions:

Cancer	Includes all cancers
Musculoskeletal	Includes physical frailty and other musculoskeletal problems
Lung Disease	COPD (chronic obstructive pulmonary disease) and asthma
Metabolic and Heart Disease	Diabetes, strokes and TIAs, hypertension, coronary heart disease
Mental Health	All causes

NB Figures come from GP reports, and are thus likely to be under-representative of the population as a whole.

This is where a difficult old age lies – not in the risk of death, but in limiting conditions.

The diagram (facing page) highlights the major causes that limit our old age. However, you will notice at once that in about 15% of the population, these conditions appear before people are even thirty years old. Today, these are not really diseases of ageing as much as preventable diseases caused by unhealthy living. We tend to place the responsibility for lifestyle lapses firmly on the shoulders of the individual but, as you will soon read, that is far from the case.

Diabetes has been bracketed with various types of heart disease because the prevailing opinion is that many of these conditions are causally linked. Obesity, malnutrition and lack of exercise feature large in the hallmarks of all these diseases. Fortunately for the unwary, the drug Metformin, as well as blood thinners and statins, can help reduce the more alarming symptoms – but they are not a cure.

Lung diseases are often linked to pollutants in the atmosphere, and there is a need to push governments to reduce pollution, but we must also ensure that we don't self-pollute. Both smoking and alcohol can, of course, exacerbate the risks.

Note how prevalent musculoskeletal problems are, and how early their onset is. Causes of early onset can include injuries and accidents, but later onset causes may include anything from mild arthritis to serious osteoporosis.

Cancer rarely becomes a chronic condition, unfortunately showing up more often as an acute illness that results in surgery and a cure, or early death. A grain of comfort can be found in the fact that the older you get, the less aggressive and the less deadly it becomes.

While all the common comorbidities are strongly linked to lifestyle factors, such as obesity, malnourishment, lack of exercise and addictions, we should not conclude that lack of self-care is the sole cause. In 2015, health life expectancy for males in the North East was 59.6 years compared to the average in England of 63.4 years.[13] In South Tyneside, male health life expectancy was only 56.8 years.[14] The figures show that inequality, particularly financial inequality, plays an important part.

It isn't your fault

Society, government and big business all bear some responsibility. The extent to which we can make personal changes is inextricably linked to the social, cultural and economic condition that we find ourselves in. Throughout this book you will come across examples of age prejudice, government indifference and commercial zeal that can trip all of us up. If you have the strength, now might be the time to start pressuring for the changes in our society and culture that would make living a happy and healthy old age much better for more people.

Reducing the risks

An unhealthy and premature old age is not an enjoyable prospect. Sadly, type 2 diabetes can give a 40-year-old the impaired eyesight of someone twice their age. Smoking can bring debilitating breathing difficulties to a 30-year-old. Drunk driving killed or injured an estimated 8,680 people in 2018. About 30% of those injured were under the age of 24. [15]

Smoking

Smoking was, until recently, considered the most aggressive killer. Even more than his claret, Rumpole's fogging cheroot is right up there in the high-risk category. The more tobacco you smoke and the longer you have smoked it, the more vulnerable you are to cancers and heart disease. The data reveals a pretty clear relationship between smoking and illness. Smoking is so dangerous because it applies heat to dangerous substances. The added heat energy is a catalyst, transforming the products of combustion into even more damaging toxins, which are difficult to track because their temperature and thus their chemical structure may change several times during the process of inhalation. For example, while smoking you inhale polluting tars that literally clog the lungs, the body absorbs poisons that inhibit natural processes, and highly reactive molecules that interfere with the microbiome and DNA. Because of this nicotine can be a very effective weed killer as well.

We all know that smoking causes lung cancer, but that is only the tip of the iceberg. Because smoking causes damage to the whole body, we find its effect magnified in many other cancers, in heart disease, in metabolic diseases (such as diabetes) and in muscle wasting. Once you have started to smoke, only total abstinence can start to repair the damage.

Studies suggest that moderation doesn't work. More than any other habit, smoking multiplies other impacts. If your life is subject to environmental pollution, you live in poor housing, or you work in a 'dirty' industry, smoking at any level multiplies the risk. And if you indulge in other high-risk activities, such as alcohol, drugs or eating unhealthy food, smoking will exacerbate the harms.

If you could only make one change to reduce your risk of early death or ill health in old age, it would have to be to stop smoking – *today*.

Alcohol

When we drink any type of alcohol, which is a toxin, it is delivered to the entire body, befuddling the brain, slowing down our reactions, tripping up our limbs and damaging our organs. Depending on how much you drink, and how often, that produces a progressively damaging effect. The challenge comes when we try to define what counts as 'excess'. While alcohol is legal, and moderate drinking is not socially frowned upon, we now recognise that there can be devastating effects from drinking too much, even if problem drinkers continue to function, holding down a job and hanging on to their spouse or loved ones. Alcohol is one of the many toxins we put inside our body that is dose-dependent; the more you take, the worse things can become.

However, we are all different and alcohol affects us differently. Some people have argued that rich red wine, taken with food, contains polyphenols that make it protective against heart disease – one of the biggest challenges for older people. Remember the French paradox? Part of the irony of French longevity is the fact that the French are quite heavy drinkers, especially when it comes to wine*.

Yet there is no denying that the bloodstream very quickly distributes alcohol to every cell in the body, and as soon as it does so, a storm of protective activity is set loose. The alcohol breaks down into a substance that is chemically similar to formaldehyde and the cells react accordingly, just as they would if you'd taken a poison like strychnine or cyanide. Normal bodily functions are halted while as much energy as possible is directed to dissipate the toxin. For example, the way fat is turned into energy is disrupted. Organs may be deprived of oxygen, as every available oxygen molecule goes to dampen down toxic oxidative stress caused by the poison. Protein-coding slows down. There won't be enough oxygen or energy to manage anything else, and this in turn reduces immunity, changes our digestion, kills off digestive microbes and may result in DNA damage. In addition, the whole metabolic system goes into crisis mode as every cell in our body tries to break down the alcohol and turn it into

---

* Since the Millennium alcohol consumption has reduced in France, in response to more stringent advertising and licensing rules, but it has increased in the UK.

something less damaging. One of the main reasons why governments and health institutions have such difficulty describing a safe dose is that in reality there isn't one. Even a small dose, under the wrong conditions, can prove damaging.

Alcohol guidelines from the UK government are pragmatic, aimed at steering us towards the path of moderation. We are advised to drink no more than 14 units per week (140g) of pure alcohol. Studies of normal, healthy, middle-aged people suggest that when the dose starts to creep up to 20, 30 or 40 units a week, they are running the risk of reducing lifespan and health-span. Angela M. Wood published a report on risk thresholds for alcohol consumption in the Lancet journal in 2018, which combined results from over half a million participants from 83 separate studies. It revealed that those who drank 35 units a week in their 40s – that's just over three bottles of wine or 15 pints of beer weekly – reduced their average lifespan by four or five years.[16]

Part of the impact of alcohol is immediate, but there are also long-term effects. It can induce pretty well every single disease on the long-term condition list above. Something that makes us feel happy and relaxed in the short term can lead to depression later on, not to mention that if we happen to be subjected to other toxins, for example pollution or cigarettes, we may find that our risk of poor health multiplies alarmingly. Whenever the body is using up energy to clear toxins, our resilience to infections and diseases is reduced.

It is not simply the dose of alcohol that must be considered. It is the effect on the mind, and on our self-control, that adds to the difficulty of giving advice. If no-one in the UK drank a drop of alcohol, the accident rate would plummet, the rate of unplanned pregnancies would tumble, the crime rate would drop and we would all become thinner and fitter.

Alcohol stimulates our appetites (including lust and greed) and reduces inhibitions. That isn't necessarily a bad thing, as it might make the party go with a swing. However, the process by which we get rid of alcoholic toxins in the body requires the body to convert the alcohol into fat as quickly as possible. Once safely broken down and stowed in our fat cells, the toxins can do no more immediate harm, but of course the long-term harm of being overweight is in itself a serious risk factor. Even Rumpole's polyphenol-rich claret is broken down by the body into super-fattening carbohydrates. Alcohol contains the archetypal empty calories, delivering the double whammy of causing unhealthy weight gain while contributing to malnutrition.

It sounds like that extra glass of claret might be a pretty bad idea.[16] However, when we try and unravel the numerous studies on alcohol, we find strange anomalies that lead us to believe that complete abstinence may not be necessary.

There may be some times in life where even one glass of red wine just isn't a good idea. For example, even the French advise zero alcohol during pregnancy; we know that small quantities of alcohol in the blood stream, flowing straight into the foetus via the placenta, can severely affect things like birthweight (a proxy for healthy development). But when we reach old age, the effects of alcohol seem to diminish.

Moderation might help. The same Angela M. Wood meta-analysis,[17] quoted above, which showed a strong connection between alcohol and life expectancy in middle age, reveals interesting counterintuitive results in older participants. Moderate drinking has far less of an effect when we get into our 80 and 90s – but we have only a vague understanding of why this might be.

Other studies have indicated that older women who drink moderately enjoy a slightly higher longevity – though I must stress that the word is *moderate*, ie. less than government guidelines in the UK. Aged drinkers may simply be survivors and stronger than the next man. When you get that old, the adage; *eat, drink and be merry* may well apply.

A study carried out in the Netherlands indicates that after adjusting for other factors, such as smoking, weight and physical activity, on average men and women aged 68-70 increase their chances of living longer when they drink a small amount of alcohol. The sweet spot is about 10 grammes of pure alcohol per day – less than that recommended by UK government guidelines. [18]

It is well documented that alcohol stimulates blood flow, and may initiate a hormetic response in older drinkers. Hormetic means the effect is only positive in moderate doses; there is a sweet spot – go higher or lower and the effect is negative. Alternatively, it may be that moderate drinking is associated with more social engagement. The commensality of going to the pub might well outweigh the negative aspects of a half of bitter. But alcohol in high doses and at any age is definitely a destructive and addictive toxin.

Other intoxicants

We rarely consider other intoxicants in lifestyle studies, but pollution, recreational drugs and prescription drugs can have devastatingly similar effects to smoking and alcohol. The common factor in all these substances is that none of them are necessary. Recent ONS figures show that by the time a young person has reached the age of 15, 74% will have tried alcohol, smoking, vaping or other drugs. Over a third of pupils at 15 will be regular users, either smoking or drinking in the last week, or using drugs in the last month.

Sadly, while cigarette smoking is reducing among adults and children, vaping is increasing.[19] Tobacco firms will try and tell you that nicotine is as safe as naturally-derived caffeine – but it isn't. There is no food that naturally contains nicotine, in the way that tea and coffee, which are safe, mild stimulants, contain caffeine.* While many are convinced by the suggestion that vaping stops you smoking, I'm not sure that ingesting very high levels of nicotine isn't instead a way of maintaining the addiction to nicotine and thus to cigarettes. What a waste.

Nicotine addiction is unlike an addiction to cream-cakes or hip-hop. Nicotine generates negative biological changes in the body and brain and causes physical withdrawal symptoms, as serious as alcoholic dependence. The results are particularly diabolical in children and young people – ask any school teacher.

Obesity

Now that so many people have given up smoking, obesity is taking over as the lifestyle factor that has the greatest impact on our health. While only about 40% of the population of the UK have ever smoked, 100% of the population have to eat. The forces that stop us leading a healthy lifestyle, eating well and exercising more are so inextricably linked to our modern obesogenic lifestyle that it is difficult to untangle the mess. Chapters five, six and seven will cover this in much more detail.

The good news is that once we've got over the hurdle of smoking, drinking alcohol and taking nefarious drugs, there isn't anything else you'll need to give up, or even moderate. Healthy living is about changing the way we eat, move and think, but it doesn't need to involve anything that feels like restriction. People say they are addicted to sugar, or butter, but that isn't a strict physical addiction like alcohol, nicotine or cocaine.

---

* See Chapter 8 for more information about artificial caffeine in Coca-Cola. See Chapter 7 for information about the benefits of coffee drinking.

The solutions are far easier and don't involve unpleasant withdrawal symptoms. Someone who is seriously overweight is highly unlikely to experience any unpleasant symptoms at all, even if they decide to go on a super strict diet. They don't need to fear feeling uncomfortably hungry; it is a very rare symptom.*

Choose to be exceptional

All this gives us a clue as to why people like Jeanne Calment managed to live so long without leading the perfect lifestyle, including continuing to drink a small glass of port after dinner, well after her super-centenary. Medical studies look at the average, not at the exceptional. Few take much notice of the extremes of the bell curve. Yet when we reach old age, we are all inhabiting something of an extreme position. The very fact of having reached a ripe old age makes each and every older person exceptional.

What we see when we flip the telescope between large-scale population studies, which seek to define the *average*, and case studies of *exceptional* individuals, is that we are flipping between the general, unexceptional bulk of humanity and the extraordinary outliers.

Wanting to lead a happy and healthy life is about seeking the exceptional. Fortunately, it may well turn out that exceptional long and healthy life is within the grasp of us all.

---

* Anyone who is overweight is likely to have forgotten that feeling hungry is a pleasant feeling we get in anticipation of the next meal. Overweight people rarely experience the feeling of hunger at all, even when they diet, because their body fat is available to provide iron rations until the next meal. However, that doesn't mean that fear of hunger, or cravings might not occur. A good nutritionist or therapist can help with management strategies.

Endnotes

1 Li S, et al. (2022) *Early life affects late-life health through determining DNA methylation across the lifespan: A twin study.* Lancet eBioMedicine. Digital publication 2022 March 14; Vol 77:103927. DOI: 10.1016/j.ebiom.2022.103927

2 Some cells like red blood cells do not have a nucleus. The nuclei are discarded immediately after dividing, transforming the cell into an even more efficient oxygen transporter

3 Gershman, Ariel et al. (2022) *Epigenetic patterns in a complete human genome.* Science 376, eabj5089(2022) DOI:10.1126/science.abj5089

4 Dhamija S & Menon MB (2018) *Non-coding transcript variants of protein-coding genes – what are they good for?* RNA Biology September 10th 2018;15(8):1025-1031. DOI: 10.1080/15476286.2018.1511675

5 Ng et al. (2023) *Antibodies against endogenous retroviruses promote lung cancer immunotherapy.* Nature, 2023. DOI 10,1038/s41586-023-05771-9

6 Quetelet, A (1835) *Sur l'homme et le développement de ses facultés, ou essai de physique sociale,* translation (2013) *A Treatise on Man and the Development of His Faculties* (1835;), (Cambridge Library Collection – Philosophy) (R. Knox, Trans.; T. Smibert, Ed.). Cambridge: Cambridge University Press. DOI:10.1017/CBO9781139864909

7 For those of you who enjoy a bit of maths, BMI is weight in kilos, divided by height squared in meters. The average healthy BMI is about $20\text{-}25\text{kg}/\text{m}^2$

8 ASH (Action on Smoking and Health) *Facts at A Glance* from; ash.org.uk/resources/view/facts-at-a-glance retrieved February 2024

9 Mortimer, J (1987) *Rumpole's Last Case* Book, Publisher Penguin London

10 Statista (2017) website; statista.com/statistics/749078/elderly-population-of-the-uk-by-age-2017-2032/

11 Alzheimer's Research UK Dementia Statistics Hub, dementiastatistics.org

12 Department of Health (2012) *Long-term conditions compendium of Information,* Report, 3rd edition

13 House of Commons (2019) *Health inequalities: Income deprivation and north/south divides* Insight Guide Published Tuesday, 22 January, 2019

14 South Tyneside Website article: *Life Expectancy from,* southtyneside.gov.uk/article/60972/Life-Expectancy; quoting ONS 2015 figures. [retrieved April 2022]

15 Department of Transport (2020) *Reported road casualties in Great Britain: final estimates involving illegal alcohol levels*: 2018

16 Angela M Wood et al. (2018) *Risk thresholds for alcohol consumption: combined analysis of individual-participant data for 599,912 current drinkers in 83 prospective*

studies, The Lancet, Volume 391, Issue 10129, 2018, Pages 1513-1523, ISSN 0140-6736, DOI: 10.1016/S0140-6736(18)30134-X

17 A meta-analysis combines results from many studies which adds to the accuracy of the findings, because of the larger number of participants and the potential to iron out anomalies in individual studies

18 Piet A. van den Brandt & Lloyd Brandts (2020) *Alcohol consumption in later life and reaching longevity: the Netherlands Cohort Study*, Age and Ageing 2020; 49: 395–402 DOI: 10.1093/ageing/afaa003 Published electronically 9 February 2020

19 NHS Digital, (2022) *Smoking, Drinking and Drug Use among Young People in England, 2021* ONS; Published 6 September 2022 at digital.nhs.uk/data-and-information/publications/statistical/smoking-drinking-and-drug-use-among-young-people-in-england/2021

3

The art and science of body maintenance

People and machines are different. Forget everything you've ever read about the similarities between repairing cars and curing people. The mechanic must make sure connections are sound and joints are leak-proof. An engineer must design an engine that lasts for years, but the human body can grow stronger naturally and repair itself. Imagine if a Mini could turn itself into a Maserati. The doctor's role isn't a mechanic's; it is more that of a gardener who sows seeds, prunes, pulls out weeds and treats pests and diseases with time-honoured cures. The reason that machine analogies don't work is because the body is not one machine, one organism, although we often seem to act as one being. In fact, the body consists of trillions of cells, each with their own role, lifespan and state of health. Because of our complexity we are more like the lawn than the blade of grass, like the forest not the tree. Consequently, and fortunately, it takes a lot to kill us. But change, growth and ageing are inextricably linked; you could say that ageing starts on the day we are conceived.

What is ageing

Since civilisation began, people have put forward various theories around growing old. The ancients wondered whether ageing was a disease that could potentially be cured, meaning that we could live forever. Then a second-century Greek physician called Galen suggested that ageing was a natural process that could be mediated by preventive measures such as diet, but not escaped altogether. Not everyone agreed, but his book *Hygiene* is considered the only surviving classical study of old age and was hugely influential in the development of Renaissance medicine.

Today we are still engaged in a similar debate. Some people (I am not one of them) advocate the following of rigorous routines. Is it just coincidence that the Ancient Greek Galen called his book, *Hygiene* and now we have a craze called 'clean' eating? Today, modern medicine often treats ageing as a disease to be cured, while at other times people have suggested that ageing is an irreversible and natural process to be modified, but not eliminated altogether. The decision to treat, or to let nature take it's course, is part of every doctor's nightmare.

Even the phrase 'to age' is now commonly used as a catch-all term to describe various processes, few of them welcome. Human ageing is often depicted in terms of an inevitable physical and mental decline and rarely associated with the positive aspects of long life, such as a rich memory, a wide network, experience and wisdom. Old people know how to do lots of things; they've seen it all before. Because of their experience they can be calm in a crisis and sensible when faced with a dramatic situation. They know that it is a waste of energy to 'get in a flap'. If you want good gardening tips, ask an old gardener – they'll have learned from many seasons of trial and error.

The dictionary definition of ageing is simply related to the passing of time and a progression of birthdays. It is we who impose cultural associations upon ageing that ignore how the decline we call, 'getting long in the tooth' is not linear – neither is it a one-way process. Every cell in the body acts differently, ageing at different rates and replenishing differently. No type of decline is ever attached to a specific age. That is why it can be so difficult to guess someone's age.

That our bodies change with time is not in dispute. As the birthdays tick by, we will all start to look different. A baby will develop stronger legs and become a toddler, a child will mature into an adolescent and eventually the brain of an adolescent will lose its naivety as the fully-grown adult emerges. You might think that after that stage it is downhill all the way – but this is not so. Cells continue to grow and divide throughout life.

The fountain of change in the body springs from a small pea-sized gland at the base of the brain called the pituitary gland. The pituitary triggers the production of many essential hormones by sending chemical signals to the adrenal (stress), thyroid (metabolic) and gonad (sex) glands. One of the most important functions of the anterior pituitary is the manufacture of the human growth hormone, a protein/amino acid-based peptide called somatotropin.* This is sent to the liver where it is transformed into insulin-like growth factor-1 (IGF-1).

IGF-1 is required by almost every cell in the body and naturally declines as we age. However, the growth hormone that is abundant in a growing child still courses through the veins of a centenarian. In an infant, a growth hormone ensures that the baby grows into a healthy adult, reaching a peak in adolescence. For the centenarian, growth hormones

---

* Somatotropin derives from the Greek *soma*, meaning body and the verb *trepein* meaning to turn.

ensure that repairs and regeneration occur in all cells. This growth hormone, alongside a cocktail of protein-rich nutrients, is necessary in order to activate stem cells, and to trigger division and regeneration in all other cells. Almost every cell in the body is primed to respond to growth hormones throughout its lifespan, which is fundamental in the maintenance of DNA. The protein strings these hormones contain is really important, made by the body in order to maintain the body.[1]

If this IGF-1 stops working, or ceases to be manufactured, the result is premature ageing; ordinary everyday repairs cease to be carried out and the system slowly declines. A lack of growth hormones, or an inability for them to do their job, is an important aspect of ageing. However, the picture isn't completely one-sided. As we age, cell replication can get out of hand. Tumour growth, an increased immune response and arthritis attest to this, suggesting that too much IGF-1 growth hormone can be as damaging as too little. As with all things, there is a sweet spot.*

What's it all about?

An influential scientist who has studied ageing for most of his life is Tom Kirkwood. In 1977, while still a young man, he entered the ageing debate with a small paper in the journal *Nature* that changed the way we think about ageing.

Today he is Professor Emeritus at Newcastle University, where he has headed the Institute for Ageing and Health for many years. In 1977 he wasn't even based at a university, but at the National Institute for

---

* Recently this idea has been challenged. Some people think that ageing is a function of too much IGF-1 in old age, and have done some studies on dogs to try and prove it. However, current research in humans points the other way; levels of IGF-1 naturally decline as we age and are associated with muscle atrophy and frailty.

Biological Standards and Control (NIBSC) in London. It was he who made sense of it all (in true Archimedean style) during a eureka moment in his bath, and was encouraged by enlightened mentors to publish.

Kirkwood saw that his peers weren't asking the right questions. The challenge wasn't to find out how we age, as we can observe that processes well enough. The real question was why we age at all, and why some age far quicker than others. Kirkwood understood, as a true geneticist, that ageing must confer some benefit to evolution – otherwise it simply wouldn't happen. According to Darwin's theory of evolution, some detrimental traits can be inherited, but only beneficial traits endure. The fact that all humans (and intelligent animals) age to some extent means that evolution has seen no reason to maintain our bodies in pristine condition throughout life. We call this 'genetic preferencing'. On the face of it the genetic mutation that allows us to age well after our childbearing years seems detrimental, but Kirkwood's hypothesis was that ageing is beneficial to survival.

Kirkwood started by looking at the sort of errors that cells make after they have been triggered to divide by growth hormones such as IGF-1. These errors are the raw materials of evolutionary change, causing both good as well as harmful mutations with every generation. Evolution requires some errors in order to improve – just not too many.

Kirkwood also thought about the differences between cells in the body. Clearly germline cells from the egg and sperm must be replicated very accurately. If a single code in the DNA strand is incorrect, the cell may not be able to replicate, endangering the foetus and compromising healthy childhood growth. Therefore, vast amounts of energy are required during pregnancy and childhood to ensure healthy development. Even after birth the super-rich diet of breast milk is packed with proteins, energy, essential nutrients and bio-active ingredients such as the mother's immune cells, to provide babies with a kick-start in life.

Sitting in his bath back in 1976, Tom Kirkwood realised that maintaining human life is rather like maintaining a city. Imagine if every time a pot-hole appeared in the road the council went out and resurfaced the entire street. That would be a dangerous waste of scarce energy and resources, when a bucket of tar would do the job. The disposable soma theory, as it has become known, is now recognised as one of the most likely rationales for ageing.

Kirkwood's theory recognised that some cells, such as egg and sperm cells, are worth preserving exactly, but that the others, known as somatic cells, do not matter so much to the individual, or the species. Perfection amongst somatic cells in the body is not essential. In the end wrinkles and grey hair really don't matter at all! We should simply consider them a mark of heathy ageing. Perhaps the disposable soma theory is another way of illustrating that nobody is perfect; worth remembering when you face the mirror in tomorrow's harsh morning light.

Think about skin. If every human skin cell replicated itself really accurately, we would possess the skin of a baby into old age. Peachy skin would be nice, but it is clearly not essential to survival; in fact, a baby's skin is not well protected against sunshine or abrasion. We who have wrinkles and liver spots are less fragile, even if our tough skin may be symbolic of the slower, error-ridden, low-energy replications that occur as we get older. Skin cells are replicated accurately enough to do the job of protecting the body remarkably well – keeping toxins out and blood and bones in – even into very old age.

For most of human existence, few of us would have lived beyond middle age. Thus, genetically a body that remained perfect throughout an even longer life would have been a waste of precious resources.

Humans who managed to survive the assaults of childhood diseases (of which there were many) would have been the ones who were inherently strong enough to use the available energy (from scarce food) most effectively. They could withstand higher levels of stress, even at the expense of jettisoning a few perfect cell replications along the way. The energy required to make perfect repairs every time something went wrong would have been a huge waste, just as the cost of shiny new roads in the city would involve massive taxes. The penalty for cellular perfection could be a diversion of energy away from vital functions and reproduction. This would have been especially important during times of famine, when the higher energy required to replace slightly imperfect cells would have diverted resources away from tackling the effects of starvation and guarding against disease. The survivors might have been a little thinner and a bit more wizened, but they lived on, their metabolism simply settling for less for a while.[2]

For me, learning about this theory was a revelation. I see things differently now, and I'm much more accepting of my own and other's imperfections.

When he was invited to give the BBC Reith Lectures in 2001, Kirkwood said this:

"Even in a person as old as 100, most of the cells are in good working order. If a cell culture is grown from the biopsied skin of a centenarian, the culture growth rate is not detectably different from that of a culture grown from a much younger person. Our bodies don't just rot. If we can understand more about the fine molecular balance between the processes that lead to damage and the processes that effect repair,

there need be no bound to what we can accomplish.
Everything we have learned about the science of ageing
suggests there is no quick fix – no fountain of youth –
but equally there is no limit. With hard work and
determination, we can keep pushing back the
boundaries of good quality life." *

_____

Growing older, growing different

The changes that we usually call ageing could be more accurately described as cellular damage limitation. A long healthy life is about continual growth and change and a continuous process of maintenance that focuses on the important things and doesn't bother so much about the unimportant things. We must stop thinking of ourselves as old bangers, all rattle and rust inevitably headed for the scrapheap, and start to see ourselves as valuable 'classics'. Every human body is a community of interrelated cells that work together to keep us strong. Whatever vintage we may be, our own bodywork will repay any care that is bestowed because human bodywork – our cellular structure – can repair itself, given access to the basic raw materials of sunlight, food, water and energy.

Our own restoration system is completely different to repairing an old croc, where replacement of entire sections is often required. Instead, our bodies grow and repair themselves one cell at a time. Quite naturally, and without medical intervention, every cell in the human body is working, all day every day, to repair damage, maintain vitality and keep us limber. Cells wear out – no-one can deny it – but unlike the bodywork of a car,

_____

* BBC.co.uk/programmes; Tom Kirkwood The End of Age.

rusty cells auto-destruct to make way, so that new and better cells can replicate and grow. Some fast-growing cells, like the ones found in our digestive system, will mutate in a matter of days in response to dietary changes. That's a really useful function, as it means that our digestive system can adapt quickly to seasonal changes in the availability of food. We can take advantage of a glut as well as manage shortages. It also helps us modify our diet for the better. For example, refined sugar is one of the easiest foods to eliminate from a diet.*

Life is a process of millions of cellular activities occurring simultaneously. As we grow older, the sum total of the assaults to our systems increases. The genes we are born with can have an impact – but don't right yourself off simply because longevity doesn't run in the family. In the long term, the impact of environment is far greater. Healthy food, fresh air, exercise and stimulating activity will ensure that these processes have a good chance of continuing for many years to come.

Our birthdays are inevitable, just as night follows day and 60 candles on the birthday cake follow 59. We might observe the past year's damage as bodily imperfections, reduced faculties or increased frailty. But we can help ourselves by guarding against early damage, slowing this process down and nurturing repair. The rate of decline is not inexorable.

---

* Before the sugar shortage of 1974, which lasted about six months, most people would take sugar in hot drinks. For me, a student at the time, the soaring costs were a trigger to give up buying and eating granulated sugar. After a week or two, I'd completely lost the taste for it. What had actually happened was that numerous sugar transporters in my gut had withered from disuse. When sugar returned on the menu, I didn't want it any more. I have never missed it since. During that year (1974/5), according to the Food and Agricultural Organisations of the United Nations, per capita sugar consumption in the UK decreased by almost 20%; it never bounced back to such highs again. We now know that these cells naturally replicate every three or four days, and if they are not needed, they simply stop replicating. We all need a few, but if their number creeps up, a few days of abstinence will result in a natural modification of the appetite.

The life of cells

In order to understand ageing – the good and the bad – we have to understand the life of cells.

The study of the living cell started with the invention of microscopy in the latter part of the sixteenth century. Early microscopes could not enlarge enough to see individual cells. It took almost 100 years for the craft of lens grinding to progress to such an extent that microscopes could enlarge enough to show us how all living things are made up. The man who first peered down one of these new improved machines with a 200 x magnification was one of their makers, the technician – not scientist – Antony van Leeuwenhoek (1632-1723).

Leeuwenhoek's curiosity knew no bounds. He put everything he could lay his hands on under his new lenses. He became so fascinated that he hired someone to draw what could be seen and began to send reports to The Royal Society in London. He is credited with discovering and describing the bacteria that lives on our bodies (part of our microbiome), the structure of blood cells, sperm cells and the array of microorganisms that we find wriggling and spiralling in pond water. School children still collect pond water and marvel at the life they see. These tiny single-celled organisms he called *animalcules*.

The human cell is a remarkably robust organism, built just as a single-celled creature is built, but endowed with the capacity to divide and change its nature at the same time. Single-celled creatures can only divide and multiply copies of themselves. The millions of cells in all higher-order animals, including humans, stem from the single fertilised cell, brought to life by a combination of egg and sperm, which then multiplies in the womb to form a growing foetus, the baby, and so on. You were probably taught that cells continue to divide and differentiate as the baby grows in the womb, and then in childhood the cells divide and grow even more to create the adult. That is where the lesson often ended. But cell division and differentiation continue throughout life as the hormones that dictated childhood growth become the hormones that dictate cellular repair and re-growth.

Biologists think that life on earth originated in single-celled units and all subsequent, more complex, creatures grew out of those single cells clustering. First, they specialised to form larger and more complex plants. Living cells are thought to have originated when two cells, each possessing different but important characteristics, combined together*.

From the simplest to the most sophisticated creature, life's building blocks have remained remarkably constant over the millennia of evolution. Living cells contain a nucleus, surrounded by a sea of gelatinous liquid in which swim tiny and delicate elements, much like small cells in their own right, called organelles. A single-celled amoeba or a speck of yeast will look rather similar under a microscope to a human cell.

It was not until the invention of x-ray crystallography and the pioneering work of Rosalind Franklin that we were able to peer further into the workings of the cell. What we could see was the ubiquitous presence of DNA strings – the double helix – that exists in every living cell, whether animal or vegetable, unlocking the close associations that underly evolution.

As electron microscopy improved scientists were able to see more and more. The most important element of a cell is its nucleus, which contains a copy of our DNA (deoxyribonucleic acid). Our genes carry the codes for thousands of different working proteins, but a lot of the heavy lifting is done by loose strands of ribonucleic acid (RNA), set free from the DNA helix, to travel outside the nucleus. These short strings of data, a

* A forerunner, but not a replica, of human fertilisation.

bit like a knitting pattern, are then sent to other parts of the cell where a whole series of delicate bits of cellular machinery use the individual protein-coding strands to manufacture all the elements of the living body, as well as the hormones that regulate their use.

Investigating the complexity of the cell often diverts our attention from this variety of cells, and from their constant mutation and division. Over time, cells change. Some, such as fat cells, can grow to collect excess fat and shrink when the fat is extracted to make energy. Some skin-like cells change and replicate every day to respond to a changing environment. These epithelial cells are widespread throughout the body. They form the covering of all skin surfaces, line body cavities and hollow organs, and are the major tissue in glands. They protect insides from outsides, and they can filter, absorb, secrete and excrete. They line our entire digestive system, managing the critically important mechanisms that absorb and distribute nutrients and discard waste products.

Other cells such as blood cells move throughout the body transporting oxygen, hormones and nutrients, refreshing the immune system and delivering their precious load where it is needed. Once the oxygen has been delivered a denuded red blood cell will be pumped straight back via the lung, to load up with new cargo and go around again.

Mitochondria

Modern methods of microscopy, combined with computer animations and DNA analysis, have led to the discovery of each cell's miniature wonderland; the array of organelles, each one like a small cell in itself, performing a really important task, sometimes thousands of times each day in order to maintain life. Different organelles have different functions and the different machinery possess a fairground of delightful names, such as Golgi apparatus, lysosomes, endoplasmic reticulum, ribosomes, centrioles and the equivalent of the Big Wheel, the mitochondria.

Mitochondria are miniscule power engines that generate energy.* The energy they produce powers the cell's replication, growth and renewal, but it also powers all human processes. In the right cell, these tiny electrical charges, multiplied hundreds and thousands of times, can power our thoughts, actions and reactions.

A cell will cease to function if it is no longer needed, or it may replicate into something slightly different. This may or may not be a good thing. The signs we observe as growth and ageing are actually the gradual build-up of millions of different cell changes, particularly changes in the energy a cell possess by virtue of the mitochondria. In youth, cell degradation is more than balanced by energetic repair and growth or re-growth. As time goes by, the decline of cells can overtake the renewal. Cells become less energetic; their replication less perfect. We start to age visibly. Wrinkles, grey hair, weaker muscles and shorter memories are the external indicators that things may be changing – but in recent years we have discovered that what we observe as decline is actually self-preservation. The body's energy is being diverted to important organs, such as the heart and brain, and other important functions, such as managing the immune system, which continues to plug away in spite of external appearances.

Protein

Most of the body's structure, including the blood, muscles and organs, are made of different proteins, which themselves are made of groups of amino acids. The proteins and their building blocks of amino acids are

---

* Mitochondria in fact do a lot more than simply generate energy, though that is their primary role.

formed within the cell, using the nutrients we find in food as the building materials. Even solid bone, which is principally made of calcium, requires specially-formulated cells called osteoblasts that chaperone minerals to the bones to shape and maintain them. While the basic structure of bones seems to last a lifetime, our bones are not fixed. Just like the rest of the body, the skeleton grows and changes over time, breaking down and building up anew.

The food we eat is broken down into its constituent parts (amino acids, vitamins, minerals etc) and transported to cells to make new proteins which in turn make new cells, that fulfil different roles in the body or repair old cells.

Protein consists of long, tightly-wound chains of 20 amino acids, some that our cells cannot make, which must come from food, together with hundreds more that the body can make by re-arranging the amino acid building blocks in the proteins we absorb through the gut. Like blocks of Lego, amino acids can all be fitted together in different ways to form different tissue, or to perform different, and often very sophisticated, functions. While protein in the body is not actually alive, in the way that a human cell is alive, it does move about quite a bit. If you examine protein under a powerful electron microscopy you can see that it jiggles around, acting and reacting by means of tiny electronic charges to its environment. People have referred to this as dancing. (Google *dancing proteins* to see what I mean). The tiny electron interchanges that go on between amino acid molecules mean that specialist proteins can perform mechanical tasks on a tiny scale, such as opening and closing valves to let specific nutrients into a cell, embracing and transporting nutrients around the blood stream, or smothering invading microbes and viruses and expelling unwanted debris. Because of the complex needs of the body, proteins are continually being broken down and rearranged into new forms in a process called protein turnover.

If we cannot get enough protein in our diet and the correct cocktail of protein building blocks – amino acids – then the rate of protein turnover can gradually lead to protein malnutrition. In older or ailing people that decline in protein can show itself in a relatively short space of time and can have a very noticeable physical impact, inducing weakness and frailty. Over time, lack of protein will result in more susceptibility to injury and disease, as well as muscle wasting and organ malfunction. You can often tell someone who is suffering from protein malnutrition, because they become drawn and haggard, looking old before their time.

While physical signs of protein loss can be stark, its effect on the mind and our feelings can be insidious. For example, serotonin (sometimes called the 'happiness hormone') is derived from tryptophan, one of the essential dietary amino acids that our cells cannot manufacture. Tryptophan is found in the protein provided by milk, fish, meat, oats, cheese and nuts. A good balance of serotonin in the brain is required at all times. People who suffer from low serotonin – for example, those with eating disorders – may find that common anti-depressants, such as SSRIs (serotonin re-uptake inhibitors) don't work.[3] Some studies have even found that depleted tryptophan in the diet of otherwise well-fed older people effects working memory and movement.[4]

But it is no good to simply focus on one nutrient or one amino acid; they all work in concert with each other. In order for the body to function it needs the full mix of essential amino acids and the full cornucopia of essential macro- and micro-nutrients. *

* In other words – a generous, balanced and varied diet.

The body of a 76 kg (12 stone) person contains about 12 kg of protein (about 1/6th of our total weight). Of this protein, nearly half is found in skeletal muscle, powering our arms, legs and torso. Structural tissues such as blood and skin contain other significant amounts. [5] Protein isn't stable. The protein packages are prone to fray and delaminate, like tagliatelle bundles in a cooking pot. Within the body, protein is forever breaking down and being replaced, sometimes due to lack of nutritional resources, but also due to muscle and organ stress. That protein is re-used for repair and rebuilding, but also – *in extremis* – protein can be used as energy, even at the cost of destroying tissue.

In times of stress, such as famine, disease and anxiety our muscles and eventually some organs may become severely depleted in order to provide energy for essential functions such as heart, lung and brain activity. We see this effect in ageing, but also in disease, cases of protein malnutrition and poisoning, including where pollution and other toxins destroy the protein-building pathways. This is a slow process: only about one per cent of our bodily protein can be broken down in a day. But over time, if we are not eating enough protein, muscles will shrink to provide energy for more vital functions. This process, known as 'catabolism', results in the characteristic emaciation we see in famine victims, the characteristic ennui we find in extreme dieters and the drawn features of cancer sufferers (where proteins are diverted to deal with the tumour) and in the scrawniness of habitual smokers (where toxins interrupt protein-building). [6]

Protein depletion is not a one-way street. Removing a stressor or pollutant, improving diet and increasing exercise can all help the regrowth process in bones, cartilage and muscle, enabling weaker areas to be replaced by strong new tissue. Muscle-builders use our understanding of this process to 'get ripped' (lose body fat) and then by exercising, weight-lifting and eating high-protein meals, nurturing stronger and bigger bodies. This process continues throughout life.

Some of our muscles are vitally important. It is enjoyable to be able to walk ten miles, or carry an infant, but at the same time that most important of human muscles, the heart, is getting a good workout as well.

Our health is inextricably linked to our consumption of nutrients, especially proteins. For example, we need a constant and diverse diet to feed the manufacture of immune cells. These are dedicated cells which build up when infections are detected, forming the correctly-shaped molecules needed to catch onto and destroy whatever alien virus or bacteria each day might bring. These antigens are broken down and remade, time and again, in response to changing needs. In addition, the cells manufacture signals and hormones that are in fact highly reactive and energetic peptides (strings of new proteins), which have the ability to travel through the body, principally via the bloodstream, and to make things happen.

Proteostasis is the complex process that regulates the absorption and use of proteins within our cells to keep us healthy. Each step in the flow of information, from DNA to RNA snippets to protein, provides the cell with a potential control point that adjusts the amount and type of protein it manufactures. Keeping the process of proteostasis vital is a way of staving off ageing. Making sure we eat enough of the right nutrients, every day at every meal, will keep us strong and reduce the risk of disease and injury. For the process to work efficiently, we need a good digestion and a healthy metabolism that can transform the food we eat into healthy new cells. That is why older people are advised to eat protein at every meal, to counteract their reduced ability to digest larger portions of protein at any single meal.

In order to make new tissue, the process of cell division must take place. DNA will pattern the new cells in a complex, highly-choreographed unfolding and separation of the double helix into two different identical packages which produce the nuclei of twin daughter cells, (living cells are always considered to be female). As time goes by, the copy of the copy of the copy can go a bit awry. The new cells can be slightly different from the original, and may become more and more different over time. These chance mutations may be beneficial, representing Darwinian evolution in action, as well as offering a way that our bodies can respond to different environmental influences. But sometimes cells mis-replicate, causing flaws.

In a healthy body, the cell is pretty good at repairing mistakes. In all the millions of cell divisions that occur within one lifetime, it is extraordinary that fingers don't turn into thumbs more often! While some flaws represent an improvement on the original, and may be absorbed into the evolution of the species, some slightly flawed cells can run out of control, triggering tumour growth. More often than not the misreplications are benign, simply showing up as subtle changes. We see them as imperfections, the first signs of ageing, though if we re-classify these changes as signs of a robust maturity, some of them might appear more welcome.

Evolution has learned that liver spots and skin tags will not kill you. So why do we waste energy on them, when renewing muscles and keeping our brains ticking over is far more important? The ways our bodies use energy and the way cells intercommunicate are all linked to the ability of the body to make the correct protein molecule at the correct time and in the correct quantity. This helps to keep our energy in balance, and ensures that the correct hormones and enzymes can travel around switching processes on and off.

All the hallmarks of ageing are a signal of how the body always places the essential above the cosmetic and show us how well cells reproduce most of the time. Even as babies, we simply don't have the energy to replicate every cell perfectly. The result of this conservation of cellular energy means that while there may be more tiny mistakes, and while processes may slow down, the basic machinery will continue to work pretty well. You may have grey hairs, but that doesn't mean that your body isn't still doing sterling work in maintaining a healthy heart. It simply reveals that your body is prioritising. The trigger may be lack of energy, toxins (such as smoking or alcohol misuse), or trauma. We see going grey as a sign of ageing, yet none of the classic hallmarks of ageing are programmed to switch on at a particular birthday, or in a particular order. While this progressive damage is a natural process we observe as we get older, it can also be induced by stress or self-neglect. Being bombed in his childhood home in Pinner during WWII almost certainly resulted in my father sporting a dash of grey hair from the age of 12. It was sixty years until the rest of his blond locks caught up.

The ageing cell

The cellular equivalent of car maintenance is replication. And so that new cells can flourish, old cells must make way. Cells die or just give up working, a process known as *senescence*, but their components are re-used in new, changed and even better cells. We will die only once, but in order to keep us ticking over for many years cells die and renew thousands of times every day. Nothing is wasted. It is sustainability in action.

Each cell is, to a certain extent, independent of its neighbour. One cell can change or die without having any effect upon its neighbour, but the body still works as a coherent organism. There exist many different types of connections and communications between cells. Information is communicated via blood vessels, nerves, hormonal stimulation and bio electrical impulses. The process of differentiation, stimulated by these intracellular communications, allows similar cells to cluster together, forming the organs of the body, skeleton, muscle, skin and so on. And very specialised cells erupt, in very specific locations, to form the minuscule complexity of the eyes, ears and tongue – each one a miracle of bio-engineering, as well as the more prosaic perfection of nutritional transporter cells in the gut that allow the transfusion of nutrients from food into the bloodstream. Our organs can repair, but they must all last a lifetime; the cells in our body may also last a lifetime, but some, such as gut transporter cells, may only last a few days.

Cells can go wrong for all sorts of reasons. Redundant cells tend to shrivel up, lose water and eventually disintegrate. This form of spring cleaning is called *apoptosis*. If a cell is critically damaged by injury, say by a cut, burn or infection, it will die. In the case of such death or *necrosis*, specialist cells called macrophage cells (part of the immune system) flow in to clean up the debris and redistribute it. Macrophage 'cleaner cells' have the effect of causing a localised swelling, which itself can infect other nearby cells.

Over life this process becomes more and more active, putting the body under stress. For example, arthritis is a chronic swelling of the joints, caused by an over-stimulation of macrophages which may be triggered by local stress, hormone interactions, infections or drugs. This over-stimulation of the immune response becomes more common as we age and is considered by some gerontologists to be the factor most involved in the frailty we associate with growing old.

Not all faulty cells die or wither. *Dormant* cells can remain alive and primed for action for years, without changing or reproducing. The cell will still fulfil its everyday role, but the DNA strands within the nucleus fail to divide in preparation for making two new daughter copies. This may be due to a fault, or maybe a healthy response to negative signals. Dormancy is in fact an important preservation strategy for the body.

If a cell contains dangerous mutations it might continue to function, but it won't replicate that damage. The exception to that rule occurs in many cancers where damaged cells, instead of remaining dormant, continue to divide, apparently unresponsive to the normal signals that control irregular growth. At first the genetic *mutations* may be benign, but over many divisions, individual carcinoma cells can amass more than 60 different mutations. Often these mutations occur in the regions that respond well to growth hormones, such as IGF-1, allowing damaged cell divisions to escalate, causing uncontrolled divisions which greedily lap up nutrients and supplies that should be destined for healthy cells. By this stage, these cell clusters start to multiply uncontrollably. Eventually the tumour may burst (metastasise), exploding its contagion into the blood stream.

Modern cancer cures look at the way the body naturally recognises and attacks damaged or infected cells. It turns out that our immune system is primed to enter infected or metastasising cells, parcel up the damaged elements and ship them out. Our own systems can deal with mutations like cancers as well as attacking foreign microbes and viruses which are called pathogens. Once the debris is cleared, the cell can continue its role. This process, called *autophagy*, is a very efficient auto-immune process because it recycles rather than discards the debris. It occurs in all life forms, from yeast to humans, suggesting that it is crucial, important and efficient.

The microbiome

Alongside ever-changing, ever-renewing cells that make up a living, breathing body, we are host to an army of microbes, cells that sit on the surface of the skin but also nestle deep inside us. Recently we have realised that this microbiome is equally important to our wellbeing, impacting everything from mood to digestion. Just like human cells, the cells in our microbiome are affected by their environment. Individual colonies can flourish or atrophy depending on the situation. Certain functions, for example the breakdown of food and absorption of nutrients within the digestive tract, could not happen without the beneficial microbes that have taken up residence there and help with the process. The microbiome is far more mutable than our own body cells. A slight change in diet, a more humid atmosphere or taking antibiotics can immediately change the structure and efficacy of our microbiome.

DNA and ageing

When scientists discovered telomeres, some thought they had discovered life's ticking time bomb. The long double-helical strands of our DNA are bundled into tightly-bound packages of genetic information called chromosomes. Humans have 46 different chromosomes, 23 from each parent, and when a cell divides, the chromosomes have to unfold in order to be copied. At this point they are far more vulnerable to damage than when they are packed neatly in the chromosomal knot.

Evolution has provided a natty network of telomeres at each end of the genetic strand to stop the whole thing unravelling uncontrollably. Telomeres have been likened to the plastic aglet on the end of a shoelace that limits fraying. They are meaningless strings of genetic code that sit at the beginning and end of a length of DNA. In their redundancy they protect the important DNA code from being accidentally broken off. But, just like shoelaces, they don't work forever. The duplication process can continue in spite of a bit of decay each time. As we age, reproduction in cells becomes more and more haphazard and the sacrificial telomeres become more and more ragged. If they break off entirely, the cell becomes incapable of dividing.

Analysis of telomere length in older animals, including humans, always displays this shortening to some extent. But you can't predict age by counting telomeres. The variations between different cells in the body are as marked as those between different age groups. They are not, after all, a harbinger of death, but a useful preservation technique.

Are stem cells a cure for ageing?

Stem cells first entered the news cycle with that famous image of a human ear growing on a mouse's back. These days we hardly raise an eyebrow at the idea that stem cell research might one day restore sight to the blind or regenerate function in human organs. Behind the headlines, human cells continue to do their job every day, as they always have. For example, every time we cut ourselves stem cells wade in to form a scar. The reason why scar tissue doesn't look exactly like the skin around it is that these hastily-summoned cells are called upon to quickly morph into functioning skin cells. In another emergency, they might have needed to become something quite different. This is why scientists are excited by what tasks stem cells might perform, given the right tweak.

Your own stem cells will be unique to you, but they have not yet taken on a specific function. Within the fertilised human egg there exists very special and powerful stem cells called germline cells, which contain the DNA code for the entirely new and unique future human. They are so important to the next generation that a large amount of energy is used up to keep them in peak condition throughout our reproductive lives.

As it happens, not all stem cells will contribute to the DNA of a new baby, like germline cells. Their fate is to continue to differentiate (to change as they divide), becoming any type of tissue that is required throughout the life of the host. In adult humans the greatest number of stem cells are located in the bone marrow, from where they can be sent through the body via the blood stream. However, they do occur in vast quantities in other parts of the body, in our teeth and most mysteriously of all, within adipose tissue. Human blubber is no longer considered to be simply padding. We now know that it contains a store of cells that are crucial to the systems that repair damage and initiate new tissue – including immune cells and stem cells. But you can have too much of a good thing. Being overweight may not greatly increase the number of stem cells in our body, but it can overwhelm the systems.

Wherever they reside, different cells are working and dividing within our bodies all the time, repairing and replicating themselves, even into very old age. But our ability to ensure stem cells accurately replicate becomes gradually impaired as we age. This stem cell exhaustion is a function of a slowing metabolism and our inability as we get older to 'stoke up the batteries' as we did when we were younger.

Throughout the 1960s and '70s, gerontologists and biologists couldn't agree on why this cell repair process gradually runs down. Some scientists thought that senescence (cell death) was genetically programmed. This theory made assumptions about when any cell might naturally die and used declining telomere length to provide evidence for the theory. But the fact is that cells have wildly varying lifespans.

Some scientists even suggested that ageing was hard-wired into our genetics as a natural way of disposing of older members of a community that were no longer fertile. Yet how could those who died immediately after their child rearing years pass on any more or any fewer genes than those who stuck around?

Today we recognise that living a long life has less to do with super-successful ageing than it does with our ability to survive childhood.

Might those of us who survive into adulthood possess a greater resilient that sets us up for a longer life?

Some people have suggested that ageing is a beneficial trait. Those who live beyond the child-rearing years will have more time and more wisdom to contribute to society. In addition, the supportive contribution of grandparents and great-grandparents to the survival chances of offspring may mean that nature wants to keep them going rather than polish them off.

We can't assume that we exist in an evolutionary system that is only governed by the so-called 'selfish gene'. Our genes may be selfish (according to Richard Dawkins) but as a species, we are not. And while selflessness is not unique to humans, characteristics such as cooperation, empathy, the passing on of wisdom and the herd instinct are arguably the hallmarks of humanity. Such characteristics benefit the whole community, and as such seem to be positive heritable traits.

Ageing as an immune response

As the preceding paragraphs have illustrated, the body responds to cellular mistakes or invading pathogens by mounting a highly energy-intensive immune response. Special cells need to be manufactured and then sent out to kill off damaged cells or neutralise invading pathogens which may carry germs and disease. At the same time the body starts to manufacture new, correct cells to replace the faulty ones and to secrete hormones that are needed to detect and deliver the appropriate signals. If the body is under attack from any form of disease or stress, higher quantities of nutrients and energy are required to mount the defence. An immune response can double or even triple our daily calorie requirement, which is why we often feel desperately tired and groggy when we are sick.

Instinctively we take more rest at such times so that the body can focus its energy on getting better.

While the immune response is well-known for its ability to fight viruses, tumours and other diseases, what is less well-known is its role in dealing with general wear and tear. Cellular repair is needed more and more as we age but, over-use of the immune response can cause a dysregulation resulting in inflammation.

We are all familiar with the type of irritation we get when we are bitten by a mosquito. The bite can easily become inflamed and itchy and sometimes forms a scab. The puss which causes such discomfort is in fact a sign that macrophage cells are working well, dispatched by the immune system to flood the bite and clear away the toxin. Thinking about the pain and general unpleasantness of a simple cut or insect bite can explain the effect of a heightened immune response in other parts of the body. As we age, inflammation can become more and more noticeable, causing muscle ache, joint stiffness and conditions such as arthritis and even dementia.

Recent research has suggested that relatively benign viruses we shake off in adulthood can cause problems later, when the immune system ceases to work so efficiently or when we are under stress. One case in point is the Human Simplex Virus (HSV) One and Two, which causes herpes.[7] We have known for some years that during relatively benign youthful infections this virus can enter the brain and lie dormant only to re-emerge in later life as the immune system starts to change. In a vain attempt to clear the infection, the immune system will form sticky substances not dissimilar to the puss we find in a pimple. Within the brain these substances are called *amyloids* and can start to interfere with normal tissue, disrupting the effective functioning of brain cells. Amyloids and tau (another type of abnormal brain protein) are closely correlated with Alzheimer's disease.

A major study funded by the US National Institute of Ageing at Columbia University is trailing the anti-viral drug Valacyclovir on the assumption that if you clear the virus, you clear the build-up of amyloids, although other companies are finding drugs that ignore the virus and simply clear the amyloids.[8] For example, in 2023 Eli Lilley reported very good results in Phase 3, human trials of the drug Donanemab, which can clear amyloid and perhaps halt the symptoms of Alzheimer's. Will prevention or cure work best for dementia?

Neither arthritis nor Alzheimer's are exclusively conditions of old age. Similarly, at any age the immune response may go into overdrive, causing fevers, tumours and infections like sepsis. Conversely the immune system can give up the ghost altogether, leaving us vulnerable to infections, disorders and diseases. But it seems that our bodies start to react more and more to these sorts of niggles, sometimes exaggerating rather than ameliorating the symptoms.

Imbalance in the immune response is symptomatic of the body's progressive inability to re-set itself after disease or injury. It is, to some extent, related to age, but it is much more related to our state of health. Some 20-year-olds have the immune system of an average octogenarian; some octogenarians don't have any problems with their immune systems at all, being able to shake off illness or injury as well an anyone. The oldest documented person to survive Covid was Sister Andre (Lucile Randon), a French nun who was 116 at the time and living in a care home in Toulon. Several of her fellow residents became infected – some died – but she had the natural immune resistance to shake off the illness, living two more years to become the world's oldest person for a time until she died in 2023.

The Fortingall Yew in Perthshire is the oldest tree in the British Isles, and is thought to be between 2,000 and 3,000 years old. We humans are built with the 'belt and braces' biology beloved of nature and inherent in cellular structure, so we can survive all sorts of assaults. We have two arms, two feet, two ears, two lungs – so if one fails, we can still breathe and get about. Brain damage in one place can be restored in another. We are omnivorous, resourceful and optimistic. The trade-off for that complexity is that we can't live for a few thousand years, like the Yew tree, or re-grow a limb, like the salamander does.

We may not be the oldest living things in creation, but our cells have extraordinary robustness and longevity. Some of the oldest animal cells on the planet exist inside the skull of a super-centenarian. Brain cells last a lifetime, endowing us with long memories, giving us time to think, to learn from one another's mistakes and to pass that wisdom on to the next generation. Inherited knowledge, which has nothing to do with DNA, has helped us develop a highly attuned sense of empathy, showing us that we can work for the good of others instead of just helping ourselves. That in turn means that our species benefits from older generations and supports the wholly positive theory that ageing well is an evolutionary bonus.

Prevention is better than cure

Healthy ageing relates to how much you look after yourself, how robust your genetics are and how the world, and your environment, looks after you. Set-backs can be reversed, the body goes on repairing and replacing cells right up to the moment that you take your final breath. Even at a venerable age we can recover from illness or injury, but in order to do so we need to consider building up a resistance to illness and preventing injury.

Is building up resistance simply a function of good diet and plenty of exercise? Will an apple a day really keep the doctor away?

For too long we have considered many diseases associated with old age to be self-inflicted. We have taken the rather rigid view that we bring disease on ourselves. Your GP will use the term 'lifestyle change', which implies it is all our own faults. But that is far from the truth.

For example, a recent survey of chronic obstructive pulmonary disease (COPD) observed that it has long been thought of as a disease that occurs in adult cigarette smokers. However, the review goes on to state that genetics and life course events can also cause, exacerbate or predispose individuals to the condition. The evidence actually shows that indoor and outdoor air pollution, occupational exposures and use of e-cigarettes and cannabis also causes COPD. It can just as likely be caused by impaired lung development during early life, by infections or asthma, and exacerbated by tuberculosis and HIV, particularly in low and middle-income countries where treatments are scarce.[9]

Like many diseases, and certainly like the 'disease' we call ageing, the causes can be complex. But we know that preventative medicine works. It isn't as widespread in the NHS as it should be, perhaps because it is difficult to persuade vulnerable groups to take part. Preventative medicine can exaggerate the divide between the educated and the naïve, and between rich and poor. We know that economical procedures like screening programmes and taking cholesterol-lowering drugs can save lives, but at the moment it's a self-selecting option. You have to decide whether you want to do the screening or take the drugs, and then whether you want to take advantage of diet or exercise programmes, smoking cessation prescriptions and addiction services.

Yet, regardless of the offer at your local surgery, preventative medicine is something we can all practice, whatever your doctor, government, friends or the internet may or may not be advising. When it's our own bodies at stake, it's worth taking control.

One of the people who changed our thinking about preventative medicine was the scientist Ancel Keys. He knew only too well, even as a young man, that he was a lucky survivor. When he was born in the US in 1904 childhood was still the most dangerous stage of life. Official figures in his hometown of San Francisco, just starting to be collected at the time, revealed that one in eight babies were destined to die before they reached their first birthday. If you were poor, you stood an even lower chance.

One of these vulnerable babies was the infant Keys. In 1906 Ancel (a name which means fortunate) was living in downtown San Francisco, the son of impoverished teenage parents. Given the odds at the time he was lucky to even reach his second birthday. Disease, malnutrition and the trauma of birth itself would have taken many of his contemporaries.

At 5.12am on the morning of 18th April 1906, Ancel's cradle was rocked by a far more violent force than usual – an earthquake. What his frightened parents would not have known is that they were living within a mile of the epicentre of what was to be one of the world's most devastating earthquakes. Three thousand people died and four-fifths of the city of San Francisco was destroyed. The post-quake horror was as terrible as the tremor itself. In their zeal to make the streets safe once more,

Ancel Keys 1961.

97

officials requisitioned damaged buildings and blew them up, shattering the gas mains and triggering yet more explosions and deaths. Fires raged for three days, depriving residents of their belongings, their shelter and their livelihoods. Baby Ancel would have heard the fire engines and perhaps seen the flames of the inferno that followed the quake. He would have heard the frightening roar as buildings that survived were dynamited and sensed the fear of his parents in the mayhem that followed.

Human empathy and community action saved the city. Extraordinarily, people from surrounding states immediately rallied to help. The homeless were fed from soup kitchens that had been hastily organised and stocked. That nourishing soup would have saved countless lives, possibly even young Ancel's life. In adulthood Ancel Keys would refer to that time in his childhood, telling people about his lucky escape and how his family survived the aftermath.

Keys turned out to be as fortunate as his given name anticipated and we, as the beneficiaries of his work, have been fortunate as well. He grew up to become one of the twentieth century's most respected nutritional scientists. Whatever his parents told him about the food dispensed after the San Francisco earthquake convinced him that a healthy diet can make all the difference. He believed in that old saying about food being the best medicine, observing that a healthy lifestyle helps to protect against illness.

In his lifetime, Keys founded not one, but three ground-breaking avenues of research. His work on diet and metabolism was forged during World War Two and perfected after the war. The way we eat today, many aspects of our health culture and the way doctors assess our eligibility for treatment are all inextricably linked to Keys' work. Using Quetelet's constant, which he re-named as the body mass index (BMI), he popularised an assessment system to map out healthy norms.

He pioneered research into diets, both the healthy and the unhealthy, and showed us why the post-war American diet of processed foods and TV dinners was so dangerous. He investigated the Mediterranean diet, which is still the basis for healthy dietary advice today.

Keys' early career was unusual. After a succession of unsatisfying jobs in his twenties, he eventually applied himself to a career of scientific research. He turned down a prestigious job at Cambridge, Massachusetts to found the Laboratory of Physiological Hygiene at the University of Minnesota, an institution that lacked prestige, but allowed him to have complete control over his work.

In the 1940s news of the shortages suffered by those caught up in WWII reached the US. Newspaper images of emaciated refugees amongst the wreckage of bombed-out cities were shockingly reminiscent of pictures of San Francisco after the earthquake. In 1944 Keys commenced a study on starvation. This experiment, conducted to assess how concentration camp survivors might be coaxed back to health, was so audacious that it has never been repeated. Ethical considerations would certainly not allow such extreme research today, even on the fully informed, healthy young volunteer pacifists who made up his study group.

The men were provided with an under-powered diet of bread, gruel and vegetable broths, similar to that which concentration camp inmates were given. Under starvation the men started to hallucinate, to become depressed and aggressive, and in some cases to begin self-harming. Keys saw first-hand how a poor diet can affect the brain as well as the body.

After a while the men could think of nothing but food. They became listless, as their energy dwindled, and fights would break out over a crust of bread or half an onion. Some became fascinated with food, cutting out recipes from magazines and replacing their Marylin Monroe pin-ups with pictures of T-bone steaks and cheesecake of quite a different kind. Even while they were still on minimum rations some of the men honed their appreciation of fine foods. They started to be able to distinguish between good food and bad; between a mere subsistence diet and the pleasures of haute cuisine. After the war, several became professional chefs. At the end of the starvation diet, Keys re-introduced healthy food and showed how the men could be brought back to good health. However, for some that were less psychologically robust, the experience was permanently scarring.

The Minnesota Starvation Study confirmed the dangers of the sort of fad diets that had become fashionable in the 1930s.[10] The Hollywood Grapefruit diet was just one of the tortures that people would put themselves through. Unfortunately, after the war quacks continued to suggest everything from cabbage soup diets, cookie diets, to high fat diets, using scant science to justify their methods. Although some people thought that Keys' starvation study was unethical – and it certainly would not be allowed today – the project pioneered an effective treatment for malnutrition and continues to save lives. Those young medics who finally liberated the concentration camps used Keys' knowledge to save lives; it made him famous among scientists, if still unknown outside the medical world.*

Keys' wartime research had also delivered to his Minnesota institute a flood of prestigious funding. He had the luxury of choosing how, where and what he wanted to study. He decided to go back to a place he loved – southern Italy – where in the early 1950s he had gone to investigate the diet of Neapolitan workers because a colleague had claimed they never had heart attacks. His hunch was that dietary habits might influence our

---

* One of those young medics was my late father-in-law, the haematologist Professor David Robertson Smith.

chances of a longer life. This trip eventually became his most influential survey, the Seven Countries Study, that compared diets and cardio vascular disease rates in the US, Finland, the Netherlands, Yugoslavia, Italy, Greece and Japan. [11]

The scale of the survey, the sheer number of subjects involved and the length of time over which he observed them, made his findings statistically very significant and potentially devastating to processed food producers. Keys showed that a Mediterranean diet, high in fish, fibre and fresh produce, but low in saturated fats, corresponded with far lower death rates from cardiovascular disease. The heart disease risk for US men turned out to be ten times greater than that of their Mediterranean brothers.

Since then, there has been fierce debate regarding which part of the Mediterranean diet was responsible for that difference. There may also have been other financial and lifestyle effects which Keys' research did not consider. He was criticised for laying the bulk of the blame on saturated fats, though if you read his work, he makes it very clear that he considered the totality of a Mediterranean diet, together with the lifestyle, to be important.* In recent years some celebrity health pundits, wishing to push their own theses, have even questioned the statistical basis of the research.

Because of Keys' work, everybody in the UK today will have their cholesterol levels routinely monitored in a blood test. If the result comes back too high, especially if you are over fifty, have ever puffed a cigarette or suffer from high blood pressure, you will be offered statins. Cholesterol is a type of lipid, or fat that is found in round nodules of lipoprotein in

---

* The typical Mediterranean diet is low fat, low sugar, low in red meat, high in fibre, with a focus on a varied range of fresh produce and fish. Typical Mediterranean people in the 50s did not own cars, walked or rode donkeys and worked in manual jobs such as agriculture or fisheries. See Chapter 5.

the blood stream. This type of fat is made naturally in the body by the liver, but it is also available in various 'fatty' foods. Cholesterol can be divided into low- and high-density lipids (LDL and HDL). The balance between the two is important for health.

Ancel Keys concluded that it was a surfeit of cholesterol that was quite literally clogging up the arteries of American males, leading to a very high rate of heart attacks and strokes. His advice, was to change to a Mediterranean diet and exercise more. These days, we are often tempted to ignore that advice and instead take hyperlipidaemia drugs that lower cholesterol levels. The global market for these drugs was forecast to reach US$22.6 billion by 2022.

These preventative drugs treat a cause; they don't treat the disease, they simply reduce the risk of getting the disease in the first place. Naturally people have varying levels of cholesterol in their bloodstreams, but we are all advised to take them if our blood cholesterol levels are above average. On a global scale these low-cost preventative medicines work well. Furthermore, if your BMI is over $25kg/m^2$ or under $18.5kg/m^2$ (subject to ethnicity) your doctor will suggest you improve your exercise and diet. It is most likely that the GP will recommend what is now termed the Modified Mediterranean Diet.[12] Modern studies show that statins work well, but lifestyle changes can reduce the risk of other diseases and conditions at the same time.

After the war America was seen as a land of opportunity. Reconstruction fuelled the economy, giving people jobs and purpose. Superior technology, like radar and the jet engine, were seen as deciding factors that had helped to win the war. People thought that technology could win the peace as well. During the late forties and fifties food, particularly in America, began to change radically. Cooking became 'food technology' and fresh produce gave way to processed, factory packaged concoctions. While undernourishment was the concern of the depression and wartime, excess became the challenge of peacetime. In 1961 Keys announced to the world that the US was experiencing a new disease – an obesity epidemic – which was a far more malevolent and manmade crisis. His Seven Countries Study made the cover of Time Magazine, whose pages reported Keys' assertion that the most common form of malnutrition in the US at that time was caloric excess. [13]

By that time, 48 million American citizens were overweight. Keys, by now a respected scientist in the eyes of the public, realised that it was not simple excess that was fuelling the epidemic. Refrigeration, automated processes and packaging aimed at reducing waste was actually starting to reduce nutritional content at the expense of added fat and sugar fillers.

America invented the TV dinner

The processed diet was born on a wave of press hype and Maddison Avenue advertising. Modern favourites such as TV dinners, long-life baking and over-sweetened confectionary might have looked like the stuff that mothers used to make, but they were far from the real thing.

Food manufacturers soon learned the taste benefits of adding shelf-life extenders such as sugar and salt. Sales, as well as profits, could swell by increasing these ingredients, enhancing the flavour and pumping up the portion size. Cheap fats, sugar substitutes such as corn syrup, emulsifiers, artificial flavourings and colourings all went into the mix. It made for low-cost, luridly attractive food that lasted well on the supermarket shelf, or in the Frigidaire – a device that every American home suddenly possessed.

Keys foresaw that this new food might not be as healthy as the real thing. He had proved that the Mediterranean diet might just have the edge on Coca-Cola, Big Macs and Krispy Kremes.

At the time, Keys would counter any criticism by retorting that his studies drew on evidence from thousands of cases. In epidemiological studies like those in Keys' work, the force of numbers helps prove the hypothesis. Today, studies can recruit hundreds of thousands of virtual subjects, gleaned from digital health records. We can use Mendelian randomisation, cheap and simple DNA testing, to even out genetic differences between study populations. Because the basic measures we use such as weight, blood lipid levels and blood glucose levels are universal (all down to Keys), we can now compare many studies. If we find agreement across many different types of populations, and many different locations, we can be pretty sure it counts as important evidence. I have no doubt that Keys research has proven valid.

But any study, however grand, is only evidence for the time being. The complexity of the topic should not stop us from refining our understanding. The answers are never simple, and one thing is sure to remain true, however much we learn: there is no 'silver bullet' treatment that will keep us young and healthy.

Keys practiced what he preached. He and his wife ate home-made Italian food most of the time and published hundreds of healthy recipes. They exercised every day and watched their weight. They spent their later years in the southern Italian fishing village of Pioppi, where they ran an institute and summer school. Ancel lived to the age of 100, working and remaining physically active well into his late nineties.

A cyclist friend visited Pioppi recently and remarked on its elevation. Perhaps in the end it wasn't just the Mediterranean diet that gave Keys and his wife an unusually long lease of life, but all those healthy hills as well.

Prevention is definitely about protecting ourselves by making what healthcare advisors call 'lifestyle changes'. Ancel Keys looked solely at heart disease, but it would be counterproductive to spend much time worrying what our own weaknesses might be. Since Keys' work was published, we have discovered that diet and exercise influence many more conditions than just heart disease. We are now aware that adopting the healthy lifestyle measures he pioneered protect us against many non-communicable diseases such as cancer, metabolic syndrome and even premature ageing. By boosting our immunity, the same measures can also help protect us when we catch communicable diseases such as Covid and can even help protect us against mental health crises, including the much-feared dementia.

In a way we've come full circle and ended up back at the beginning of medical philosophy, thinking as the Greek writer Galen did; some aspects of ageing are diseases, that we now associate as much with lifestyle and environment as we do with birthdays. Diseases can be cured, or their progress can be slowed down. For example, diabetes type 2, once thought of an incurable symptom of ageing, is now considered a disease that can be treated, beaten into remission and even cured.

So perhaps we can define ageing by knowing what it is not:

- Ageing is not pre-programmed;
- Ageing is not the same as getting older;
- Ageing is not a linear process of decline – it can be slowed down and even reversed;
- Ageing isn't completely out of our control.

Gerontologists are more persuaded than ever that our bodies are built to last. Everything is designed for sustainability; we are not a throw-away species. Seen from this perspective, ageing doesn't seem so bad.

The first signs of ageing do not spell disaster for the whole body. It is simply an indication that the body is automatically diverting energy from the cosmetic to the important bits. In other words, the system is working! We have the ability and, perhaps, a duty to assist this process by looking after ourselves, and each other.

Endnotes

1   Zhang WB & Milman S, (2022) *Looking at IGF-1 through the hourglass.* Aging
     (Albany NY). 2022 Aug 25;14(16):6379-6380. DOI: 10.18632/aging.204257.
     E-published 2022 Aug 25
2   Kirkwood, Tom, (1977) *The Evolution of Ageing,* Nature 270, 301–304 (1977).
     DOI: 10.1038/270301a0
     Tom Kirkwood's paper, published in Nature in 1977, is now very difficult to find
     for free because it was published pre-internet. Wellcome Medical History Library
     in Euston Road London can show you a copy
3   Kaye, WH et al. (2002) *Anxiolytic Effects of Acute Tryptophan Depletion in
     Anorexia Nervosa* Published online in Wiley InterScience (www.interscience.
     wiley.com). DOI: 10.1002/eat.10135 [retrieved July 2021]
4   Mace JL, et al. (2011) *The effects of acute tryptophan depletion on neuropsychological
     function, mood and movement in the healthy elderly.* J Psychopharmacology. 2011
     Oct;25(10):1337-43. DOI: 10.1177/0269881110389094. E-published 2011 Jan 24
5   Lentner (1981) *Geigy Scientific Tables: Units of measurement, body fluids,
     composition of the body, nutrition.* Book, Ciba-Geigy, Publisher 1981- Biological
     products ISBN0914168541
6   Commonwealth of Australia, (2006) *Nutrient Reference Values for Australia and
     New Zealand Including Recommended Dietary Intakes.* Endorsed by NHMRC
     September 2005; at nhmrc.gov.au [Retrieved June 2018]
7   ClinicalTrials.gov NCT 03282916 Phase II trial in progress
8   Eli Lilley Press Release. (2023) *Results of Lillys landmark phase 3 trial Donanemab
     presented.* https://investor.lilly.com/news-releases/news-release-details/results-
     lillys-landmark-phase-3-trial-donanemab-presented
9   Brusselle GG & Humbert M, (2022) *Classification of COPD: fostering prevention
     and precision medicine in the Lancet Commission on COPD.* Lancet; Published
     Online September 5, 2022 DOI:10.1016/ S0140-6736(22)01660-9
10   Keys, A et al. (1950). *The Biology of Human Starvation.* St. Paul, Minnesota: Book,
     Published by University of Minnesota Press, MINNE edition. ISBN 978-0-8166-
     7234-9
11   thesevencountriesstudy.com [retrieved April 2023]
12   Trichopoulou A, et al. (2005) *Modified Mediterranean diet and survival: EPIC-
     elderly prospective cohort study.* BMJ. 2005 Apr 30;330(7498):991. DOI: 10.1136/
     bmj.38415.644155.8F. E-published 2005 Apr 8
13   Editorial (1961) *Medicine: The Fat of the Land,* Time Magazine, Friday, Jan 13,
     1961

4

The rhythm of life

The Rhythm of Life is a powerful beat,
Puts a tingle in your fingers and a tingle in your feet,
Rhythm in your bedroom,
Rhythm in the street,
Yes, The Rhythm of Life is a powerful beat... *

Imagine sitting by a country river on a summer's day. The sun is shining and fluffy white clouds amble across a pale blue sky. Beside the river, pastures grow luxuriantly. Cows graze in wildflower meadows amongst tufts of white and purple and pink. Insects buzz while going about their business. Birds dive for midges above the river's tranquil margins. Below you can just make out the glimmer of a trout, her mouth opening and closing as she samples the clear water. Ancient oaks punctuate hedgerows in full leaf. White umbels of cow parsley fringe a winding trackway. A hare runs out, glances around and then lollops back across the field.

What your mind's eye is observing is an idyllic vision of life. The movement, the growth, the flow are all defined by the word life and they are all ruled by a cellular process we call *metabolism*. We are all

---

* From the musical *Sweet Charity*, 1966. Lyrics: Dorothy Fields. Music: Cy Coleman.

living things – plants and animals – operating in a natural and abundant environment. The classical definition of life encompasses performance and reproduction. Biological performance, or activity, requires continuously varying supplies of energy. A lot of my research has revolved around discovering how we garner energy, how age influences our vitality and whether we can do anything about it. A closer understanding of how our metabolism works and how we can re-energise ourselves becomes more and more important in later life.

The bar we should set for ourselves is a high one. This ambition, not simply for longevity but for enduring vitality, may be new to many readers. We all know that the heart beats, that we breathe, eat, sleep, think and move. But we also know that a satisfying life is a whole lot more than that. Living should not be defined by the mere absence of disease, but by vitality, *joie de vivre* and by the prolongation of healthspan rather than lifespan. In order to attain a long and happy life, we need to understand what brings everything together. One of the most important factors is energy; where it comes from, how the body uses it and how it is regulated.

Solar power

On Earth, solar radiation is the only original source of energy we possess. But sunshine is erratic and unpredictable. The very existence of any plant or animal depends upon the ability to store and manage energy and to adapt to whatever energy may be available at any time. This biological process of energy-generation and expenditure is called the metabolism, and it is metabolism that supports the healthy rhythm of a life. If the body can manage our energy requirements well and can ration and balance energy needs, we will not suffer the negative effects of ageing so much. Energy translates into high levels of immunity and resilience, including strong muscles, heart and lungs, and an alert mind.

Every scintilla of energy we use to power our bodies has originally emanated from the sun. The diagram below shows how *photosynthesis,* or the absorption of solar energy, is the way plants gather energy and convert it into glucose in order to grow larger and more luxuriantly. By contrast, as animals breathe their cells *respire,* generating *metabolic* energy from *glucose* gleaned from their diet.

The twin actions of photosynthesis and respiration are worth a moment's attention. The first thing you might notice in the diagram is

 SOLAR ENERGY

Photosynthesis: $6CO_2 + 6H_2O \rightarrow C_6H_{12}O_6 + 6O$

Solar Energy + carbon dioxide + water → glucose + oxygen

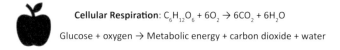

Cellular Respiration: $C_6H_{12}O_6 + 6O_2 \rightarrow 6CO_2 + 6H_2O$

Glucose + oxygen → Metabolic energy + carbon dioxide + water

 METABOLIC ENERGY

Respiration and photosynthesis: the energy merry-go-round.

that the chemical formulae for both processes contain three elements: Carbon (C), Hydrogen (H) and Oxygen(O). You can see by looking at the formulae how important carbon is to our metabolism. Our tissue contains high proportions of carbon, as does the food we eat. People often look at these formulae and conclude that to gain energy we must eat sugar or carbohydrate, a molecule that is high in carbon. But in fact, carbon is just as present in fats and proteins. Cellulose, the scaffolding of plants, and DNA owe their basic structure to the way that other elements and molecules can easily bind to carbon's four free electrons in the atom's outer shell and, once bonded, remain strongly engaged.

Earth is one of the few locations in the universe where oxygen exists on its own. In most situations the attraction between the four free electrons in a carbon atom will be too strong and carbon dioxide becomes the common atmospheric gas.* But photosynthesis of plants use energy from the sun to break down carbon dioxide to form carbon-rich plant material. Oxygen is superfluous to the process and, over the millennia, its presence has risen from almost zero in Earth's atmosphere to its current composition. Air contains about 21 % pure oxygen and it is that oxygen that keeps us alive. The scientific assumption is that a planet without oxygen is a planet without life.

---

* A carbon atom is extremely stable at ambient temperature, and thus forms the backbone of many beneficial and life-giving, as well as toxic, compounds. It has four available (covalent) bonds, which means it can attach to itself to form long molecular chains, while still pulling other atoms towards it. Sugars, fats, some vitamins and alcohol molecules also contain bonds with oxygen (two bonds) and hydrogen (one bond). In organic chemistry carbon is often found in molecules containing nitrogen, sulphur and phosphorus, where it can form antibiotics, amino-acids (the building blocks of protein) and DNA. Carbon also forms the basis of hydrocarbon fuels, such as oil and the universal cellular 'fuel' adenosine triphosphate ATP, to be explained later in this chapter.

Plant photosynthesis is a chemical reaction that forms molecules of carbohydrate, combining carbon, hydrogen and oxygen to manufacture strong plant growth and thus provide nutritious food for animals. One of the reasons fruit and vegetables taste so good is because of their stable carbohydrate, i.e. their carbon (C) + water (H_2O) structure, which provides a sweet taste and a satisfying bite. Pollinators are not attracted to flowers because they need the pollen; that is incidental. Bees and insects brush against stamens, picking up pollen on their way to get at the carbohydrate-rich nectar deep within the floral axis.

Animal respiration, or breathing oxygen, gives animals several advantages over plants. Our energy input is not controlled by daylight, but by breathing in oxygen and grazing. Thus, our energy can be stored for long periods of time. Animal cells possess the ability to generate vast amounts of energy in a process called respiration. Respiration is another miraculous, but simple chemical reaction that goes in the opposite direction to photosynthesis. The twin processes of photosynthesis and respiration form a neat balancing act where nothing goes to waste. Animals breathe oxygen-rich air that plants have exuded, they drink water and eat carbon-rich food. This releases the plant energy that was once captured from the sun's rays during photosynthesis. The bi-product is carbon dioxide, which animals breathe out, and is then once again available to plants to start photosynthesis. Carbon dioxide gives plants a spurt of vitality, just as deep breathing does to humans. We love to be beside the seaside, because ozone (O^3), a super-rich oxygen gas occurs naturally in sea air. Simply pump carbon dioxide into a sealed greenhouse for a week or two and you will observe the plants shooting up like giants. It's a secret all Chelsea Show gardeners know. Medics know that if you pump extra oxygen into a ventilator the patient will revive. Mario Puzo's novel, *Fools Die*, suggested that Las Vegas casinos pump oxygen into the rooms, to keep people awake and gambling for longer. Though it might work, it is an urban myth and would constitute a serious fire hazard. The oxygen we breathe in – day in, day out – is in fact highly combustible.

All living cells, whether animal or vegetable, are subject to exactly the same chemical, physical and biological laws. The trillions of cells within the human body have each inherited their energy-producing mechanisms from the first life on earth. Their similarities help them work together, as clusters that grow, act and react interdependently as well as independently. Alongside energy development for growth there sits a defensive operation, protecting cells from negative influences such as toxins and pathogens and clearing away damaged or dead cells, replacing and renewing individual cells and sometimes whole systems. Humans possess a complex system of hormonal sensors, nerve responders and electro-chemical conductors that stimulate our conscious actions while performing millions of unconscious functions. All this activity is regulated by metabolism, a sort of 'volume control' on activity.

Inside the human cell

In the last chapter we looked at how the body can be considered as a group of cells, and how cell replication and repair is an important aspect of maintaining health and youthfulness. In this chapter we are going to look inside the cell to discover where the energy for life originates.

Our metabolic heath is an important clue to longevity, helping us understand why some people age far better than others. *Homeostasis* is the process that regulates our metabolism. It is the energy balancing-act, regulating energy all day, every day. It is what the Chinese call the ying and the yang.

There are examples of this type of energy balance everywhere in nature. If left to its own devices any stretch of wild countryside will create a flourishing, balanced ecosystem. Whether we observe an entire region, a single plant, a flock of birds or a well-trained athlete working at peak performance, they all develop a level of energy sustainability. It is as vital to the continuation of life as the balance of payments is to our economy.

Homeostasis is an internal cellular process, but human cells don't work alone and don't exist in isolation. Responding to our environment is part of the cellular equation, balancing the ebb and flow of abundance and scarcity. Change and adaptation is as much an integral part of a successful life as stability and conservation of energy. A successful ecosystem or a healthy individual body must be able to adapt to new situations and re-stabilise.

The biggest life-change of all is procreation. It expends vast quantities of energy but childhood growth, puberty, recovery from illness and intellectual maturity all expend high levels of energy as well. If you are escaping from a wild animal or working for a PhD, energy is required, either in short bursts for running away or more prolonged stints for problem-solving. We are all aware that we need energy to grow, but we sometimes forget that we also require energy in the form of vitality to innovate, to garner the resilience to fight disease and retain reserves to adapt to different circumstances. Something we don't always appreciate when we plan for old age is that adaptations become harder to deal with, not because we can't appreciate them intellectually, but because we may not have the energy to address them. Major life changes, such as retirement, bereavement, winning the pools or moving house all require energy and resilience. A healthy metabolism, something that happens on a multitudinous but minuscule scale inside every active cell in the body, is therefore key to maintaining energy resources and to nurturing enough resilience to enable us to deal with whatever life throws at us. Our current dilemmas regarding worldwide energy resources highlight how important sustainability is to each of us, on many levels. Nature has found its own way to remain sustainable. Climate scientists, politicians and urban designers all talk about resilience, and clinicians use exactly the same word. Resilience means elasticity, the ability to get back into shape after some form of stress. Human resilience means the ability to recover easily and quickly from illness or hardship, but also from exertion or a period of intensive work. It is a physical and intellectual issue as well as a resource one. At the root of human resilience is a healthy metabolism.

Fortunately, our bodies and our psyche are made to bounce back. All living things possess this ability. We are successful as a species because we are particularly flexible and adept. Homo sapiens are uniquely favoured in having higher levels of consciousness than other animals. We are rather good at learning from experience and planning for the future. Like squirrels, we store things up for rainy days; like puppies, we play and jump and run to exercise our growing limbs; and like all great apes, we will go to great lengths to seek out the choicest fruits of the forest. We have ingenuity, foresight and a prodigious memory. For humans, resilience is an amalgam of thinking ahead, keeping fit and attending to any issues promptly. Yet we don't need to do it on our own. Health requires a daily, even moment-by-moment vigilance. Our bodies need to be stoked up with healthy foods to fuel the chemical processes that run the system and we need to keep moving to aid digestion, repair tissue and gain strength. Oxygen provides the propellant that generates the energy we need to move our limbs, to keep the heart beating and our minds sharp. The brain requires a constant supply of oxygen and glucose *every second of the day* to maintain our consciousness.

Every time we choose to socialise, to go outside, make ourselves a cup of tea or do the crossword, we are exercising our metabolism. For example, if we choose to walk instead of drive, we can improve our physical strength (as well as reduce pollution and lighten the planet's carbon dioxide load). When we are on the move, even at quite low speeds, our metabolisms will be running at a more efficient level, exercising our mind and our body, making ourselves more open to social interaction and becoming more curious about the world around us. We will be building up our own resilience.

Overall, people who possess a healthy metabolism feel and look younger. They are more energetic and brighter. They have a greater chance of living a longer and a healthier life. A healthy metabolism is worth striving for.

Getting going

Food provides us with the energy we need to live, as well as almost all the nutrients we need to keep our body in good working order. The energy we receive from food represents the supply side of the homeostasis equation; the flip-side is balanced by activity. It isn't simply an equal balance between 'energy in' and 'energy out'. Activity increases the efficacy of the input side as well. Our metabolism is re-booted by bouts of exercise, as long as they are interspersed with relaxation and refeeding. Our motivation, our mood, what makes us get up in the morning, and our sense of satisfaction as well as the quality of our sleep all contribute to and are regulated by our metabolism.[1] It all happens right inside our cells – not in our brains. This is why we have little control over our appetites for energy and our need for relaxation.

If we wish to give ourselves a fighting chance to get things back on track, we should stop thinking about fad diets and gym fees and instead consider the far broader question of metabolic balance, which is another kind of work/life balance. The work some people do in hitting the exercise machines, or starving themselves in order to reach physical perfection, misses the point. Metabolism requires whole body maintenance; energy in – energy out; mental as well as physical.

In a healthy person our cells are able to flip between slow and fast metabolisms in seconds. Normal changes in activity such as walking and sitting, eating and sleeping all require very different metabolic states. If the 'on-off switch' within each cell is not working properly then our bodies go into a progressive decline. Diseases such as diabetes type 2 are known as metabolic diseases because they are always associated with changes in energy balance and a modification of metabolic rates. But this loss of vitality isn't a one-way street called ageing. More and more studies are showing us that a healthy metabolism can be regained, and that lifestyle changes can rekindle vitality.

Mitochondria

Energy is generated within the plant or the animal cell by special *organelles* called mitochondria. The scale is so small that cellular biologists are still not really able to see what is going on inside these minuscule cells, within cells. Instead, they find out by observing the product of tiny electro-chemical reactions and by using computer models to replicate them.

Our ability to see inside the cell is new and can be as exciting and tantalizing as space exploration. Since 1953, when George Palade published the first electron microscope images of the mitochondria, the race was on to understand these little worm-shaped beasts that have so much impact on our lives.[2]

It wasn't until the 1970s that scientists unlocked the secrets of mitochondria and their production of energy. And it is only since the noughties, that we have been able to join up all the dots with regard to their function as 'nature's power-houses' and begun to realise the full contribution of the mitochondria.[3]

Bio-power stations

Plants require daylight to make sugar, which is then transported to the plant mitochondria to re-generate that solar energy. Animals have the ability to store glucose, the principal nutrient that produces energy and can thus manufacture energy at any time, simply by breathing in and out. Within the mitochondria this process of *oxidative phosphorylation*, dubbed OxPhos by bio-scientists, means that animals can regulate their own energy use without any immediate external energy input. All we need to create a spurt of energy is to breathe in a little harder. We are neither rooted to the ground in order to absorb nutrients, nor trained to face the sun to absorb light energy. It means we can move about. Making the decisions about where and why to move has arguably made us both more adaptable and more insightful.

Mitochondrial organelles in humans have a marvellous symbiotic relationship with their host cells. The host absorbs fuel and oxygen from the blood stream and delivers it to the mitochondrion, which manufactures energy to donate to the cell so it can fulfil its function. In some cells mitochondria float free. In muscles, mitochondria cluster, tightly packed amongst tensing muscle fibres to provide the intense burst of energy required to move our limbs. In sperm, mitochondria form strings which encase the swimming tail to provide the jet propulsion required to reach and fertilise the egg. Some cells have few mitochondria. Heart and liver cells, which are working all the time, have a huge number. The actual work of generating the energy is done by elegant microscopic atomic turbines that populate inner walls of the mitochondria, ramping up electrical capacity each time they rotate.

Mitochondria use a raw material derived from glucose and oxygen called pyruvate, which in turn is *metabolised* to form *adenosine triphosphate* (ATP), a molecule that is easily used by all cells as a source of chemical energy. Hundreds and thousands of these energy pumps in each mitochondrion work constantly, together generating enough energy to power the mind of the genius and the exertions of the athlete.

Mitochondria are so small that electron microscope images of them are rather disappointing. You can't see anything happening. Even 3D animations of a whole mitochondrion make them look like fat worms, or floating sea cucumbers. All the excitement goes on inside their cellular casing. The real magic occurs at the atomic level.*

Since the 1970s studies of mitochondria took a nose-dive. The intense efforts to establish how energy was produced clouded our appreciation of all the other things that mitochondria actually do. If mitochondria were mere biological power-stations, then once the biochemical reactions had been unravelled, there was nothing more to discover. The clue that they might do more than facilitate OxPhos came via the curious collection of proteins that are within the mitochondrion. This organelle is unique in possessing its own store of mitochondrial DNA (mtDNA), which is inherited solely from the mother. Unravelling this DNA shows protein-coding genes that have absolutely no role in producing energy. What are they doing there?

Metabolism and longevity

In the human body, homeostasis, the balancing of energy input to energy output, helps to divert energy to different parts of the body. Certain

---

* If you are interested there are some delightful animations that show how the whole thing works. Look up the 'Electron Transport Chain' video by *BioVisions at Harvard University* on YouTube

parts of our bodies, not least our brains and vital organs, must remain ticking over the whole time. Our bodies must also maintain a functioning immune response, attending to cell damage and infection. Homeostasis balances this ever-present energy need with the equally important, and sometimes very high, energy requirements of activity; working, sensing, and responding to dangers and stresses. The surplus energy that these microscopic organelles generate for us give us the strength to do much more than simply run our bodies. Humans have the surplus energy to think and to plan, to spend time creating a better environment and addressing challenges in the world. Very few, if any other creatures look outside their own environmental bubble to try and change the world, but such is the miraculous nature of human energy that we have both the intellectual and physical capacity to think about and help others as well as ourselves.

In a car, the bodywork is simply a wrapping for the interior. The engine powers the wheels and a few gismos – nothing else. But in humans, homeostasis helps to apportion the available energy between keeping the engine running, keeping the lights and wipers on, and running the repair shop that keeps our own 'bodywork' in good order.

At cellular level, the human body is constantly fighting off myriad assailants. The classic diseases we see as the signs of ageing all feature a gradual running down of the metronome of life, a gradual reduction in the efficiency of the metabolism, which are sometimes triggered by age but also by diseases and toxins such as smoking and alcohol and often by obesity and lack of exercise.

It was only recently, when we began to reassess the role of the mitochondria, that scientists began to see a closer relationship between metabolic health and ageing, over and above the simple process of energy balancing.

It is now thought that mitochondria are an important part of a cell-specific and dynamic organellar network that regulates a wide range of functions central to cellular life, death, and differentiation. When the mitochondria go wrong, particularly when there are inherited errors within the mitochondrial DNA (mtDNA), it contributes to a growing list of common disorders, including type 2 diabetes, neurodegenerative diseases and cancer. What is becoming very clear is that the mitochondria regulate far more processes than energy production and are probably central to our understanding of the ageing process.

Metabolic syndrome

If maintaining a healthy metabolism turns out to be crucial to healthy ageing, then it provides us with a clearer target for our lifestyle changes and medical therapies.

We look at the diseases we dread in ageing, such as heart disease, diabetes or dementia and tend to think of them as independent diseases. We look at failures in the system, such as cancers, communicable diseases and auto-immune diseases, such as arthritis and rheumatism, and see them as having discrete causes; smoking causes cancer while eating too much sugar causes type 2 diabetes. But that is not really the case. Cancer can be *caused* by over-eating, just as much as by smoking, while smokers are 30-40% more likely to develop type 2 diabetes than non-smokers.[4] What links these causes is that they all disrupt a normal metabolism. That the biggest culprit for years has been smoking has masked the negative impact of a whole series of other environmental pollutants and toxins. Now that fewer people smoke, we can see the wood from the trees and observe how obesity can also seriously disrupts a normal metabolism.

A faulty metabolism is defined as a syndrome. *Metabolic syndrome* is the word we give to conditions where the balance between the energy that comes in and energy that goes out has gone awry. Sometimes the cause is within the cells themselves – a general loss of energy – while sometimes the cause is external. More often than not symptoms are exacerbated by a messy build-up of fat cells; our on-board energy stores. Our adipose tissue, where we store the different fats that the body uses, contains a lot more than simple fat cells.* The fat harbours macrophages, specialist cells that attack invading pathogens such as microbes and viruses that carry disease. Fat cells grow in number as we grow, making childhood obesity a particularly difficult condition to treat. They look like tiny balloons under the microscope; they grow and shrink easily, but their number is virtually impossible to reduce except through surgery.

Over the years, quite a bit of rubbish inevitably builds up in and between mature fat cells and the resulting bio-active secretions can over-excite the immune response and contribute to a range of diseases such as heart disease, strokes and type 2 diabetes. Obesity generates a constant background, over-energetic, inflammatory response. One danger is that inflamed macrophages in the adipose tissue may start to release tumour-response hormones** These hormones have a really important role in attacking cancerous cells, but they are also pretty efficient at killing off healthy cells as well. This can lead to serious dysregulation within the immuno-metabolic system and may signal one of the reasons we find such a strong link between obesity and many different types of cancer.[5]

High blood glucose levels are a symptom of diabetes type 2, but these days doctors don't think that they are the fundamental cause. Recent studies reveal that diabetes type 2 is triggered by a build-up of visceral body fat that can interfere with our metabolism, blocking up insulin

---

* Mainly but not exclusively triglycerides – a very large fat molecule.
** For example, necrosis factor alpha (TNF-α) and interleukin-6 (IL-6)

glands in the pancreas.[6] What we now know for sure is that clearing away some of that fat, by dieting, improves pancreatic function astoundingly well.

As we age, the balancing act of homeostasis can become a little shaky. Studies have shown that, on average, the older we are, the less energy we can generate. The system becomes gradually less and less efficient, and with that drop in efficiency, the body starts to become a bit slap-dash in some processes. That's when signs of ageing start to creep in. After middle-age our bodies simply don't have the energy to repair and renew as much as they did when we were younger.[7] We now know that the trusty mitochondrion also contains the wherewithal to switch off energy supplies to cells that are no longer needed and thus regulate cell death – an inevitable aspect of ageing. In addition, we now realise that mitochondria are more closely associated with other organelles called *endoplasmic reticulum* within the cell that manage calcium storage, protein synthesis and lipid (fat) metabolism.

Calcium deficiency has long been noted as an issue in ageing. While the mineral calcium is fundamental to maintaining strong bones and teeth as well as being critical to blood clotting, its charged ion (Ca^{2+}) triggers muscle contractions and regulate normal heart rhythms as well as organ and nerve functions. Pagliarini and Rutter, in their review of mitochondrial functions, comment that:

"It is difficult to overstate the significance of Ca^{2+} signalling in the regulation of eukaryotic cell biology, as it plays a role in almost all aspects of cell function."

We now know that the mitochondria have a preeminent role in maintaining calcium for the purposes of energy production, but in so doing may also have a subsidiary role in managing calcium distribution across the entire body and in particular in maintaining a whole series of functions that are associated with ageing, not least frailty. If our metabolic systems are so important, and if activity levels are fundamental to maintaining a healthy metabolism, and thus healthy mitochondria, then rather against the odds the same sort of self-care (in particular diet and exercise) could really help us guard against many of the diseases of old age – not just metabolic syndrome and diabetes type 2 but cancer, heart and lung diseases as well as frailty brought on by osteoporosis, muscle weakness and dementia. In fact, this is exactly what the correlational studies of ageing show. Whichever of these diseases you look at, the same lifestyle factors are implicated in all of them.

The workings of the cell are as complex and as varied as the stars in the universe. Just as we require stronger and stronger telescopes to even glimpse their splendour, so larger magnification in microscopy, alongside a host of modelling and experimental techniques, are helping us glimpse the wonders of the human body. Delving into the minutia we find the health of the cell to be critical. And delving even more deeply into the cell we find that the mitochondrion is far more than the power-house of the cell, but its own vital organ.

Keep the rhythm going

A healthy metabolism is largely within our own control. Healthy ageing requires us to take a little more care of our own bodies, making what is called in the medical profession lifestyle decisions.

Maintaining a healthy metabolism means maintaining a healthy diet and enjoying adequate exercise. These should not be seen as strictures, and there is no need to consider most of these lifestyle changes as anything other than pleasant. Some may be more difficult to achieve than others, but without exception, the outcome is extremely pleasant. When planning your future, think in terms of retaining a zest for life that will make eating healthily a pleasure and continuing to be active a delight. Make sure your future plans take you somewhere where you can continue to eat well and exercise easily, whatever happens. Make sure you are not inadvertently limiting a heathy metabolism by relinquishing too much daily activity, too much agency or faith in your ability to look after yourself and control your own destiny.

Endnotes

1   Marcheva B, et al. (2013) *Circadian clocks and metabolism.* Handbook of Experimental Pharmacology. 2013;(217):127-55. DOI: 10.1007/978-3-642-25950-0_6

2   Palade GE, (1953) *An electron microscope study of the mitochondrial structure.* Journal of Histochemistry & Cytochemistry 1953 1:4, 188-211

3   Pagliarini DJ & Rutter J. (2013) *Hallmarks of a new era in mitochondrial biochemistry.* Genes Dev. 2013 Dec 15;27(24):2615-27. DOI: 10.1101/gad.229724.113.

4   www.cdc.gov/tobacco/campaign/tips/diseases/diabetes. [retrieved April 2023]

5   Coelho, M., Oliveira, T., & Fernandes, R. (2013). *Biochemistry of adipose tissue: an endocrine organ.* Archives of Medical Science: AMS, 9(2), 191–200. DOI: 10.5114/aoms.2013.33181

6   Gerst, F (2019) What *role do fat cells play in pancreatic tissue?* Molecular Metabolism 25(11) May 2019 DOI: 10.1016/j.molmet.2019.05.001

7   Ravera, S, Podestà, M, Sabatini, F et al. (2019) *Discrete Changes in Glucose Metabolism Define Ageing.* Sci Rep 9, 10347 2019. DOI: 10.1038/s41598-019-46749-w

5

The gourmet

Our glorious summer of old age must include a glorious summer diet. Eating is not simply a task to be undertaken with the minimum of fuss; it is part of our culture, is inextricable from our social lives and is vitally important to our mental as well as our physical wellbeing. I became a clinical nutritionist because I recognised that a healthy diet is one of the real fundamentals of a heathy life. These days an unhealthy diet, manifest by a rise in eating disorders and obesity, is the most important cause of ill health, having taken over from smoking some years ago.[1] These days only about 12% of the population smoke, but 100% of us eat and commentators believe that almost 100% of us eat an unhealthy diet. This is less of a lifestyle choice than something forced upon us. Whether we are in the supermarket or the local café, we often find that healthy food is difficult to come by, forcing us to eat innutritious, processed food that is often more akin to garbage.

The mistake we often make is to conflate healthy eating with cutting down. Food fanatics don't live longer than the rest of us. Eating well is not about cutting down quantity or cutting out various food groups.

It is about eating enough of the good things to really fill you up and satisfy you, and rejecting foods that are high-calorie and lacking in nutrition. Don't reject good, healthy foods such as potatoes, eggs, bananas, bread, milk or rice. Someone might have told you that they have a high glycaemic index, or a high fat content, because they might contain lactose, or because gluten is bad for you. You might think they are fattening, but they absolutely are not. What they all are is filling and so don't need to be eaten in huge quantities. (The wholemeal variety, the fresh and the freshly made, are the best.) We know today that what really makes us gain fat is the habitual eating of low-nutrition foods that include packeted and shop-bought refined cakes, buns and biscuits, ready meals, take-aways (from most chains), confectionary, crisps, packeted snacks, sugary drinks and alcohol. A little bit of what you fancy won't do you much harm, it is the habitual poor diet that we need to steer clear of. There's no doubt about it, that can be difficult and sometimes expensive. The secret of a healthy diet is to throw away the packets and the boxes. Become a gourmet. That shouldn't be an impossible task, but we all need a bit of support, accurate health information and government legislation to save us from ourselves.

Your image of a gourmet might be rather distorted by the avuncular persona of Monsieur Bibendum. The Michelin Man, as he came to be known, was invented by the cartoonist Rossillon in the 1890s to sell beer. All spare tyres and jocularity, he was named after a Latin saying, *Nunc est Bibendum* – let's drink! The cartoon character was rejected by the beer manufacturer, but when Rossillon offered the cast-off little man to the founder of the famous tyre company, Andre Michelin recognised in this portly middle-aged bon-viveur a perfect fit for this new tyre market. Since then, the Michelin Man has been synonymous with the Michelin Guides, which in themselves have become the world leader in recommending fine dining. But inevitably, the corpulent little tyre man has made us associate eating well with over-consumption and with his original purpose – over-imbibing.

If ever you've known a true gourmet, they do not overdo it. Elizabeth David, the famous food writer, summed it up very nicely when she described summer cooking in terms of enjoyment: [2]

"Summer cooking means the extraction of maximum enjoyment out of the produce which grows in the summer season ... it means catching the opportunity of eating fresh food, freshly cooked."

A 'glorious summer' indeed, but few food writers were as brave as she was in calling out her era's 'gourmet catering'. Very few of us have the pleasure and time to cook every meal we eat.

Let's get this clear from the outset: putting on weight is not a symptom of laziness or stupidity. So often it is simply a result of a lack of focus. In life we must deal with the here and now, attending to whatever is thrown in our direction, and the need to eat healthily can often be cast aside. If you are in a rush, where do you eat healthily? Restaurant food is more often than not as bad for you as processed food. In the deli and in the dining room, taste is so often augmented by salt and rivers of cheap oil, quality is obscured by sugar and spice, and the exotic, imported and processed is often passed off as superior to simple, local and fresh. Even some really expensive shops and restaurants sell fattening food. But of course, it so often looks attractive and benign. Do not be seduced by glossy images and purple prose. Even respected restaurant critics can be misled by clever marketing and hype.

Yet there are food writers and chefs who take the time to question. Jamie Oliver has become a sophisticated healthy food commentator. In launching his child obesity plan in 2018 he highlighted the fact that we have managed to change cultural norms in anti-smoking drives and seatbelt use and that both were initially met with anger or confusion. "But with effort, optimism and inspiration, we've seen seatbelts and smoking restrictions become the norm," he said.[3]

Surely, we can create a society and a food system that doesn't foster diet-related disease, obesity and type-2 diabetes? Jamie Oliver is one of a long line of gourmets who have been unafraid to speak their minds. For example, the food writer Roy Andries de Groot, in his 1966 book *Feasts for All Seasons* defines his approach to food as one of respect – for one's body, for one's guests and for the food itself.

> "It is the responsibility of the gourmet to demonstrate in every possible way that the public does know the difference [between good and poor food] and to demonstrate respect for the good taste and intelligence of the consumer..."

He considered it his duty to complain if he encountered something of poor quality. He maintained high food standards for himself and would always call out the compromises made by food manufacturers and restaurants simply to make more money.

A true gourmet is nothing like the little tyre man. He or she savours small portions of the very best-quality food. Eating well, by which I mean eating healthy, tasty and satisfying food, is the very best prescription for a long life. And as long as you aren't really overweight*, then eating healthily is a better long-term plan than a crash diet. If you are overweight or obese, do not despair, in almost all cases, obesity can be tackled.

Protein

Gourmets always make a bee-line for the protein in a meal. This is a sound strategy. As time goes by, our bodies become less efficient at metabolising or processing all the nutrients we require to fight disease and rebuild our strength. In order to redress the balance, many nutritionists advise that older people increase the protein content of their meals. Yet in the UK, official dietary advice does not recommend food of higher nutritional density for older people.[4] (I tend to have a sneaking suspicion that this lackadaisical approach is tolerated because it allows hospitals and care homes to continue to provide cheaper meals. It is the protein in a meal that costs the money.)

If we decide to increase the protein we eat, we need to re-balance our diet by reducing the number of calories we consume from fats and carbohydrates. That's not difficult, because protein is a particularly satisfying food and fills us up quite well. But the corollary is that we simply cannot afford to eat as much processed foods like factory-produced breads, cakes, fizzy drinks, pies and burgers in the quantities that we might have done in former years. This rebalance occurs gradually over the years as we age.

The cost of food often bears no relation to its nutritional quality. Even an artisanal loaf can be innutritious if it is made with refined flour, swimming

---

*   The definition of obesity for adults (18-65) is $30kg/m^2$ i.e. weight divided by height^2 in metres. This is BMI, discussed later in this chapter. But I don't advise embarking on a diet until you have taken professional advice. You may not need a diet at all, it may simply be a matter of eating different foods.

in oil or stuffed with dried fruit. The flour will be underpowered, lacking the rich mix of vitamins and minerals found in wholemeal flour, as well as lacking vital fibre. There's nothing wrong with a little olive oil or a spoonful of raisins, but any cooking oil is one of the fattiest products on earth and raisins one of sweetest. It is nice some of the time, but not a substitute for simple bread. The main reason why we get these fancy breads in restaurants is that they are cheaper than protein. They fill you up so much that you don't notice the meal hasn't really satisfied you.

When you are really hungry you will find that a healthy chunk of lean protein will be satisfying in the long-term and give you the energy to face the rest of the day. The gourmet might choose something traditional like Sole Bonne Femme, or Chicken Casserole, or a modern vegan option such as a Tandoori Tofu (soybean) or a Lentil Bolognese.

Protein is required by all living cells, to enable the cell to build itself, to function and to replicate. When we eat a piece of fish, or a chunk of tofu we are eating long strings of highly complex and chemically-active molecules. Each protein chain consists of blocks of different amino acids which are broken down by the digestive system to be re-built into all the

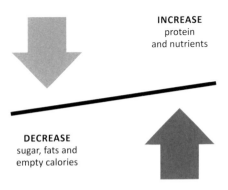

INCREASE
protein
and nutrients

DECREASE
sugar, fats and
empty calories

How our diet needs to change as we age.

different proteins that the body needs. DNA is protein; muscle is protein; hormones and antibodies are all different types of proteins, made by cells within our own bodies from foods that we eat.

Perhaps one of the reasons that protein is under-represented in our diet is because it is expensive to buy and perishable. Meat, fish, dairy products and eggs are also off the menu for increasing numbers of people on ethical grounds, meaning they must make a special effort to consume sufficient protein from cereal, nuts, seeds, legumes and other alternative sources. In the case of plant-based diets, protein from cereals becomes an even more important source of protein than in an omnivorous diet.

Protein, whether derived from animals or vegetables, is the most important food group for older people. As our ability to metabolise protein recedes with age, we often need more than in middle age.

How much protein?

Many countries, with more progressive nutrition policies than we have in the UK are taking notice of recent research and altering their advice. The reason they are doing so is because the power of evidence is mounting. For example, the PROT-AGE Study was commissioned in 2013 by the European Geriatric Medicine Society to review the data and consider new recommendations, that might be different to the 0.8 grammes of pure protein per kilogram of body weight per day ($g/kg/d$), as recommended in most EU countries at the time. In the UK that figure was – and still is – 0.75g/kg/d. The study concluded that to help maintain and regain lean body mass (everything but fat) older people should increase their protein ingestion by up to half as much as a younger adult to 1.0-1.2g/kg/d. If they are active and exercising, then the protein intake could be increased further to 1.5g/kg/d, i.e. up to double the UK recommendation. In a healthy 70kg (11 stone) person, a 1.5g/kg daily protein ration would mean eating over 100g of pure protein each day, the equivalent of 400g of white fish or 1kg of cooked lentils.[5]

In the UK, the Government's Scientific Advisory Committee on Nutrition (SACN) observed that 27% of 65 to 74-year-olds and 33% of the 75-and-over age group had a protein intake below even the modest UK recommendation.

Ironically, regardless of their findings, SACN concluded that protein recommendations for old people should not be increased, or even encouraged.[6] This counter-intuitive decision was based on our old friend the 'average' person. According to SACN, the average person in the UK eats too much protein. But no special case was made for older people, even though the report religiously records the outcome of respected medical research that suggests that protein intake and muscle mass and strength are correlated.

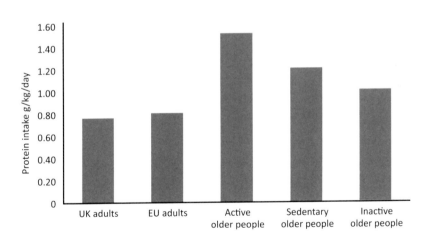

Comparison between UK and EU protein recommendations and portions recommended by the European Geriatric Medical Society for active, sedentary or inactive older people.

Perhaps the committee were cognisant of other research that links eating too much meat protein to climate change, as well as other research that links processed meats to stomach and colon cancers. If that is so the report does not mention it, merely suggesting that further evidence is required.

The gourmet in me would suggest eating far less processed meat, increasing the variety of proteins and going for quality. That means quality and sustainability of production as well as product. The recommendation to eat more protein should not be a licence to eat meat pies, packeted lasagne and fatty cuts of bacon. Neither should they be seen as a requirement to eat nothing but T-bone steak. There are many more sustainable and healthier types of protein to consider, as well as cheaper sources of protein to choose from. The data shows that on average, older people eat less protein than their middle-aged peers. In order to save the planet, we don't need to cut out all meats; we can just change the type of meat we buy and the frequency with which we eat it. We shouldn't be cutting down on protein, but we can seek plant-based as well as animal sources.

Older people often experience a gradual loss of appetite, a slowing metabolism, a reduction in activity and thus a resulting breakdown of body protein stores. This gradual decline is sometimes augmented by misinformation and economic considerations. It triggers a condition of protein loss called *proteolysis*.

These big discrepancies between advised and actual protein consumption in the UK, sometimes *too much* in adulthood and almost always *too little* after 65, as well as the massive differences between nutritional advice across the developed world, should, at the very least, raise eyebrows. If some younger people are eating much more protein without noticeable harms, why do we concern ourselves so little with almost a third of our old people who are eating too little? And that is by the meagre UK standards. Much more protein is advised by other countries.

For over 15 years the Australian government has suggested that older people should eat far more protein than their younger neighbours: [7]

"Men and women aged 70+ years require approximately 20% more protein each day than those aged 19–70 years. Even higher rates of protein intake have been recommended for [some] older people..."

Nordic countries have also responded to the increasing volume of evidence around quantity and regularity of protein diets for older people. This may seem counter-intuitive, because old people aren't *growing*. But in fact, their bodies require more regular repair at a time when the capacity for repair may be waning.

We know that chronic diseases are more frequent in the elderly. This can lead to periodic temporary losses of body protein through *catabolic* muscle-wasting, exacerbations of disease, temporary periods of bed rest or a loss of appetite. Even healthy older people tend to exhibit a natural loss of muscle mass and strength with age, which is called *sarcopenia*. The cure is more protein, more often, combined with strength-appropriate exercise.

As an example, the Australian recommendations are given below. You will note that it isn't just protein dosage that is under-emphasised in advice from the UK. The Australian government recommends more vitamin B12, B6, D and calcium in diets when we get to our 70s. [8]

Australian dietary guidelines illustrating increased recommended dietary intakes (RDIs) per day with age. Here protein is measured in grams of pure protein.

Men	Vitamin B2	Vitamin B6	Vitamin D*	Calcium	Protein
19-50	1.3mg	1.3mg	5µg	1000mg	64g
51-70	1.3mg	1.7mg	10µg	1000mg	64g
70+	1.6mg	1.7mg	15µg	1300mg	81g
Women	Vitamin B2	Vitamin B6	Vitamin D*	Calcium	Protein
19-50	1.1mg	1.3mg	5µg	1000mg	46g
51-70	1.1mg	1.5mg	10µg	1000mg	46g
70+	1.3mg	1.5mg	15µg	1300mg	57g

* Vitamin D does not have an RDI but an AI (adequate intake) value

A challenge for the UK's one-size-fits-all strategy is that people don't age at the same rate, their diets are hugely different, their levels of activity are hugely different and as we age a simple weight check becomes irrelevant. Once you retire, reach menopause or the age of about 65, your GP should not simply assess whether you are overweight. A diligent GP will also wish to assess where fat has formed and whether muscle mass or strength has declined. That can't be done with a standard pair of waiting room-scales. Your BMI gradually becomes irrelevant.

We all know about the danger of gradually eating too many calories, illustrated by adding up those of an extra digestive biscuit each day, leading to serious weight gain over a year. But under-eating even smaller amounts of healthy protein, can have an equally, sometimes more devastating effect over time. If you are tired of counting calories, a basically healthy person only really needs to monitor one thing – which is the amount of protein eaten each day, at each meal, and observe how much better it feels.

Fortunately, there's an easy answer, if you are under-eating protein. Just add milk! Taking a cappuccino, a bowl of Greek yoghurt, or an evening glass of hot chocolate may be all that is required to turn an underpowered diet into a healthy one. Milk is a convenience food, economical to buy and to store. Contained within natural milk are long strings of complex proteins and amino acids that do far more than simply feed us. They contain ready-made amino acid building blocks that the body can use to make antigens, supply our hormonal needs and trigger enzyme reactions. Alongside easily digested protein, milk contains beneficial carbohydrates, fats, minerals and vitamins, in just the right balance and structure to be readily used to boost our immunity, repair damaged cells and keep body and brain firing on all cylinders.

Vegans, or those who don't enjoy drinking milk, should beware. It is impossible to manufacture the complexity of nutrition in any milk substitute, even if the factory-produced milk substitute is packed with added supplements. These additives might read well on the label, but don't really tell us about the complexity of nutrition that real milk provides. Most milk substitutes contain too much sugar, too little protein and different proportions of amino acids. That is why new mothers are encouraged to breast-feed – formula milk just doesn't do so well for babies. Similarly for adults, I'm sorry to say that oat milk, almond milk or coconut milk, though a delicious drink and a very useful alternative to soft drinks, just doesn't offer a real nutritional substitute for fresh whole milk. Unsweetened, fortified soy-milk is probably the best alternative. But don't kid yourself. You'll be missing out on so much.

Milk is particularly useful for those of us who might suffer from a reduced appetite, a lack of interest in food, or an impaired ability to consume protein-rich foods. In addition to protein, milk products provide a good source of calcium, vitamin B2, B6 and B12, which are all important for bone health. A take-away cup (330ml) of whole milk contains approximately 11 grams of protein. A fresh cappuccino coffee, or hot chocolate made with pure cocoa powder (not the sugary version) can provide an excellent booster. You do not need to resort to expensive protein bars or shakes – they are processed foods and if you don't agree, just glance at the contents list, or take a sneak Google peek at the factory where they are made.

The link between protein and muscle mass is no secret – ask any body-builder. But it has taken us a long time to recognise that muscle loss is a critical aspect of ageing, and we've taken even longer to understand that modifying our protein intake can protect us. By the 2010s a series of studies had revealed that higher dietary protein ingestion was beneficial to support good health, promote recovery from illness and maintain functionality in older adults. Geriatricians were coming to the conclusion that the one-size-fits-all dietary protein recommendations found in most national guidelines might be wrong. It is not only older people that can benefit from a higher protein diet; studies have shown that low-protein diets can reduce our mood and induce depression*. And in contrast high-protein diets are now also recommended for adolescents, to boost brain development, during pregnancy and while breast-feeding.

Don't forget that as well as animal-derived products, we get a lot of our protein from legumes and cereals, which also contain high quality protein without too much fat. Wholemeal wheat is one of the most nutritious protein sources. Cereals provide about a quarter of the protein in an average UK diet. Good bread is quite literally the stuff of life. [9]

Carbohydrates and fats

Most nutritional tables make a big division between *carbohydrates and fats*, but in fact their chemical structure isn't so different. The body can

---

* A lack of tryptophan, one of the essential proteins the body cannot manufacture, is implicated in depression and in a reduced effectiveness of anti-depression medications such as selective serotonin reuptake inhibitors (SSRIs).

derive energy from fat or carbohydrate, breaking down anything that you eat to extract the basics: carbon, hydrogen and oxygen in all its concoctions. The nutrients so extracted zip around the blood stream to provide energy to every cell in the body, or convert these three elements into molecules of glycerol, which can be stored in the liver or into triglycerides (fatty acids) which provide a long-term energy store in our fat cells.

We talk about *bread and butter* as a way of describing something basic. Coincidentally this simple dish contains healthy portions of carbohydrates and fats as well as useful protein. A balanced diet must include carbohydrates as well as fat. Fats provide vital cellular building blocks as well as a means for energy storage, cushioning to joints, an aid to waste elimination and a sustainable store of fat-soluble vitamins. Carbohydrates provide energy. Carbohydrates, proteins and fats all carry different mixtures of vitamins and minerals to complete the balanced diet.

Both fats and carbohydrates provide texture, smoothness and flavour to foods. I think so many people fear fats and sugars in their diet simply because their flavours and textures make them extremely 'moreish'. Sometimes they are difficult to resist and *boy* can they be can be intensely calorific. 100g of olive oil contains 884 calories, and 100g of granulated sugar contains 384 calories. It is easy to splash oil about, and habit-forming to sprinkle food with sugar, but there are less calorific ways of enjoying carbohydrates and fat. Butter, because it has a higher water content, is actually 19% lower in calories than olive oil, and grapes, the sweetest of fresh fruits, contain only 67 calories per 100g portion.

Sweetness and flavour are to be found in all carbohydrates, not just sugar. The gourmet knows that the complex flavours in fruits and the lactose in milk possess a more subtle but equally satisfying sweetness.

The carbohydrates in cereals, root vegetables and legumes all possess a gentle sweetness. Think of the sweetness of a fresh carrot, caramelised onions or peas.

You will have seen the nutritional information on many products, where fats are divided into the saturated and unsaturated categories and carbohydrates are defined by their sugar content. But a balanced diet is not achieved simply by monitoring the proportion of glucose found in carbohydrates, or the types of lipids in fats. Different fats and carbohydrates have different effects. It is unhelpful to think of these as all bad or all good. It is the mix of different carbs and fats that we need to keep a watch on. Some types of carbohydrates (for example fruit juice sugars) provide an easily-absorbed energy bomb – that's why astronauts drink orange juice before a flight. It gives them the boost of energy they need to resist the astonishing G-forces at lift-off. Other types of sugars, for example those found in fruit and cereals such as oats or rice, are bound up in plant material. They distribute glucose to the bloodstream more slowly, maintaining our energies for longer periods of time.

A healthy diet includes quick-release and slow-release sugars. Fast-release sugars, found in items such as fruit, give an instant energy boost and are thus excellent for breakfast and in deserts at the end of the mid-day meal in order that we can quickly get back to working (or playing). Digestion takes up a lot of energy, which is why we tend to feel tired after a big meal. If you are planning a feast, make sure you commence with a good protein and vegetable main course, supported by some slow-release carbohydrate and dietary fibre. This will satisfy most hungers and make you less likely to raid an attractive, but probably over-sweet, dessert trolley. Traditionally, and correctly, we have called the meat or fish (protein) course the main course; desert should definitely be the smaller course.

Fats come in all shapes and sizes. There are saturated fats and unsaturated fats, low-density and high-density lipids. There are long-chain fatty acids and short-chain ones. There are creamy whole-milk fats that are delivered in large globules (which seem to be helpful to the body) and high-cholesterol meat fats that can very quickly build up fatty deposits in the blood vessels. There are unhealthy trans fats, now banned in many food products, which have been modified by high-temperature cooking.

In spite of what you might read in magazines, neither carbs nor fats are 'bad' for you. They are both *essential,* but some are far better for you than others. Oats contain slow-release sugars that provide long-term energy, making foods like porridge an excellent breakfast dish. Add a little fruit to your porridge and you will get a little quick-release energy as well to wake you up.

Over time, our digestive systems become sluggish and some people may find high-fibre foods, or fibrous vegetables, more difficult to digest. Fats can help the digestive system work efficiency and reduce constipation. Our ability to swallow may become impaired, making solid foods more difficult to eat. That tends to push us towards eating softer (refined) foods and sugary deserts – but fruit puree and vegetable 'mashes' need not be adulterated. While glucose from any sugary substance, from honey to Battenberg cake, is essential for life, and white flour is a good source of protein and is, by law, fortified we should favour wholemeal cereals, fresh fruit and vegetables.

The greatest different between wholesome or wholemeal produce and the fortified variety is the difference in fibre content. Our friends at SACN have observed for years that very few of us eat the required amount of fibre – 30 grammes per day. Yet no-one seems to take a blind bit of notice in care homes or hospital settings. Restaurants and bakers are oblivious. Strange, because lack of fibre is very strongly linked to one of the most prevalent and aggressive cancers we can develop – colon cancer.

Plants

It has become very fashionable to talk about a plant-based diet as if it is something new. Fruits, vegetables, legumes and cereals have always been the mainstay of a healthy diet. Forget about five portions of fruit and vegetables per day; it is the vegetables you ought to concentrate on, and 10 different types of fruit and veg each day is now considered a better target. A very large meta-analysis in 2017, conducted by epidemiologists from Norway, Imperial College and Harvard concluded that the lowest cancer risk was observed at those with an intake of 600 g/day (7.5 servings/day), whereas for coronary heart disease, strokes, cardiovascular diseases and general mortality, the lowest risk was observed at those eating 800 g/day (10 servings/day). That's a level of intake that is double the five servings per day (400 g/day) currently recommended in England.[10]

As well as five-a-day, some people advise us to steer clear of starch and high sugars (such as orange juice); however, even starchy vegetables like potatoes contain a lot of Vitamin C, and bananas are packed with potassium and vitamin B6, so this larger allowance means you can add a few extras into your target, ensuring you don't stint on the starchy and fibrous content which is also important. Neither should you get hung up on portion size. Your 10-a-day can include smaller portions of tasty elements like garlic, a sprinkling of chilli or a spoonful of jam.

Dietary fads

People who advocate a plant-based diet often eschew cereals because of their gluten content, which is perceived as a negative. Dietary fads, such as eliminating sugar, lactose, high glycaemic index foods or gluten (a protein) can all play havoc with the digestive system. Such diets can very easily reduce the amount of fibre we eat, which in turn can lead to food intolerances, allergies or irritable bowel syndrome. It often requires specialist nutritional advice and time to get the digestive system back to tolerating these foods if they have been frivolously abandoned. The best advice is to never cut any wholesome food out of your diet unless advised to by a registered and qualified nutritionist or the hospital dietician.

If you think you are addicted to sugar, then think again. Many people don't realise that sugar cravings are very easily cured because the gut is so mutable. Those sugary treats may be calling to you now, but if you stop buying processed sugary foods for a week or two you'll soon be free of their spell. The sugar transporters in your gut will have withered away, and with them much of the craving. Of course, malevolent food manufactures will still put a lot of effort and money into trying to lure you back again, so your body may get over it, but your mind might still be seducible. Be on your guard.

Water

You might think that I'm insulting your intelligence by mentioning water in a book about long life. Of course, we need water. The question is how much. Myths abound regarding the correct amount of water and the form in which it should be imbibed. It is definitely true that drinking plenty of water is especially important during heatwaves and periods of fever or disease, when the requirement for water increases. Unless you are suffering from heat stroke, your thirst will always be the most efficient indicator. If you feel thirsty, you need to drink. Don't allow habit to limit your intake. As time goes by, we may become more aware of urinary urgency and concerned about little accidents. The worry, rather than the reality of the situation, can slowly dissuade us from keeping a glass of water by the bed, or by the desk. Yet one of the most vivid signs of ageing is wrinkles, and they can be very successfully mediated by regularly drinking liquids.

It is also quite normal to feel a greater urgency to pee as you grow older. However, beware the costly and uncomfortable trap of incontinence underwear. Most of us simply need a good pair of cotton knickers most of the time. Incontinence and urgency, if it is regularly occurring, can also be treated very simply with pills. Please don't reduce your water drinking because you are worried by urgency. Please do not start buying those awful plastic knickers until you have exhausted other avenues.

Any liquid, even caffeinated tea and coffee, contributes more H_2O to the diet than their caffeine content takes away from it. There is nothing wrong with a double expresso, although you should note that the Italians always serve a small glass of iced water with a black coffee.

Soups, fresh fruit and vegetables all possess a high water content. Fresh tomatoes are 95% water. Once inside the stomach it is all H_2O and all equally useful to biological processes. If you decide to embark on a fat-loss diet, water will help you to feel full, even if the calorie count is lower than usual.

Carbonated drinks are not such a good idea, even if they contain zero calories. This is because the acid in sodas and soft drink flavourings can corrode teeth and damage bones, extremely effectively, in the presence of carbon dioxide (that's what the bubbles are made of). And because they are also high in sugars, colas, are also associated with bad tooth decay and osteoporosis. Caffeinated soft drinks, such as colas and energy drinks are manufactured using highly processed chemical caffeine, which provides an artificial chemical high, and in my view does not compare with the flavour and aroma of a really nice cup of fresh coffee. Steer clear.

Sauces, made with a mixture of watery stocks mixed in with fats, adorn many of our classical dishes. The humble white sauce is an emulsion of butter and water, or butter and milk, which is itself an emulsion of curds (casein protein), milk fat, water, lactose and whey protein. These mixtures all absorb and enhance the flavour of more subtle foods, such as mushrooms or parsley, and soften the flavour of sharper foods, such as mature cheddar or anything from the onion family.

Too rich for me!

All this talk of the enrichment of food may have you reaching for the dyspepsia tablets. Irritable Bowel Syndrome (IBS) often accompanies old age or stress of any kind. The gasses released as a natural part of digestion can exacerbate wind, which people find very embarrassing, and the way liquids, fibres and spicy foods interact with the digestive tract can cause diarrhoea and/or constipation. However, I must stress it is perfectly normal to fart and belch twenty to fifty times a day. Generally, it goes unnoticed by everyone around. While they can be an indicator of disease, they are also commonly found quite naturally in older people, along with other gastric irregularities such as slow absorption. The cause is more often than not a sluggish digestion. Food doesn't go through the gut as quickly when we are older. If we can increase the efficiency of our digestion, then we are more likely to be able to cure the consequences. Simple remedies can all help. Try drinking water (not alcohol) with a meal, chewing more conscientiously, sprinkling ground linseeds on morning cereals and allowing a big meal to digest for 15 minutes before taking a post-prandial stroll.

If such solutions don't work, then a FODMAP diet, administered by a trained and registered nutritionist, can help. This is an elimination diet, but must be followed up by a gradual re-introduction of foods one by one until the culprit is identified. No food should be eliminated for good, but some may need to be rationed. If so the nutritional implication of reducing that food must be well understood and alternative supplements added to the diet.

Diet and culture

Each culture has its own cuisine, but by comparing the dishes of different nations it soon becomes quite easy to distinguish the staple foods in each diet. The staple is traditionally the local cereal that makes up the dominant part of a population's diet. Food staples are eaten regularly – even daily – and supply a major proportion of a person's energy and nutrition needs.

Some foods contain a mixture of protein, carbohydrate *and* fat. Milk products are particularly favoured, which is why most nutritionists would give them a separate classification. Because of the fat content of milk, and because it is so nutritious, you don't need to go overboard. 100-200ml/day is an adequate minimum.

Whether you take your milk as Bulgarian yoghurt, from Indian Yaks, British cows or Greek goats, you will be eating one of the most delicious and varied foods the world knows. As a gourmet, you will need to get to know just what milk products are available in your area. Supermarket milk is cheap, but that's really all it has going for it. Look for brands that say they are grass-fed (producing a milk far better than the cereal-fed sort), organic (of course) and raw or as lightly pasteurised as possible. Pasteurised milk breaks down the milk fat molecules that occur naturally in raw milk, changing flavour, changing the way the gut processes the fats and destroying the creamy top of the milk, which for me is always reserved for breakfast porridge.

Cereals are different, but essential, across the world. They contain important quantities of carbohydrate, fibre and protein with little fat, so they fill you up and aid elimination without leading to weight gain. For example, in the UK we tend to see high protein wheat-bread as our staple cereal, while Asian cooking is based on rice and sometimes chapattis, while Mediterranean cooking uses different wheat grains which have adapted to growing in hotter climes. Think about the high-quality durum wheat pasta beloved of the Italians, or North African couscous. They are all cereals, and while they contain different proportions of nutrients, they are all classed as staples because they provide a healthy source of carbohydrate, fibre, protein, B vitamins and minerals.

Micronutrients

While protein, carbohydrate and fats are considered the three main constituents of a healthy diet, and described as macronutrients, they are actually the tip of a delicious and health-giving iceberg.

The full gamut of vitamins, minerals, trace elements and phytochemicals which make up the category of *dietary micronutrients* can only be found by eating a wide range of wholesome foods. The gourmet always seeks out the freshest local delicacy, with different flavours, colours and textures that reflect their different nutritional content.

Micronutrients are rarely required in quantities of more than a gram or two each day, but they possess powerful biochemical gearing. In the body, vitamins and minerals act as catalysts, making beneficial reactions happen, or inhibiting the wrong reactions. Essential micronutrients cannot be made by the body itself, so must be ingested or absorbed, mainly, though not exclusively, in our diets. (Vitamin D famously needs access to sunlight, but is also available in some foods.)

There is a pill for every one of these micronutrients; but the best (and cheapest) approach is to eat plenty of fresh, healthy foods.

Trace elements

We only require tiny amounts of the principal dietary elements, such as zinc, copper, iron or selenium; hence they are called trace elements. However, each and every one of these trace elements are vitally important to bodily functions. Some such as fluorine are required to maintain strong teeth and bones. It might come as a surprise that some metals such as copper, zinc and iron are nutritional requirements. We tend to consider them as poisonous, which they are in high qualities. But copper and zinc are present in many of the body's enzymes, hormones and genetic material. They have powerful molecular qualities, helping to stabilise the folds and twists of bio-active proteins and enabling tiny protein valves and hooks to function. They contribute to the way proteins dance!

Iron is essential for a healthy blood circulation. Within each haemoglobin (red blood) cell, iron atoms pick up four oxygen molecules in a bio-active embrace, and convey them, via the bloodstream, to every part of the body. Having delivered their load, the haemoglobin molecule then returns to the lungs to pick up a new quartet of oxygen atoms. Eating iron-rich food confers flavour as well as supporting the blood oxygen supply and protecting against the paleness and tiredness that is such a visible sign of anaemia. It is not necessary to eat meat in order to derive iron, but plant-based (non-haeme) iron is less useful to the body, so we require almost double the level of iron if it's solely derived from plant-based foods.

Mineral salts

In previous decades, vitamins and trace elements were discussed way before we were urged to think about *mineral salts*, another sub-group of essential elements. But in my view, salts have gained an unfairly bad reputation simply because some people, particularly those with certain types of heart conditions, need to moderate their intake of sodium. Indeed, when we talk about salt as a baddie, we are invariably talking about sodium chloride, or table salt. Yet that's not the whole truth.

Salt is actually quite a good thing. Mineral salts that are naturally present in the food we eat confer piquancy and also play a vital role in controlling the water and acid-alkali balance in our body. In particular sodium, potassium, calcium, magnesium, chloride and phosphorus are able, when mixed with water, to conduct tiny currents of electricity. These are called electrolytes and work in the body in a similar way to electrolytes in batteries. Dietary salts provide the mechanisms that switch on the enzymes and hormones that trigger things like nerve signals and muscle contractions. Important mineral salts such as calcium and phosphorus are stored in bones and teeth, and require constant topping up, even when we have grown to maturity. Calcium, which is the most abundant mineral salt to be found in the body, is easily absorbed from milk and dairy products and is one of the reasons dairy foods are considered an important component of a healthy diet. Calcium in the form of chalk is often added to plant milks as a fortification and a colourant, but is arguably a poor substitute.

Other mineral salts such as potassium, magnesium, sodium or sulphur are derived from the soil that plants grow in, the water these plants absorb or where animals graze. Once again, a varied diet that includes fresh farm produce will mean that most of these elements are easily available. Unless advised to cut down on medical grounds, most of us will be able to moderately season our food right into our dotage. Again, someone with a gourmet mindset has the edge when it comes to a healthy diet. A foodie will always relish a different flavour. And if taste-buds become jaded, then pepper, chilli, garlic, herbs and spices are a pleasant addition to what can seem less tasty fare. They all contain high quantities of beneficial mineral salts, plus a lot of other good stuff, such as vitamins and phytochemicals.

Vitamins

The word vitamin derives from the original nomenclature *vital amines*, when all essential vitamins were thought to be amino acids and vital to life. All vitamins fulfil important functions within the chain of processes that allow life to thrive. Many are amino acids, but some are not. They are all termed 'essential', because the body cannot make them from the diet. Some, such as vitamin C (ascorbic acid) are water soluble, which makes them fragile and subject to degradation if stored for a long time, chopped or heated. We love our citrus fruits and lemony flavours, but most other mammals are perfectly able to manufacture vitamin C internally. Your dog or your cat simply won't be interested in eating an orange, but humans, apes and bats can't make Vitamin C – and consequentially we all share a liking for tangy fruit.*

Other vitamins such as A, D, E and K, are fat soluble, found in the fats of dairy, meat, fish and vegetables and can be stored in the body for longer. This is one of the reasons why a fat-free diet would be dangerous to sustain – as well as very dull. Without fat to store and distribute vitamins, we'd end up with serious deficiencies.

The way we derive vitamin D, which is also fat soluble, is slightly different, in that we absorb this nutrient from sunshine as well as from some foods. Ultra-violet sunlight is absorbed through the skin and provides the stimulus for converting 7-dehydrocholesterol, an unsaturated fat and a product of natural cholesterol production in the body. It is found in abundance in healthy skin. The vitamin is further transformed by the liver and kidneys into forms that the body can use. Vitamin D plays an important role (alongside calcium) in preventing osteoporosis and regulating muscle function. In addition, we are beginning to find more

---

* See Chapter 8, for the story of Vitamin C, as a supplement.

and more ways that vitamin D can benefit our immune systems and dampen down the inflammatory response. In some quarters it is seen as a miracle anti-ageing drug. My own view is that it is an essential aspect of many different human functions, and takes an active role in various metabolic processes, but in isolation is unlikely to be the silver bullet. It is necessary, but not sufficient.

Useful quantities of vitamin D can be found in oily fish, red meat, liver, mushrooms and egg yolks. As we mature, our skin gets dryer and the natural absorption of vitamin D from sunlight becomes less efficient. We also tend to bare our bodies less and become more cautious about sun bathing. Over time, a variety of causes might reduce our natural synthesis of vitamin D, and impede our health. These days vitamin D supplements are recommended for all older people, even if you can't always get them on prescription – but don't stop enjoying a little fresh air and sunshine.

Skin cancers, one of the most prevalent cancers in the UK, can be caused by too much sun, but going the other way and covering up too much can also be dangerous. 15 minutes a day out in the sun between April and October without sun block is all that is needed. However, a vitamin D supplement is now recommended for all adults during the UK's dismal winters. Not all advisory bodies agree on the ideal level of various vitamins. For people over 70 years of age, for example, Australia recommends 50% more vitamin D than the NHS in the UK.[11] Vitamin regulators have to steer a fine line between prescribing too little and too much. Too little will reduce or even nullify the effect, while too much can in some circumstances be dangerous, and in other cases simply wasteful. Remember, it is the government – in the guise of the NHS – that has to foot the bill. The difference in cost between the NHS recommendation of 10 micrograms – a unit of mass equal to one millionth (1×10^{-6}) of a gram – and 15 micrograms of vitamin D is negligible for one person, but starts to add up when you consider the large number of people who are prescribed supplements. Because it is stored in fat, it can build up and overdoses could be dangerous.* The only way to really check whether your supplement dose, your sun exposure and winter diet provide enough vitamin D is to have a blood test in the autumn and in the spring of each year.

Cobalamin (vitamin B12) is also required to protect against nerve damage and pernicious anaemia, where red blood cells cease to be manufactured in bone marrow. Lacto-vegetarians need not be concerned, but the Vegan Society advises that all vegans should take B12 supplements (as well as vitamin D, iodine and selenium) to counteract deficiencies in a vegan diet[12]. Because of the variation in some of these elements in the natural environment, everyone must take a bit of care. For example, not all Brazil nuts are a good source of selenium (it depends where they are grown) and not all milk contains adequate iodine (it depends on where the cows graze). A simple eating diary would immediately tell a nutritionist if you were under eating enough variety, and thus getting enough nutrients. But as we age, the challenge is not always diet. It can be very hard to diagnose malabsorption of micronutrients and even harder to put things right.

If you get your nutrition from a varied diet, and you do enjoy being outside in the sunshine, you are far less likely to suffer deficiencies or overdoses than you might if you were getting your nutrients from a bottle of pills. Supplements should never be seen as a first line of defence. We simply don't yet know enough about the minutia of vitamin absorption and metabolism to rely on pills long-term. The market research company

---

* Even quite large overdoses of water-soluble vitamins such as all B vitamins and C will simply flush right through you. But beware, even benign water-soluble vitamins have their limits.

Mintel reported that the vitamin and mineral supplement market grew to £568 million turnover in 2023; vitamins and minerals within food come free.[13]

Phytochemicals

Phytochemicals are *amuse bouche* to the gourmet. The term is a catch-all to describe the complex chemical compounds that grow with the plant, helping it respond to its unique environment. For example, evolution has helped plants accumulate brightly coloured flowers to attract pollinators, bitter flavours and aromas to deter nibbling pests or to infuse insecticides and fungicides into the seed to protect the reproductive process. A few phytochemicals can be super harmful to humans too, but generally they come in such small doses that they simply add sharp, spicy, zingy or hot flavours, as well as different and enticing colours.

People have known for millions of years that plant extracts provide potent curatives. It is only recently that the role of the phytochemicals we eat in our food has been shown to help regulate our metabolism. Eating a healthy variety of food, full of different phytochemicals, can revitalise our metabolic system while donating helpful anti-inflammatory, anticoagulant and antioxidant qualities.

It is easy to understand why a healthy and varied diet could keep us young, and why an unvarying, dull and processed-food diet could contribute to ageing. It is the phytochemicals in fruit and vegetables that contribute to the received wisdom that variety as well as quantity is important.[14] The real value of different phytochemicals in the human diet is often overlooked; not because they aren't important, but because as yet we have scant idea when, why and how important they are. There are no *recommended daily allowances* (RDAs) as there are with most vitamins and minerals, and no reliable lists to tell us whether phytochemicals are essential. There are far too many types and sub-types to have yet been catalogued. There are thousands of edible plants, and many of those plants that we know to be beneficial have hundreds of varieties, with each one containing a slightly different cocktail of phytochemicals.

Monks and physicians have used plant extracts for centuries and modern medicine has often successfully mirrored these extracts in artificial versions. Many of the most potent medicines we use today, such as Aspirin, Metformin, Digitalis and Morphine were originally derived from plants, but are now synthesised in the lab.

Food scientists are still only scraping the surface, often cherry-picking phytochemicals we already know that have established human effects. For example, some commentators are convinced that the abundance of phytochemicals in red wine and chocolate might outweigh their negative influence on our diet. But even with these front-runners, there is little convincing evidence to back up what would be delightfully pleasant findings. All I can advise is that eating many different flavours and colours of fruit and vegetables will provide a rich mix of nutrients as well as helping gut microbes to flourish, letting nature do its best. Until more research is completed, it is best to emulate the gourmet, use all the senses, and value variety, enjoy flavour, aroma and colour and do not shy away from more acquired tastes which might be spicy, bitter or tangy due to important phytochemical benefits we have yet to decipher.

Caffeine is just one of the phytochemicals that have become important to our lives since the importation of coffee to Europe in the early seventeenth century. While individual tolerances differ, most of us can and should enjoy coffee every day; it provides a great kick starter in the morning to wake us up and can help to restore a sluggish metabolism. It appears in the contents list of many weight loss pills, but I advise my clients simply to enjoy an expresso every so often.

Can you eat too much?

It is not necessary to exclude any particular food from a healthy diet, but if you wish to shed some fat, it will be necessary to eat fewer calories overall. Concentrate on wholesome, low-calorie, nutrition-dense foods, which can be eaten in generous quantities. Foods like wholemeal bread will satisfy your appetite after only one or two slices, while the white processed version feels far lighter and can be eaten by the bucket load, though both types of bread contain almost exactly the same number of calories per gramme. Wholemeal bread is not only satisfying to eat, it contains lots of extra goodies like dietary fibre and nutrients that come calorie-free. These nutrients signal to your stomach that you've eaten well. Eating food of low nutrient value may not turn off the hunger signals, as the body can sense when some nutrients are missing, even though you might have recently eaten a very large but innutritious meal.

We are faced with many poor food choices in shops and restaurants, so much so that you should not become too downhearted if a simple diet doesn't work. Blame the commercial food industry. Processed foods contain a dizzying mixture of unnatural chemical substitutes, such as artificial caffeine in cola and high-fructose (very sweet tasting) corn syrups. In addition, artificial colourings and flavourings are moreish, but innutritious and are thought to be a cause of ADHD (Attention Deficit Hyperactive Disorder) in children. There is a growing body of scientific literature that shows eating ultra-processed foods (UPFs) is associated with an increased risk of diet-related obesity and non-communicable diseases.

Some countries, notably Brazil, have done a lot of work to wean their populations from processed food back to natural and wholesome home-style cooking. So good is Brazil's dietary recommendations that you can easily find them in English – among nutritionists they have become a worldwide phenomenon.[15] Studies have shown that ultra-processed foods are habit-forming, habituating the brain to crave them, but they do very little to satisfy our nutritional needs. They are the perfect foods to make money from. Packaged, processed foods have a long shelf-life, they are easy to transport, the ingredients are cheap and you can eat a lot without feeling full. And when you select them in the supermarket you aren't choosing between different foods, but selecting from an array of brightly coloured packets and enticing studio photographs. We eat with our mouths, but we shop with our eyes. The inevitable outcome of habitually eating ultra-processed foods is that THEY MAKE YOU FATTER but they also lead to malnutrition – the worst of double-whammies. The chances are that you'll still feel peckish, even after you've gorged yourself. Protein, fibre, cereals, dairy, leafy vegetables and high water-content fruit will all fill you up with goodness, without the need for intensive sweeteners, artificial stimulants or poor-quality fats.[16] And the more your diet improves, the less you'll be tempted by cravings and binges.

In February 2020 the brilliant food writer Bee Wilson described Brazilian food guidelines in The Guardian.[17] She observed that the biggest departure for the Brazilian public health service, compared to UK guidelines, was to treat food processing as the single most important issue in public health. No longer were people advised to take notice of the nutrients in their food, but instead to observe the degree to which it had been processed, recognising that preservatives, emulsifiers, sweeteners, colourants and other additives all reduced the nutritional quality of the food, while at the same time increasing its calorific content. No government diet guidelines had ever categorised foods this way before.

One benefit of using such guidelines is that it becomes quite easy to self-educate. Instead of slavishly reading through the small print of ingredients, we simply need to stop buying packaged foods. In fact, packages are the only place you'll find small print. You don't find nutritional content on a tomato, a fresh egg, a newly baked loaf of bread or a fillet of fish. That's because by law, little can be done to adulterate the food. You can decide for yourself by simply looking, whether it is good food or not.* Bee Wilson also points out that the new-style advice condemns *at a stroke* many foods which have been reformulated to seem health-giving, from low fat margarines, to vitamin-fortified breakfast cereals, protein shakes and vegan substitutes. Although eating fresh food implies you might have to spend more time in the kitchen, Bee's cookery books are there to guide you through her cooking philosophy that (for most meals) simple is best.

Some people have even gone so far as to suggest that our obesogenic society is re-formulating our minds as well as our bodies. I have a lot of sympathy with the views of Dr Chris van Tulleken. In his excellent book *Ultra Processed People,* he suggests that it is not simply the food we eat, but our acceptance of the need for constant economic growth that has fuelled our excess consumption;[18]

"...our phones and apps, our clothes, our social media, our games and television. Sometimes these can feel like they take more than they give. The requirement for [economic] growth and the harm it does to our bodies and our planet is so much part of the fabric of our world that it is nearly invisible."

* Sadly, gone are the days when we can squeeze fruit, smell fish or tap a loaf.

Over to you

Fresh food is the result of complex natural processes that produce hundreds of nutrients in many different forms. Natural foods are so varied and so complex that it would be impossible every day to ensure that you were getting each of the many different nutrients that were required for every part of the body to run smoothly. It is easier to rely on traditional healthy diets which we have come to realise work remarkably well, in a symbiotic evolutionary process that has gone on for 3.7 billion years, since life first emerged. Some of our traditional diets, such as the Mediterranean diet or the Japanese diet, have been keeping people healthy for millennia. They tend to be low on red meat, moderate on dairy and fruit, higher on fish, wholemeal cereals and highest in vegetables and legumes. All foods can be sweetened by fruits and root vegetables, enriched by dairy and eggs, and enhanced by fresh herbs, spices, and augmented out of season by fermented and dried foods. No packets, no additives and no supplements are needed.

Unlike the restrictions placed on alcohol or cigarettes, healthy eating is hardly touched by regulation, and in our modern world it is becoming more and more difficult to achieve. Unscrupulous food companies can spend millions persuading you to eat anything – however unhealthy – as long as it doesn't contain poison or narcotics. Politicians rarely seem to care. They are, of course, influenced by big business and perhaps subconsciously influenced by their own poor diets. Politics has rarely been seen as a healthy profession.

Our diets influence us more fundamentally than we might imagine. Our digestive system isn't simply a glorified food mixer. The gut is often called the 'second brain' because of the complex network of neurons and nerves that supply it, and due to the very close relationship that digestion and appetite have to mood and decision-making. Gut/brain communications can be mercurial, mysterious and insidious. On the other hand, our 'gut feeling' might be signalling an important but more literal truth to us.

When it comes to the food industry, money talks. A study in 2007 revealed that the lobbying industry in the UK was estimated to be worth £1.9 billion and employed 14,000 people.[19] The report also suggested that some MPs are approached over 100 times a week by lobbyists. No wonder so few government programs are aimed at steering us in a better direction. In spite of the fact that all packaging must be labelled, there is no law that restricts poor quality, high calorie and innutritious foods from being sold everywhere, including to children. Though sometimes the tax system and advertising standards do provide a nudge in the right direction.

UK Government food recommendations influence things like the Eatwell Guide, the bible for food provision for Meals on Wheels, in hospitals, care homes and day centres.[20] The advice is rather simplistic, aimed I'm sure at poorly-trained chefs and naïve care staff. As such they can become anathema to well-trained chefs and knowledgeable carers. Poor dietary advice also poses a risk for people still caring for themselves who might have spent a lot of their life trying to cut down their calorie consumption, but who have inadvertently reduced nutritional consumption at the same time. One study of older women in Australia found that the majority of participants believed that their need for protein would reduce as they got older.[21] It doesn't.

Government advice to the public on healthy menus is scant and misleading. The Eatwell Guide has spawned a handy single-page image called the 'Eatwell Plate' (a misnomer if ever I saw one), that is used in institutional canteens and rarely backed by regulation. Thus, even the government's meagre recommendations are not mandatory. There is so much misinformation in the government's current recommendations that in my view the Eatwell Plate should be called 'Eatbad'.

Government advisors would no doubt respond that fresh food is simply too expensive for some people, particularly those who may not have the time or skills to prepare it. Brown bread costs more than white sliced and fresh fruit costs more than tinned and perishes more quickly. These well-meaning people have tried to develop a sort of compromise diet, not too unhealthy and not too dissimilar from the diet they assume most people will recognise. The Eatwell Plate used to be brimming with tins, boxes and packets. Gradually in response to criticism, these packets have disappeared or been given more detailed labels. All breakfast cereal is fortified, so a box of cornflakes used to suffice. Now that box is labelled wholegrain cereal, a product that is actually quite difficult to find if you are looking at the cornflake shelf in a shop. But the rice, the spaghetti and the bread are all unlabelled and shown as white. The slices of brown bread look decidedly like a supermarket granary bread – which is not a wholemeal bread at all.* A big carton of orange juice has now been removed in response to the realisation that orange juice is as bad for our teeth as sugary cordial. While the image shows fresh fruit, the text still suggests that tinned, frozen, dried or fruit juice will suffice. Yes, tinned

---

* It is almost impossible to buy 100% wholemeal bread in the UK. Just look at the ingredients of Hovis Granary Bread. It is brown to look at, but contains zero wholemeal flour. Starred ingredients add the brown colour: Wheat Flour (with added Calcium, Iron, Niacin, Thiamine), Water, Original Granary Blend (Malted Wheat Flake* (13%), Toasted Wheat*, Toasted Rye*), Wheat Protein [probably added gluten], Yeast, Salt, Fermented Wheat Flour*, Vegetable Oil (Palm, Rapeseed), Caramelised Sugar*, Soya Flour, Granulated Sugar, Emulsifier: E472e, Flour Treatment Agent: E300. Ingredients are listed with the highest content first. Retrieved from Hovis.co.uk, November 2023

fruit is better than no fruit – but cheap fresh fruit should not be hard to come by. In some studies, tinned fruit is excluded from the healthy fruit and veg basket because its consumption is a contra-indicator to cardio-vascular disease. In extremis, people can exist on an Eatwell diet, but it is in no way optimal and looks pretty dull.

The standard Eatwell plate is also decidedly home-counties English, in a bad way. It ignores delightful local specialties like 'neaps' in Scotland or Welsh-cakes from Wales. So irrelevant is the plate to other ethnic groups that the Diverse Nutrition Association has devised an African and Caribbean Eatwell plate that looks to me far more appetising than the UK government equivalent.[22] The tins and packets are still there, but they have lost their prominence to make way for a far wider variety of fresh produce, including yams, soursop, okra, roti and tiny bright red scotch bonnet chillies.

Yet neither the government's version, nor the diverse alternatives, address the issue of an ageing diet. They all recommend semi-skimmed milk, low-fat margarine instead of butter and pay only lip-service to wholegrain and fresh produce. There isn't a lot of evidence to support the use of low-fat alternatives for adults, but there is a lot of evidence to suggest that during youth, pregnancy, illness or old age *moderate* quantities of full fat options (200ml milk or yoghurt and 50g/day cheese) are more healthful and actually more protective against heart disease.

One study, led by Dr Annalisa Giosué at the University of Naples, points out that current nutritional recommendations for cardiovascular disease (CVD) prevention in adults are mainly informed by the belief that saturated fatty acids in dairy products contribute to high blood cholesterol levels, which in turn increases cardiovascular health risks. However, recent data indicate that not all saturated fatty acids have the same metabolic effects, and those present in natural full-fat milk, yoghurt or cheese seem not to effect health as much as other saturated fats. This may be because of the rich mix of beneficial fats within natural milk, as well as the complex nature of nutrients within a natural product. Just as it is a false economy to feed yourself packaged and processed foods at any age, it seems to be a false extravagance to pay extra for processed, low-fat options. The study concludes that, [23]

> "Overall, the available evidence does not support a detrimental effect of dairy consumption on plasma lipids [fats in the blood stream]; conversely, there are consistent indications that consumption of dairy enriched with probiotics can ameliorate the plasma lipids profile and, in particular, reduce total and LDL cholesterol in people with hypercholesterolemia [high cholesterol levels].

Hospitals and care homes will argue that institutional budgets do not provide enough money for a really healthy diet – yet the facts don't support this assertion. Hospital care costs over £500 per day on a general ward.* That's a lot of money, but a minuscule proportion is spent on food. A 2022 analysis of hospital spending in the English NHS by the Tax Payers Alliance revealed that some hospitals were spending less than £2 per meal on in-patients.[24] It is difficult to imagine how such meals can be healthy as well as appetising. Improving food to a level where it might actually help you get better would seem to me to be a very cost-effective move. [25]

---

* This equates to average cost of a bed, per day on a general ward in 2016/17, excluding operations and treatments.

And while some hospitals were spending five times that amount, patient surveys showed that there was absolutely no relationship between the cost of food and its perceived quality. Whether you are trying to prepare something wholesome at home or in a canteen, it is rarely the cost of raw food that bites – it is the preparation time or staff costs. Whether you are travelling, enjoying a snack at your office desk or invited to a slap-up meal, the food might look better, but it will be more expensive than home cooking and chances are it won't even be as healthy as hospital food.

If you only follow up one aspect of this book, I highly recommend that you become a gourmet; a critical eater, a scrutiniser of labels and a dedicated user of good, wholesome, home-cooking recipes. For most of us, eating well is not about dieting. It is not about cutting out, or cutting down. It is actually about discovering what healthy food is, and going to some effort to ensure that we eat it. Becoming a gourmet will help you 'cut through the crap' of fast, processed, over-hyped foods. It will encourage you to widen your tastes and include variety in your diet, whether by tasting some of the heritage varieties available at a farmers' market or trying something from a completely different culture.

After a while, you'll be able to detect how bland and unsatisfying the processed version is compared to the real thing. Once you develop a more discerning palate, you will find that you can eat out very easily, selecting dishes that possess some real nutritional value. Nutrition and flavour go hand in hand. Only innutritious, unwholesome food needs to be smothered in oil, sugar or salt to make it palatable. You might find that you change the café you frequent and the shops where you buy your food. Being a gourmet doesn't start with the loaded spoon; it starts in the kitchen and on the farm, respecting the chef and knowing the provenance.

Does weight matter?

This whole chapter is about encouraging you to eat well by embracing a more nutritious life-long regimen. Eating good food will make you stronger. Making do with a poor-quality, unbalanced diet and a lot of processed food will tend to increase weight and decrease health. And if you can improve your dietary habits, you may very well find you gain energy, become more active and lose a bit of that *flab*. But there is no getting away from the fact that the more fat you are carrying around with you, the less likely you will be to enjoy a long and healthy old age.

As we age and our metabolism reduces, our activity slows down and we can find ourselves gaining weight. The effects of over-eating just a little or under-exercising every day have a long-term, enduring effect.

This doesn't mean you have to deprive yourself of enjoyment. For example, choosing a slightly different biscuit with your mid-morning coffee can easily save 50 calories per day. Theoretically that is 18,250 calories over a year or about 2.6 kilos of extra weight. Adding a 15 minute walk every day to your normal routine can increase the strength and quantity of muscles, including that all-important heart muscle. However, in all honesty I should point out that it isn't as easy as that. If we eat less our metabolism tends to compensate by reducing our activity a bit, and conversely, if we exercise more, we find our appetite increasing, so that we eat a little more as well. Serious attempts to lose weight must include bringing eating into the conscious part of the mind and cannot be achieved by exercise alone.

We've known for some time that the overweight, or under-weight, are more vulnerable to a whole series of deadly conditions including non-communicative diseases like heart disease and cancers and communicable diseases or infections. A few years ago, it would have been impossible to investigate the relationship between obesity and risk of death in isolation from all the other things that dent our health. The sheer quantity of other variables that have a very real impact include smoking, economic deprivation and gender, and would demand a statistical accuracy only available if millions of subjects were followed, for decades. Ansel Keys boasted that his studies had powerful statistical significance because he counted his subjects in their thousands. Today, similar studies are able to follow millions of people living in the UK for long periods of time, thanks to a digital breakthrough that started in the early 1980s when computing was still in its infancy A GP, Dr Alan Dean, decided he would like to develop a patient record system for his practice in Essex. He managed to persuade IT staff at the local BATA shoe factory to help him, including the Czech programmer, Jan Boda. Gradually he recruited other nearby practices to join in. He began to realise the potential of these records. If the pooled and anonymised data could help pharmaceutical companies track the efficacy of their drugs, it could also help public health agencies track new diseases and help individual GPs target high-risk patients. He formed a company called VAMP. In return for anonymous healthcare data, VAMP Ltd offered GPs £500 a month. The system grew rapidly. By 1988 the databank comprised 57 practices and 543,100 patients. By 1990 the databank had more than doubled and by 1995, when it was taken in-house by the Department of Health, the database consisted of more than 4.4 million patients. While the data was gold-dust, Dr Dean didn't become a multi-millionaire. The Department of Health decided *they* owned the data, not the GPs. Under NHS auspices, the data from the NHS Clinical Practice Research Datalink (CPRD) is now sold under license to pharmaceutical companies and has become one of the world's most useful tools for epidemiological studies.*

---

* According to their recent annual report, the CPRD database is a not-for-profit part of the NHS, netting £166 million in 21/22 but spending every penny somewhere!

How big data works

Recently the NHS Clinical Practice Research Datalink, was used to follow 3.6 million patients for up to 18 years. A tried and tested statistical process called Cox regression analysis was used to examine associations between weight, mortality, and the cause of death. By taking account of variables such as people's gender, whether they smoked or drank alcohol, their age, whether they had diabetes or experienced economic deprivation, the statisticians were able to show an astoundingly clear relationship between weight, disease and cause of death. The outcomes may seem startling. Whether we look at smokers or non-smokers, men or women, old or young, rich or poor, their weight stands out as a consistent predictor of diseases caused by diabetes or heart disease.

What is even more astonishing is that death from communicable diseases, injuries or accidents also show the same correlation. All the results in the study show the same relationship in a graphical form that is sometimes called a hockey stick curve or J-shaped curve. The sweet spot, in the graph, with the lowest-recorded deaths from different causes, always occurs when body mass index (BMI) is somewhere between 20 and 30 kg/m², ie. between a healthy weight or slightly overweight. On both sides of this, the risks rise sharply for underweight individuals (generally defined as under 18kg/m²) and those who are obese (over 30kg/m²). This study is interesting because healthy BMI levels may vary between ethnic groups. I am always a little skeptical that weight alone is a good marker for health or ill-health. The BMI figures quoted here are for white British. GPs are trained to be aware that BMI safe zones are different for other ethnicities.[26]

For the first time, because of these massive databases we are seeing very close correlations between weight and health, confirming results from hundreds of smaller, more focused studies. The results above confirm what other weight analyses have found: we don't necessarily need to get right back to svelte in order to see a health benefit. Many other studies have shown that even a 5 or 10 % drop in weight can have a beneficial effect. Moderate change will provide long-term benefits and can encourage you to make further advances.

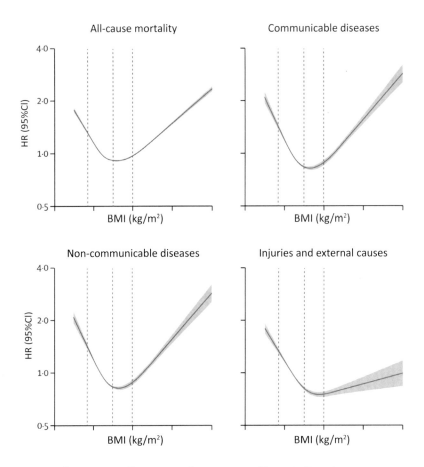

All-cause mortality compared to cause-specific mortality outcomes in a study population of 3,600,000 patients. HR=hazard ratio.

If you find yourself over or under those weights, there is now a real incentive to do something about it. That *something* is to get checked and find professional support to recalibrate your weight.

Does weight watching work?

But when we are older, it is no good simply going on a weight-loss diet. Muscle mass is too valuable to lose. For people who are diagnosed with heart disease or type 2 diabetes, the imperative to diet seriously is important. It can save your life. For example, in people newly diagnosed with type 2 diabetes, we know that a short, sharp low-calorie diet, alongside food education and increased exercise, can re-boot the metabolism, inducing such a successful remission that blood sugar-lowering drugs, such as Metformin, become unnecessary.

While the newspapers might be telling us every day that obesity is inextricably linked to non-communicable diseases such as diabetes and heart disease, we are less aware of the links between obesity and communicable diseases. However, doctors are only too well aware that diseases such as influenza and pneumonia are also more acute among obese *and* underweight patients. This was displayed very vividly during the Covid-19 pandemic, when a stark public spotlight illuminated the extra risks to the frail and to the overweight. This study also highlights how frailty, demonstrated by those who are underweight, is an equally dangerous situation.

What the BMI categories fail to highlight is the different fat to muscle balance an underweight or obese patient may have. Fat people tend to have stronger muscles as they are used to carrying around a lot more weight. Losing weight cannot be achieved without reference to maintaining and increasing muscle mass while losing fat mass.

I make no apology for using the word 'fat' in these pages. It would be cruel to use it in a social setting and even in a clinical consultation, yet its technical meaning should be clearly explained. I am concerned by the fashion for people to wear their weight with pride. I think it stems from the belief that being overweight is not the fault of the individual – and to a certain extent that is true. Often, we can't decide where we eat, how much we pay for our food, or where we buy it. Over-work and underpay may be deemed the frontline causes of obesity, to which I would add an uncaring government, an over-stretched healthcare system, greedy food manufacturers and inadequate food education from primary school to retirement. Sadly, if you put on weight (and it probably isn't your fault) it is only you who can do something about losing it. And what you need to do is to lose fat – not muscle. That is why I find the word 'fat' the simplest and most accurate diagnosis of the issue.

There is a belief that there are people who eat healthily, exercise a lot and have no chronic health problems, but are still 'chunky'. Athletes do have higher than normal BMIs because muscle weighs more than fat. But being over-fat is highly unlikely to be healthy in the long term, even where no health issues are evident today.

Fat shaming is appalling. It can lead to dangerous eating disorders for young and old alike and it is simply unfair to blame someone or single them out. We all have a tendency towards becoming obese or going the other way and ending up over-picky and underweight. In either case the duty of friends, family and clinicians is to support people when they ask for help, without judging in any way. The overriding message must be that it isn't their fault, but if they wish to make changes, there are treatments and regimens that will help.

What we are experiencing has been dubbed an 'obesity epidemic', although that term ignores the thousands of people who are underweight, or who present as a healthy weight, but in fact suffer from low muscle strength (*sarcopenia*). The fact is that our NHS and especially our primary healthcare system cannot afford to help people properly. For example, a GP surgery is highly unlikely to own a bio-impedance weight scale, or even bother to weigh its patients on an ordinary pair of scales, or measure their waist circumference, which is a very economical (if rough and ready) indicator of the presence of visceral fat.

Adverts on TV that show happy obese people jogging, underscore the dangers of timid government messaging. Countless studies show that diet or exercise alone can improve our health a bit, but long term, the best prescription is both. Surely it is cruel to lull people into a false sense of security?

A recent study that focused on the over-65s concluded that weight loss plus exercise improved physical function and ameliorated frailty (bone and muscle weakness) more than either weight loss or exercise alone, although each of those was beneficial to some extent.[27] The study highlights that for older people it is not always about losing weight, but losing fat mass.

By all means start with exercise, but there is no kind way of saying this: obesity – as opposed to simply being a bit overweight – increases the risk of early death and worse still of long-term illness. The caring approach is to help people improve their diet and exercise.

Obesity is a condition of modern life, and rarely a signal that we are weak, or greedy. Often it can be a sign that we have spent too long looking after and caring for others, instead of attending to our own health. The 'cure' is education, self-care, and knowledgeable support that can frame the situation holistically. I have learned through experience that it is no good putting someone on a diet if their self-esteem, their finances, their work, their relationships and their mental health isn't also addressed at the same time.

Some people who are very overweight are attracted to the concept of surgery or pharmaceuticals in order to regain their health. What is often forgotten is that the studies which show fantastic success with gastric bypass surgery and appetite suppressants all require a very strict diet as well. For example, the pre-bariatric-surgical *liver diet* lasts for a month or six weeks and is *very* rigorous. Appetite suppressants simply don't work, and can be dangerous, if the old over-calorific diet isn't replaced with a healthier diet. Whichever weight loss avenue you decide to pursue, the challenge will always be the same. You must be prepared to follow a healthier diet for life. The fat cells don't die-off – they simply wither, waiting to be recharged, making you fat again as soon as your healthy diet is cast aside.

Gastric bypass surgery, while much improved these days, removes parts of your stomach or gastric tract that do an important job in absorbing nutrients. Once removed, you will never be able to return to eating what you did before, and you are destined to take nutritional supplements for the rest of your life. Surgeons perform such surgery because if you are morbidly obese (a BMI of greater than $40kg/m^2$) or if you already have obesity related issues and have a BMI of $35kg/m^2$ you have increased your risk of chronic illness or death to such an extent that something must be done.

Take me away from my appetite

The most recent 'slimming' injections, which are notorious due to the Hollywood celebrities who take them, are called *GLP-1 agonists*. These are chemicals called *semaglutides* which augment the feeling of satiety that our stomach hormones naturally secrete after a good meal. They will put you off food – good healthy food as much as unhealthy food. Appetite suppressant tablets must also be taken alongside diet re-training.

Otherwise, you are likely to put all the weight back on – and more – the minute you stop taking the tablets, or self-administering the jabs.

These drugs can have worrying side effects, such as stomach and bowel disorders, vomiting complications during routine surgery and may trigger depression or suicidal thoughts.* One study assessed the absolute risk of serious complications at 1% per year of use. Because they are so new, we have no indication of the long-term effects. But they have been released earlier than you might expect because of the 99% of people they can safely help, right here, right now.[28]

None of the weight loss interventions are a quick fix. And why should they be? It has most likely taken you decades to reach the weight that you are. In comparison, for those of you who are moderately over-or underweight, I recommend a simple healthy diet, together with ratcheting up your exercise (see Chapter 6). It is the best long-term option, attracting little pain, few side effects and low risks.

It is a very specialised diet that allows us to lose fat, especially if we were fat as children, fat as adolescents and fat in middle-age. The hard truth is that getting back to a normal weight is a long slog for most overweight people, but it almost always pays off. For all those people who have dieted and seen the weight come back on, there are hundreds who have got back to a normal weight and maintained it. Many will talk of the transformation in their lives that losing weight can achieve. It can feel like a new lease of life, effecting mood and confidence as well as improving vitality and body image. By losing a bit of weight, people naturally become more animated and actually feel like exercising more. Diet a bit first, then increase activity and food intake, and so on, until you are back to a healthy regimen and a healthy *forever* diet. Part of the

---

* But remember, being obese can also have serious mental and physical side effects.

purpose of dieting is to learn. There is no point in losing weight only to have it all loading back on as soon as you stop dieting.

If you think you are in this situation, get help. You'll find it very hard to achieve your goals alone. Study after study reveals that losing weight *for good* is a lifestyle change that requires sympathetic support, technical know-how and careful monitoring. Even the best diets can fail if the monitoring is inadequate. Beware of charlatans. If the advisor makes no measurements of your fat and muscle mass, politely bow out. If you are not questioned about your mood, your job and your social life, then the advice may be too limited. If you are advised to cut our whole food groups, then walk away.

Low moods can trigger comfort eating, and there is no diet in the world that can cure comfort eating without also addressing the underlying discomfort. Eating is one of the most important and pleasantly social activities we can enjoy. If those activities are taken away from us, for whatever reason, our mood will be affected. The commensality of eating is therefore as vital to healthy eating as it is to good mental health. It makes sense to nurture your inner gourmet, and share your enthusiasm for good food with your friends and family.

That old adage *you are what you eat* has never been so true.

Endnotes

1 Ho, FK, Celis-Morales, C, Petermann-Rocha, F et al. (2021) *Changes over 15 years in the contribution of adiposity and smoking to deaths in England and Scotland.* BMC Public Health 21, 169 2021. DOI:10.1186/s12889-021-10167-3

2 Elizabeth David, *Summer Cooking.* Preface to 1965 edition. Publisher Grub Street, 2011 Edition

3 jamieoliver.com/features/jamies-plan-to-tackle-childhood-obesity [retrieved September 2023]

4 Public Health England (2016) *Government Dietary Recommendations: Government recommendations for energy and nutrients for males and females aged 1 – 18 years and 19+ years.* August 2016. gov.uk/government/publications/the-eatwell-guide [retrieved February 2024]

5 Bauer J, et al. (2013) *Evidence-based recommendations for optimal dietary protein intake in older people: a position paper from the PROT-AGE Study Group.* Journal of American Medical Directors Association 2013; Volume 14: pages 542–59.

6 UK Scientific Advisory Panel on Nutrition (2021) *SACN statement on nutrition and older adults living in the community.* Jan 2021, Published online at: gov.uk/government/publications/sacnstatement-on-nutrition-and-older-adults-living-in-the-community [retrieved July 2021]

7 Brownie S. et al., (2015) *The 2013 Australian dietary guidelines and recommendations for older Australians.* Australian Family Physician Volume 44, No.5, 2015 Pages 311-315

8 Brownie S et al. (2015) *cf*

9 McKevith, B (2004) *Nutritional aspects of cereals.* Briefing Paper British Nutrition Foundation, Nutrition Bulletin, 29, 111–142 nutrition.org.uk [retrieved July 2021]

10 Aune D, et al. (2017) *Fruit and vegetable intake and the risk of cardiovascular disease, total cancer and all-cause mortality – a systematic review and dose-response meta-analysis of prospective studies.* International Journal of Epidemiology 2017 Jun 1;46(3):1029-1056. DOI: 10.1093/ije/dyw319

11 Commonwealth of Australia, (2006) *Nutrient Reference Values for Australia and New Zealand Including Recommended Dietary Intakes.* Endorsed by NHMRC September 2005. nhmrc.gov.au [Retrieved June 2018]

12 vegansociety.com

13 Mintel (2024) UK *Vitamins and Supplements, Market Report* 2023 available to purchase at store.mintel.com/report; Summary report free online. Written by Claire Finnegan [retrieved February 2024]

14 Taylor C et al., (2020) *Fruits, vegetables, and health: A comprehensive narrative, umbrella review of the science and recommendations for enhanced public policy to improve intake.* Critical Reviews in Food Science and Nutrition, 60:13, 2174-2211,

DOI: 10.1080/10408398.2019.1632258

15 Ministry of Health of Brazil, Secretariat of Health Care, Primary Health Care Department (2015) *Dietary Guidelines for The Brazilian Population* fao.org/nutrition/education/food-based-dietary-guidelines/regions/countries/brazil/en [retrieved April 2023]

16 Monteiro C A et al. (2017) *Household availability of ultra-processed foods and obesity in nineteen European countries* Public Health Nutrition. doi:10.1017/S1368980017001379

17 Wilson B, *How ultra-processed food took over your shopping basket.* The Guardian February 13 2020

18 van Tulleken, Chris (2023) *Ultra Processed People.* Book, published London 2023 Penguin, Randon House UK

19 Parvin, P (2007) *Friend or Foe? Lobbying in British democracy* Hansard Society. Archived from the original (pdf) on 2008-12-21.

20 Public Health England (2016) *The Eatwell Guide* Public Health England in association with the Welsh Government, Food Standards Scotland and the Food Standards Agency in Northern Ireland; Available at gov.uk/government/publications/the-eatwell-guide [retrieved February 2024]

21 Brownie S, Coutts R (2013) *Older Australians' perceptions and practices in relation to a healthy diet for old age: A qualitative study.* Journal of Nutritional Health and Ageing 2013; Issue 17: pages 125–29.

22 diversenutritionassociation.com [retrieved September 2023]

23 Giosuè A, et al. (2022) *Consumption of Dairy Foods and Cardiovascular Disease: A Systematic Review.* Nutrients. 2022 Feb 16;14(4):831. DOI:10.3390/nu14040831

24 Cook S (2022) *An analysis of Hospital Estate spending in the English NHS:* Tax Payers Alliance May 2022 taxpayersalliance.com [retrieved 2023]

25 Guest JF, et al., (2019) *Modelling the annual NHS costs and outcomes attributable to healthcare-associated infections in England.* British Medical Journal Open 2020 Jan 22;10(1):e033367 DOI: 10.1136/bmjopen-2019-033367

26 Krishnan B et al., (2018) *Association of BMI with overall and cause-specific mortality: a population-based cohort study of 3·6 million adults in the UK.* The Lancet, Volume 6, Issue 12, p944-953, December 01, 2018. Published: October 30, 2018 DOI: 10.1016/S2213-8587(18)30288-2

27 Villareal DT, et al. (2011) *Weight loss, exercise, or both and physical function in obese older adults.* New England Journal of Medicine. 2011 Mar 31;364(13):1218-29. DOI: 10.1056/NEJMoa1008234

28 Ruder, Kate (2023) *As Semiglutide's Popularity Soars, Rare but Serious Adverse Effects are Emerging.* American Medical Association Medical News: Published online November 15 2023.

6

The dancer

Definition of animated:
Adjective: Full of vivacity and spirit, lively; characterised by movement, activity; animate, possessing life*

Movement is an essential facet of life. Our ability to get from A to B, to reach up to pick fruit from trees, or to bend down to cradle a kitten, proves that we are not dumb plants, rooted to the spot – we are animals. We are animated. Look at the dictionary definition of 'animated' to check if it sounds anything like your mode of life. If you've ever observed children, great apes, ponies or puppies, you will see that we are all born with oodles of liveliness.

Unfortunately for the human race, children are often chastised for running about. They are required to sit still, keep quiet and stay calm. That may make teaching mathematics to five-year-olds an easier task, but it petrifies us into submission as adults. After school sports, very few of us ever run again except to catch a bus, often lumbering ungainly, tripping over inappropriate shoes and dragging too much baggage. If you are a woman, the problem is even worse. High heels hobble, our clothes

* Collins online dictionary. www.collinsdictionary.com

hinder and propriety inhibits us.

If you work in an office then you are doubly cursed, tied to a desk and monitored in case you leave your keyboard untouched for too long. These days we tend to use a car, we pick fruit from the supermarket website and only admire animals on Instagram. Our physical experience of the world is declining, reduced to touching screens, yelling commands at unresponsive voice recognition apps and slouching behind power steering wheels that self-guide. Is it really too much effort to tweak the wheel in order to remain in the correct lane?

Along with this decline in activity has come a decline in strength and in health. But the cure for this decline is not to be found in the gym, or on exercise machines. An hour's exercise three times a week (as advised by most governments) doesn't compensate for a sedentary life. It is normal, every-day activity, the sort humans have engaged in for millennia, that makes the difference.

Gyms don't work

Movement uses up energy and speeds up the metabolism while strengthening the heart, lungs, muscles and bones. Understanding the metabolic shifts that the body makes is fundamental to understanding how to remain healthy throughout life. Even the healthiest diet won't work so well without exercise, but that doesn't mean that you need go anywhere near a gym. I think that gymnasia, exercise bikes, rowing machines, exercise couches (yes, they really do exist) are all part of the marketing world's desire to promote expensive things that we think we might need – even though they are optional, not compulsory.

The relationship between health and activity isn't linear. If you are sedentary, just a small increase in the volume of daily physical activity can produce important health and functional benefits. The diagram from

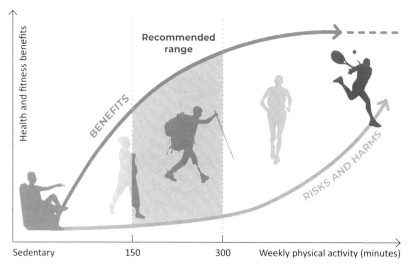

Health and fitness benefits

Recommended range

BENEFITS

RISKS AND HARMS

Sedentary   150   300   Weekly physical activity (minutes)

Dose response curve for exercise: World Health Organization.

the World Health Organisation above demonstrates that getting out and about doesn't mean being attached to a machine. Walking, hiking, swimming, playing tennis etc., is more fun and reduces the danger of injuries. It isn't so much intensity of activity- for many people; it is simply some activity.

We don't have to go rushing round like mad things to get enough exercise. A recent study concluded that currently inactive or insufficiently active people should be encouraged to engage in physical activity of any intensity, including those of light-intensity.[1] A lot of us discovered this for ourselves during lock-down, when thousands of people found their normal routines destroyed overnight. Some resorted to Zoom classes but most of us were forced to be much more sedentary than usual. In a normal day most of us will spend several hours relatively actively – this might include getting dressed up and going out, walking up and down the shop floor or along the High Street, meeting friends, playing games and having fun. We missed those social activities not simply because they were social, but because they were healthful. The 300-400 extra calories-worth of energy used up in an hour's exercise cannot compensate for normal active life, where 200 calories per hour of lower intensity activity might be engaged for five, six or even eight hours every day.

Perhaps you've never thought of a morning's shopping trip as exercise, but if you are walking about for four hours, you are likely to be using up just as many calories of energy as a solitary hour in a lonely gymnasium.

Exercise isn't about beating yourself up. Think of kittens or puppies – no-one is standing over them with a stop-watch. They play until they are out of breath, then they flop down and rest. Learning to leave the car at home, to escape the rigid employment that makes us desk-bound, and to take pleasure in being out and about, is really all we need, especially as we grow older.

There is nothing better than walking for half an hour every day. It will improve fitness, heart rate and contribute to fat loss. You can build up to it if you like. After a few weeks you'll feel lighter and more active and you'll find you actually want to take part in more strenuous activities. Your metabolic rate will have risen and you will have freed your mind.

Before long any activity will ensure that beneficial changes start to occur in the body and in the brain. One of the most important changes is to the metabolism. This happens quite naturally when we are vigorous and healthy. The exercise of skeletal muscles, whether we're talking a brisk hike or pruning the roses, will have an immediate and beneficial impact on the mitochondria (the power stations of the cell) that cluster alongside them, generating the energy for movement.[2] These tiny mitochondria* within each muscle cell, provide the bio-chemical power to move our

* See Chapter 4 for a full description of how mitochondria power our bodies.

muscles, at the same time as regulating muscle breakdown and regrowth.

Throughout life, skeletal muscle mitochondria are highly adaptable, their density within the muscle fibres changing according to physical demands. The more activity we engage in, the larger and stronger our muscles become and the more flexible our metabolism. Muscle strength has implications far wider than simply strengthening our arms and legs. When we engage in activity and movement, we are strengthening our muscles, including the heart, reducing fat, and at the same time driving blood and nutrients towards rebuilding our bones. Animation changes the entire body – and the mind.

Yet, it is a myth that exercise builds muscles. In fact, during exercise muscle tissue breaks down. Muscles are quite literally torn apart by movement, so that old cells can be flushed away and a newer, stronger collection of muscle fibres can be re-built. The restructuring of muscle occurs during periods of postprandial*, post-exercise rest. It is during the lie-down after lunch, or a good night's sleep when new muscle is built, but nothing will happen unless old muscle has been broken down by exercise first. A similar process occurs with bones that are also continually degrading and re-forming. Maintaining a positive balance between the atrophy of exercise and the regeneration of tissue during periods of rest can help to maintain a healthy body; bones as well as muscles all improving in symbiosis.

Over and above the vital importance of physical activity in maintaining muscle and bone, movement also exercises the heart and lungs, increasing the heart rate, the rate of breathing and thus the metabolism. There had been some concern that increasing exercise in older people might over-tax the heart or might increase oxidative stress, which can lead

---

* Postprandial means after meals.

to an increase in the release of pro-inflammatory cells. However, what we actually observe is the increased release of anti-inflammatory cells, which overwhelm any inflammatory processes. That may be one of the reasons why activity is linked so strongly to longevity. While all this is happening, the body can use the metabolic increase to flush out excess fat, toxins and waste products. Within the digestive system, movement also helps food to progress through the stomach and intestines, enabling its efficient breakdown and elimination.

We all know the prescription for exercise – or perhaps we think we do. Aerobic exercise (*with oxygen*) is the sort that increases our breathing rate. Around the world, weekly targets for aerobic exercise are:

- 150 minutes of moderate aerobic activity such as cycling or brisk walking

OR

- 75 minutes of vigorous aerobic activity such as running or a game of singles tennis

However, the advice has always been that healthy adults should also seek more strenuous exercise, called resistance exercise, where we exert more pressure on the muscles by pressing against them or lifting heavy objects. The classic resistance exercise is weight-lifting, but dancing, a game of tennis or gardening, as well as carrying shopping and doing the vacuuming, can all be beneficial. The advice is that healthy adults should aim for exercises on two or more days a week that work all the major muscles (legs, hips, back, abdomen, chest, shoulders and arms).[3]

What is exercise

Aerobic exercise burns fat, so is an excellent addition to a new gastronomic regimen. Many studies have shown that aerobic exercise, alongside diet, works much better in weight reduction than either do separately.[4] During exercise, breathing more heavily results in an increased heart rate, which in turn increases the metabolism and thus uses up more energy. Hormones in the body are dispatched to the fat stores where complex fat molecules called triglycerides are released and broken down so that they can be used by the body to generate more energy. But it would be counter-productive to replace the fat by eating more as soon as it is used up. The activity has started to use up fat stores, but there will still be plenty of energy left until the next meal. Some studies have shown that by triggering fat burning we actually stop thinking about eating so much. Counterintuitively it reduces hunger pangs.[5] Furthermore, energy exerted after a bout of exercise is likely to continue to burn off even more fat stores. Thus, the walk home from the court is almost as good for fat burning as the vigorous game of tennis.

It is not necessary to flog yourself in any department in order to increase your energy levels and metabolic rate. For example, there is no need to increase your step count to 10, 15, 20 or even 25,000 steps a day, as some misguided souls have done. Studies have shown that the sweet spot is more like 7,000 steps per day. And any activity, even a five-minute walk to the shops, can be helpful.[6] It all counts as aerobic exercise. You know when you're walking briskly enough, because you will be able to feel your quickening breathing and heart rate.

Resistance exercise, where we exert more stress on our muscles, is the precursor to building new muscles, breaking down the bonds of the old ones. For several hours, if not days, after muscles are stressed, the body makes use of growth hormones and foods such as proteins and glucose to 'build back better'. A rest period and a healthy protein-rich diet are as important to muscle-building as exercise. That is why advice suggests strenuous resistant exercise two or three times each week, with periods of rest in between, but aerobic exercise *every* day.

Exercising the older body

The basics of exercise don't change as we get older. However, the periods between rest and between high-protein meals become shorter. The advice for people over 75 who are involved in any type of strenuous exercise, is to rest between bouts and to ensure that all three main meals each day contain protein. There should be no meal-skipping.

With time, the muscle structure changes and thus the appropriate exercise regimen changes as well. We develop less fast-twitch muscles, which are mainly used in bouts of resistance activity, and more slow-twitch muscles that are used in aerobic exercise. Thus, the balance of aerobic to resistance exercise also needs to change as we get older. Systems do de-generate and the hormones that trigger muscle-building do deplete. But our ability to exercise muscles and re-build them never leaves us. Despite the fact that there is a massive difference between individuals at any age, it really is never too late for anyone. People can build muscles into their 90s, given the right diet and the right activity.[7]

While these well-known resistance and aerobic exercise prescriptions have become the gold standard for adult physical fitness, they take no account of capacity, age or gender differences. Neither do they do much for the relationship between movement and mood. We've all seen someone who is overweight, sweating and pounding round the park in the mistaken believe that if it's not hurting, it's not working. However, the opposite is true. The activities we most enjoy are those that will see us safely into our dotage.

Exercising for its own sake, for hours at a time, is a solitary and, I would argue, a rather selfish act. It is far better to engage in something more social, or to sign up for something where the exercise is part of a voluntary activity. At home, or in the office, try to become one of those people whom we would describe as animated. Be the first to leap up to answer the door, or put the kettle on. Short bursts of regular activities, even simply getting out of the office chair every so often, add up to a big change in metabolic health. The difference between obsessive solitary exercise and jumping up to put the kettle on is that you're doing it for someone else. Psychologically you are immediately rewarded by the warm feeling of being helpful or hospitable.

We don't have to go out of our way to find opportunity for exercise. In any case, most day-to-day activities provide a mixture of aerobic and resistance work. You only have to think of carrying shopping back home, or a day's hiking, to understand this. But the comparison of a chore such as the weekly shop with a pleasure like walking in the hills, provides further clues for how to maintain that healthy, limber and lithe body. Movement should be part of everyday life – motivating and enjoyable. Exercise is rather like dietary supplements. With vitamins the watch word is 'food first'. With exercise it is 'life first'!

Mind and body

Physical exercise isn't just about exercising the heart and lungs, or stretching muscles and strengthening bones. One day we may laugh at such a confined definition of healthy exercise. Activity is as essential for mental health as it is for the body. Social, outgoing, outdoor activity is a highly effective treatment for low mood, as well as an important support to treatments for depression, anxiety and cognitive impairments, not all of which respond well to anti-depressants. You might say that activity can reach the parts that anti-depressants cannot.[8] The irony is that the exercises that help the whole body, including the mind, have very different characteristics to aerobic and resistance exercises you might prescribe for an athlete to help them win a medal. It is the difference between real life and being a lab rat.

We can observe all sorts of good and bad things happening when we study exercise in the laboratory, but it is really only through life experience that we find activities to engage us as individuals and help us live our unique best lives. For example, there is a school of thought that strenuous exercise should be avoided as we age as it might act as a stressor. But while exercise does tax the body, it seems that pushing yourself a bit further triggers a whole series of useful processes within the body and the brain, which helps our immune systems. Just as exercise promotes new and stronger muscles and bones, it also increases cerebral blood flow and triggers a neurotransmitter release, a sort of mental 'letting go', which is the precursor to generating new thoughts, laying down new memories and nurturing original thinking.[9] Repetitive exercise of just one type can be as ineffective for the mind as it is for the body. If you find yourself caught up in its grip, you may need to examine your motivation. Even mildly strenuous jogging will only exercise certain muscles and if you jog on tarmac, the long-term effect may well be leg and knee strain. The watchword is cross-training, exercising different muscle groups in different ways. An exercise machine, which is designed to exercise one muscle group at a time, can enhance an athlete's training if well-supervised. But these machines are notoriously problematic if an inexperienced user experiments at home or in a poorly-supervised gym.

Michael Rosen tells us in his fascinating book, *Getting Better*[10], about a time when he used to go running round Hackney Marshes. At first it cheered him up but soon it became an obsession. Then one day he was boasting to someone about how much further he might run next time. He was shocked by their response, *"If I were you, I'd worry less about where you're running to and think about what you're running from."*

How the mind works the body

Not one finger can be raised without the brain imagining a movement and then issuing the instruction, so that signals can be delivered via nerves to the muscles. The sequencing of movement seems to have a particularly strong association with health and it may be why dancing, music and movement programmes achieve consistently good results, over and above their ability to make us feel good.

There is something about the rhythms, the cadences and the complex, almost mathematical structures, that make musical activity so enjoyable. While research is in its infancy, there is evidence that dance classes where the students are able to extemporise using a pre-learned series of movements, or choreograph a unique response to the music, can be particularly powerful. Working with music doesn't have to be strenuous, though some dance classes are! Singing can be hugely beneficial, as can yoga to a gentle musical accompaniment. You might not consider these active enough to count as exercise. But they are; such endeavours still possess all the elements that make up a healthy activity. Singing is perfect for everyone and anyone; even beneficial among people who have had strokes or dementia. Some people might find it difficult to string spoken sentences together, they may still derive much joy from remembering an old song. The brain seems to be able to remember more words when they are set to music.

Let's dance!

Practitioners are beginning to realise that dance classes have the edge on exercise as we get older, and that one type of dance exercise – ballet – stands head and shoulders above the rest.* It isn't the most intensive of exercises; many of the moves are downright simple, but the discipline has all the components of successful exercise. For a start, the music quite literally moves us! By using our very robust musical memory pathways and attaching movements to the music, we can strengthen and prolong both physical and mental agility.

Ballet does so much more for the body than many other types of dancing. Any type of dancing is good for the body, but it is only classical ballet that combines complex sets of gestures that require precise movements using and having control over the whole body – from head to toe. And it requires quite sophisticated concentration, where we must engage memory, emotions and logic. Mastering a slightly tricky ballet move provides the student with an important feeling of being in charge of their physique; that feeling of agency can rub-off on other parts of our lives too. For example, research in Australia, undertaken by the Queensland Ballet Group, found that older dancers reported improvements in self-confidence, self-esteem and coping strategies.[11]

In another study, older female dancers in Melbourne, who joined the Fine Lines Contemporary Dance Company, have been shown to have stronger social ties, and feel less marginalised by continuing their ballet practice. These studies have shown that however impaired our movement is, there is a ballet class that will work.[12] As one member of the Fine Lines Contemporary Dance ensemble for mature bodies in Melbourne commented:

---

* In the interests of openness, I should explain that I'm a personal devotee.

"If you can breathe, you can dance."

Staying upright

Ballet in its strictest form is about very precise poses and movements, and it is worth examining in some detail why these are important to 'Silver Swans', as they call ballet aficionados over 50.

Studies of ageing show that it is loss of stability, balance and a lack of sure-footedness that is a very potent precursor of frailty and even death. Part of the correlation between falls and death is due to the fact that once we become frail, we aren't so good at staying upright. If we do topple there is a very short period of time in which we can take action; extending a leg to minimise impact or grabbing onto something. We need to be able to perform rapid movements of the feet to re-stabilise the body.

My 90-year-old mother was given foot flexes and tip-toe tapping when she was recovering from a pelvic fracture. Hers were armchair exercises, but the foot movements were exactly the same as the exercises I now do in every ballet class.

The ballet pose has an even more direct relevance to the prevention of hip fractures, which are the injury most closely linked to the onset of frailty. For a long time, we assumed that the catastrophic falls that cause major fractures were due to bone loss or osteoporosis. But clinicians now realise this is very far from the truth. In one study in California, females 85 years and above were found to be 18.73 times more likely to sustain a hip fracture than those aged 65–69.[13] Yet, their bones were nowhere near 18 times weaker. The missing factor was loss of muscle strength and mass. Falls are quite literally a slippery slope all older people walk. As people become frailer, their co-ordination changes and near-misses occur, transforming the brave into the timid. This in turn reduces the exercise we get, reduces strength and induces hypotension (dizziness on standing up). Resistance to falls is in fact related to the way muscles and bones work together; gain muscle strength and corresponding bone strength will improve, and vice-versa.

The ballet turnout

In ballet, the turnout exercises certain muscle groups that are critical if we are to retain a resilience to falls. This stance, crucial to almost every ballet step, requires a professional ballet dancer to stand, heels together, feet turned out at an angle of 180° away from each other, achieved by rotating the thigh bone in the hip socket. The knee, calf, ankle and foot work in dynamic partnership, following – not leading – the pelvic level movement. In leisure ballet the feet will most likely be placed at 90°, but even the gentlest turnout will stretch all the leg and hip muscles, including the deep lateral rotators, six small muscles that arise from different points around the hip area, connecting and strengthening the bones of the pelvic girdle.* These muscles all terminate at a prominent bony knob on the outer face of the thigh bone, thus strengthening the vulnerable hip pivot-point. In addition, by tensing the backside and thigh muscles we are building-up the 'padding' that will help to protect our hip and pelvic bones if we fall on them. This stance also exercises other muscles and tendons that stabilise the leg and knee.

---

* The six small muscles of the deep lateral rotators include piriformis, superior gemellus, obturator internus, inferior gemellus, obturator externus and quadratus femoris.

By strengthening hip and leg muscles during ballet, people can retain a more upright stride in normal walking while also improving confidence. If we fall while we are moving forwards at pace, momentum will propel us forwards onto hands and knees, incurring nothing more than grazes; but a fall while walking more hesitantly can mean we fall backwards instead. It is far more difficult to protect ourselves, and stop the fall. If we do topple backwards, the point of impact is likely to be near the hip, increasing the risk of a serious fracture.[14]

Shake a leg

Battements or leg movements stretch the leg in all directions in turn, changing the body's balance point. *Battements tendu* involve a quick flexing of heel and toe. For example, in the *Battemens en cloche* exercise the dancer swings the leg back and forth, mimicking a bell. While they might sound difficult, these steps are practiced at the *barré or* ballet bar, rendering them very safe. By no means strenuous in themselves, speed and accuracy have a certain *caché* among dancers mature or young. If a skilled dancer trips, their reactions, honed in *battements tendu* and *en cloche* steps, can help them regain stability without ever hitting the ground. Regular practice could save any of us in a trip or slip.

In many types of movement, from ice-skating to line-dancing, much of the skill is associated with repeated gestures and balance. The student is encouraged to engage both arms and legs in any movement across the floor. Dance, yoga or acrobatics teaches us to become more aware of the body's position in space, straightening and lengthening the spine, while using the limbs and the head to adjust the balance. This is described in ballet as *aplomb*; a term ascribed to the famous Russian teacher Agrippina Vaganova.[15] It is a great confidence-builder, as well as a strengthener.

Agrippina Vaganova in 1910.

"Look at life all around; everything is growing, everything is moving forward. Therefore, I recommend keeping in touch with life and with art"

Agrippina Vaganova[15]

The heart

A heart beats faster in any pose or dance step where the hands go above the shoulders, providing an excellent cardio-vascular work-out. Many household tasks, such as pruning, reaching up to high shelves or even talking animatedly with friends in a café involve such arm movements. In dance the *ports de bras* or 'carriage of the arms' presents the classical ballet arm positions, but also leads into the flowing moves that create graceful and expressive gestures. Even people who may have difficulty walking or standing can derive exercise benefit and pleasure from some of the classical arm routines.

While these movements are generally gentle and easy to perform, they raise a heart rate a reported 20 % higher than leg exercises can achieve, at lower levels of exertion, or where it simply isn't possible to stand for any length of time.[16] There is a touching video doing the rounds on the internet which shows an elderly Alzheimer's patient listening to ballet music. In a matter of seconds her mood lifts, she starts to perform the graceful arm movements of the ballet. She is visibly transported.*

For Silver Swans of any age, ballet offers an almost perfect balance between conviviality, good exercise and maintaining poise and gracefulness that is so easily lost or forgotten.

I find ballet excellent, and because of that I've taken the time to research its efficacy in older cohorts. But ballet is not unique. Each person can find their own perfect match. Many activities can help maintain muscle and bones, and they are by no means limited to formal exercises or classes.

---

* Alzheimer's Research Association YouTube Video *Former Ballerina with Alzheimer's Performs* 'Swan Lake' *Dance*; youtube.com/@alzheimersresearchassociat2883/videos [retrieved February 2024]

Life is movement

Almost any activity you can think of involves exercise of some kind. Owning an allotment means physical work, gastronomic pleasure and social activity. Volunteering can be hard work, but enormously satisfying. Ring the changes, do different things, so that you exercise a different set of muscles, bones and brain cells. Because life is exercise, you will never need to see the inside of a gym.

Some people consider exercise as an adjunct to life, to be added as a separate activity, needing to take place in a special location, to be learned anew and requiring a whole new wardrobe. And I admit that dance classes come into that category, but I would maintain that they teach a style of movement that can be translated into everyday life.

But classes are not the only way to engage in exercise. Far better that we see activity as an integral part of life. We no longer have to strive to catch or grow our own food. Machines wash our clothes and clean our houses. We've grown up seeing wealth and success linked to more leisure time and reduced physical activity. In the 1950s we swapped the push bike for a little car, and bought labour-saving devices for the home. We have now progressed to home cinemas, remote controls, voice recognition and chairs that declare themselves Lay-Z-Boys. And a whole service industry has sprung up to ensure that any physical activity, from lifting a vacuum to taking the dog for a walk, can be accomplished for a small fee, by someone less busy or important than ourselves. I am always amused when I see some high-flying (and usually male) executives followed by a (usually female) assistant, carrying the files. It is the dutiful assistant who is benefitting from an incidental bit of strength exercise, while the executive strolls, unladen, towards his first coronary.

It may be a little surprising to encounter my advice that everyday tasks, like cleaning and DIY, shouldn't be outsourced. They can keep the body agile and save us money. Habitual activity can become dull. Even so, regular tasks, such as putting out the rubbish or doing the dishes, actually help to regulate our lives, giving us a feeling of agency as well as providing incidental exercise. More constructive tasks, such as cooking or decorating, exercise the creative muscles in the mind as well. Often these are all lost – at one fell swoop – if we move into a care home.

Imagine the mental and physical activity required if you invite a friend to tea. You might write a note or make a call. You'll need to decide what to prepare, perhaps go shopping, make a cake, cut some bread, do a quick clear up, or get out the best china. Then finally, after you've enjoyed their company, chewed the cud and had a few laughs together, you'll have to clear away, wash up and possibly store all that gossip in the long-term memory in case you want to pass it on to another friend. At any age, that sort of incidental activity can provide a surprisingly potent amount of mental and physical exercise. It is what we lost in lockdown and what many of us are striving to get back to.

Most geriatricians say that however little exercise we are capable of, we should in all cases try to reduce sedentary behaviour. Though we do tend to favour a comfy armchair as we age, it is just as important to get out of it and move around when you are 90 as when you are 30. Yet care-homes abound with lounges, TV rooms and conservatories, where older people are positively encouraged to sit down and be quiet. It's a bit like the way we pacify five-year-olds in order to teach them.

It is very easy to let household activities become too bothersome. It is also very easy for well-meaning friends or family to start to lock-down such activities, to protect the older person from becoming tired, or falling. But instead, we should encourage each other to do more, not less. Don't always rush to make the tea when you go round to see an elderly relative. Be observant – do they really want you to do it? The longer such activities can be self-managed, the better. Studies have shown that everyday activities, such as using the stairs at home, can have a radically better effect on physical health than the same exercise in a gym.[17] It doesn't really matter what interests you, as long as you stay interested.

Exercise aids

When we get older, we should make reasonable adjustments to new circumstances. Do not reject walking aids, such as sticks, walkers, or folding chairs, that help us to walk for longer distances. The Nordic or hikers stick is becoming commonplace on any public footpath you care to follow. A rolled-up umbrella suffices for some people.

Do not reject pain killers that allow you to keep moving during bouts of low-grade muscular or joint pain. Do not complain when a rug needs to be rolled away, if it becomes a trip hazard. Think of it as an exercise aid. While increasing safety, they help us continue to engage in all sorts of activities and thus remain independent, staying physically fitter and mentally more agile. Ageing is not a one-way street. Those special or routine activities can help us maintain *and* regain health. At the same time, it is plain common sense to reduce trip hazards by ensuring that floor coverings are safe and steps are well illuminated. Rather than expect an old person to simply sit down or take the lift, why not ensure that handrails and banister rails can make moving about the place easier to manage?

The most important exercise aid is a buddy.[18] Walking groups are springing up all over the place.* Creativity, especially if it involves some socialising, is a special part of exercise because it provides a work-out for the mind as well as the body. There is also some evidence that manual dexterity alongside mental effort might be beneficial. Think of activities

---

* Visit the Ramblers Association website ramblers.org.uk for groups in your area.

such as drawing, painting, and craftwork. Even quiet pass times like knitting can be good for us, especially if the pattern is challenging or the conversation of the knitting bee is stimulating. Don't kid yourself that knitting is an old lady's game. These days it has become positively fashionable after the Gold Medallist Tom Daley was seen knitting poolside in the Tokyo Olympics.

Different activities will be available in different areas. You may enjoy meeting people at a shed. The men's shed movement, which started as a way to encourage macho Australian men to connect, converse and create, is now running in the UK.* Some of the sheds are open to women as well. Whatever your interests, a little research should find a suitable local group. If you don't find exactly what you are after, in your neck of the woods the organisation will support you to start a group for yourself.

Anything that involves creativity, even if it couldn't be classed as exercise, will be beneficial. In particular when we join a class or group, we can find a new set of like-minded friends. The social aspect must not be under estimated: those who attend creative classes tend to feel that they gain more assertiveness, more *voice, visibility,* and *validation.* A 30-year follow-up among British patients indicates that a weekly or even a monthly class or formal exercise is adequate to maintain and prolong health.[19]

Dancing may not be your thing – and it doesn't have to be. Remember organised activity is only part of the activity you need to keep healthy. Experiment; get to know new things about your body, and at the same time expand your mind and your social circle. Find your own groove and above all, enjoy!

---

* www.menssheds.org.uk

"If there were a drug that could do for human health everything that exercise can, it would likely be the most valuable pharmaceutical ever developed."

Neurologist Mark Tarnopolsky[20]

Endnotes

1 Füzéki E, Engeroff T & Banzer W (2017) *Health Benefits of Light-Intensity Physical Activity: A Systematic Review of Accelerometer Data* of the National Health and Nutrition Examination Survey (NHANES). Sports Med. 2017 Sep;47(9):1769-1793. DOI: 10.1007/s40279-017-0724-0.

2 Gregory D Cartee, et al. (2016) *Exercise Promotes Healthy Ageing of Skeletal Muscle.* Cell Metabolism. 2016 June 14; 23(6): 1034–1047. DOI:10.1016/j.cmet.2016.05.007

3 NHS Live Well Website; nhs.uk/live-well/exercise

4 Colleluori G, Villareal DT (2021) *Ageing, obesity, sarcopenia and the effect of diet and exercise intervention.* Experimental Gerontology. 2021 Nov; Issue 155:111561. DOI: 10.1016/j.exger.2021.111561.

5 Colleluori G, Villareal DT (2021) IBID

6 Tudor-Locke C, et al. (2011) *How many steps/day are enough? For adults.* International Journal of Behaviour Nutrition and Physical Activity; Published 2011 Jul 28. DOI:10.1186/1479-5868-8-79

7 Deer, RR, & Volpi, E (2015). *Protein intake and muscle function in older adults.* Current opinion in clinical nutrition and metabolic care, 18(3), pages 248–253. DOI:10.1097/MCO.0000000000000162

8 Deslandes A, et al.: (2009) *Exercise and Mental Health: Many Reasons to Move.*

Neuropsychobiology 2009; Issue59: pages 191-198. DOI:10.1159/000223730

9   Dan L, et al. (2023) *Systematic Review: Landscape Characteristics Correlated with Physical Activity of the Elderly People*, Land, 2023; 12(3): page 605. DOI:10.3390/land12030605

10 Rosen, Michael. *Getting better: Life lessons on going under, getting over it, and getting through it*. Published by Ebury Press. 2023

11 Ali-Haapala, A (2018) *Ballet Moves for Adult Creative Health*. Stage One Research Report. Queensland Ballet in association with Queensland University of Technology. Available from queenslandballet.com.au [retrieved February 2024]

12 Southcott, J & Joseph, D (2019) *If you can breathe, you can dance*: Fine lines contemporary dance for mature bodies in Melbourne, Australia. Journal: Women Ageing, 1–20 2019

13 Sullivan, Kristynn J et al. (2016) *Demographic factors in hip fracture incidence and mortality rates in California*, 2000-2011. Journal of orthopaedic surgery and research vol. 11 4. 8 Jan. 2016, DOI:10.1186/s13018-015-0332-3

14 Nevitt MC et al. (1989) *Risk factors for recurrent non-syncopal falls*. A prospective study. JAMA. 1989 May 12; 261(18):2663-8. DOI:10.1001/jama.1989.03420180087036

15 Vaganova, A (1948) *Basic Principles of Classical Ballet*. Translation Dover Publications. Reprinted Jan 1969. ISBN 9780486220369

16 Osawa Y, et al. (2014) *Effects of 16-week high-intensity interval training using upper and lower body ergometers on aerobic fitness and morphological changes in healthy men: a preliminary study*. Open Access Journal of Sports Medicine. 2014 ;5:257-265. DOI: 10.2147/oajsm.s68932

17 Michael E, White MJ & Eves FF. *Home-Based Stair Climbing as an Intervention for Disease Risk in Adult Females; A Controlled Study*. International Journal of Environmental Research and Public Health. 2021 Jan 12;18(2):603. DOI: 10.3390/ijerph18020603.

18 Xu X, et al. (2023) *Social relationship satisfaction and accumulation of chronic conditions and multimorbidity: a national cohort of Australian women*. General Psychiatry 2023;36:e100925. DOI: 10.1136/gpsych-2022-100925

19 James S, et al.; (2023) *Timing of physical activity across adulthood on later-life cognition: 30 years follow-up in the 1946 British birth cohort*. British Medical Journal; Journal of Neurology, Neurosurgery & Psychiatry Published Online First: 21 February 2023. DOI: 10.1136/jnnp-2022-329955 https://jnnp.bmj.com/content/early/2023/01/24/jnnp-2022-329955 [retrieved March 2023]

20 Tarnopolsky, M (2016) *The New Science of Exercise* Time Magazine September 12, 2016 time.com/4475628/the-new-science-of-exercise [retrieved March 2023]

7

The thinker

Know your body, know your mind

The last thing you should do if you are overweight or under-active is to embark on a rigorous diet and exercise regimen without first asking yourself some serious questions about your motivation.

Without motivation and focus your efforts may well backfire. It certainly takes knowledge and support from others and it takes some courage to resist the pressures that are all around us. Sometimes we can employ fate to bounce us out of our complacency. A new job or moving to a new home can be an excellent trigger for ditching old habits and making changes.

When we talk about lifestyle changes, we are talking about changes that we make ourselves, sometimes consciously, but often unconsciously. Positive change most often comes when our conscious mind, firing on all four cylinders, observes, questions and then decides to change a habit that we've been following, unconsciously, for years. Often it takes professional help to get us in the right frame of mind.

Consider an airline pilot, responsible for steering an aircraft through thousands of miles of travel. Most of the time sitting in the cockpit is plain sailing, but the pilot is constantly on the alert, able to re-set the compass or tweak the controls to take account of new conditions. A good pilot is well-informed, well-trained and keeps an eye on the instruments, knowing the machine they fly. It is a responsible job. You are the pilot; the aircraft is your body and the journey is life.

Feelings of empowerment and control are not to be found in even the most virtuous of salads or rigorous of workouts. Good health is as much a mental issue as it is physical. Recognise and identify the voice in your head that asks, 'Why bother?'.

Don't ignore that voice; you won't be able to block it out. Bring that voice right out into the open, examine what that voice means, discuss with professional supporters and friends, and consider where that voice comes from. It is so often the case that the voice that tempts you to eat when you are not hungry, or chooses to avoid activity, originated years ago. The voice is the bit of you that feels dejected, rejected or unloved.* We all try and ignore that voice; there is pain behind it. Psychologists advise that it is better to embrace those feelings than ignore them. Working on mind and body together will have far greater benefits.[1] Freud called the voice of temptation the alter ego, while the psychologist Phil Stutz calls it his shadow. Stutz says that we should recognise and accept those inner voices as part of ourselves, even to the extent of conjuring up an image of a shadow and accepting it into our lives. He sees this as the path to self-expression and confidence.[2]

Consider your work environment, your home environment and your

---

* That voice can also represent a part of us that avoids social contact, the introvert within us or the one that tends towards paranoia.

leisure pursuits. Issues might include relationships, work stress or self-esteem. Often, all we want to do when we are stressed is to collapse on the sofa and consume a ready meal. We've all done it. From such a position, any new resolution simply won't work.

Get help if you need it. Remember the goal isn't simply life-long health, it is life-long happiness as well. It is worth spending a little effort to get it right.

Thinking and stress

When we are distracted, overthinking, worrying or ruminating we call it stress. The body deals with stress – whether it is mental or physical – in exactly the same way. Body and mind have a limited range of bio-chemical responses, which can be traced right back to our earliest animal ancestors. Your systems can't tell whether the problem is lack of food, danger, over-exertion, sickness or heartbreak. Whatever the cause, the same major stress hormones, adrenaline, cortisone and nor adrenalin will start coursing through your veins, triggering symptoms that feel like butterflies in the stomach and cause increased heartrate and hyperventilation.

Whatever the trigger, we tend to react to stress in a series of totally predictable ways. We start eating anything and everything (in case the stress is caused by starvation and needs feeding), we feel exhausted (in case the stress is caused by energy depletion and needs rest), and we feel anxious and charged (in case the stress is caused by an external threat and we need to fight or run away). If one of these quick fixes doesn't relieve the stress, we may get locked into a long-term use of a short-term responses, which in themselves are very bad for our health. Problems such as binge eating or anorexia nervosa often start as a reaction to stress. Unfortunately, because humans are endowed with a 'belt and braces' biology, for which evolution is famous, they tend to react to stress by over-eating, exhaustion *and* feeling on edge. Modern-day problems, such as stress at work, don't require any of the aforementioned responses; a trip to HR or a quiet word with colleagues might be all that is needed. Thinking it out before you react is always a good policy – but it requires conscious thought, when often all we want to do is to push that underlying stressor to the back of our mind. Over-eating, ennui or abusing alcohol and drugs are all forms of self-harm and should not be seen as a quick-fix. At the very least it is an amber light.

The ability to cultivate a healthy and active mindset establishes good groundwork for a long life. Confidence (a learned skill) helps us commit to decisions and summon the self-belief required to embark upon a physically healthier lifestyle. The philosopher Descartes wrote, back in the seventeenth century, '*Cogito ergo sum*' – *I think therefore I am.** It is also useful to tweak Descartes' wisdom to read *I am what I am thinking*. Clear away a few of those brain cobwebs, put the past behind you and re-focus your thinking on enjoying the present, however imperfect it might seem, while planning for a better future. To some people this will require a 180 degree turn, from looking back to looking forward. We can't change the past, but we can start, right now, to change our future.

The most common response to looming mental health issues is to ignore them. Yet rumination can escalate, manifesting as chronic anxiety, stress and tiredness which, if unaddressed, can lead to depression and contribute to more serious mental health problems in later life. Far better to find ways of treating a minor illness before it overwhelms us. You wouldn't ignore a fractured bone, so why ignore a troubled mind?

---

* Descartes, 1644, from the book, *Principles of Philosophy.*

One in six of us, in any given week, at any age, will be suffering from one of the more common mental health problems. It may not reach clinical levels, but this negative *drip-drip-drip* can do real damage to our life-chances. Treating a mild depression can reduce the risk of obesity, addiction, self-harm and unhealthy or reckless behaviour. It really does make a difference to act as soon as you feel things are going a bit awry. A study in Canada randomly selected a large cohort of people, interviewing them in 1952, 1970 and 1992. When they looked again in 2011, they discovered that depression at any time over the intervening 40 years was associated with a heightened risk of mortality. Some people had not sought treatment for more than 20 years. However, those people who had attended to their depression when it arose had regained their natural life expectancy.[3]

Such studies highlight the strong association between mid-life depression and dementia in later life.[4] It is easy to over-focus on this – especially when we are feeling low – so let's be clear; dementia is not a normal or inevitable part of ageing, and neither is it an inevitable result of long-term depression. Only about 4% of the over-65s are diagnosed with dementia of any kind, and only about 2% will go on to develop symptoms that require treatment. Furthermore, dementia is manageable in the vast majority of people, for the vast majority of their lives. However, while dementia is treatable, depression is curable. The wise will seek early therapy.[5]

What happens in a brain?

We are often told that the secret to avoiding dementia is a form of brain exercise – *use it or lose it*. That isn't the whole truth. We need to delve into the physiognomy of the brain to understand a little more about thinking and mental health.

Thinking is dependent upon filaments in the brain called dendrites. These make the connections between banks of neurons that we perceive as thoughts, triggering actions, responses and memories. A typical brain cell looks a bit like an octopus, with the neuron at its centre and a few or many dendrite tentacles growing out of it. At the end of each dendrite is the synapse, where tiny bio-electrical impulses momentarily bridge the microscopic gap between adjacent dendrites, sending signals between neurons. Neurologists used to imagine that if we could map the brain, we could find the root of consciousness. These days we don't think that thoughts are triggered by one dendrite signalling to another. The dendrites form complex tree-like structures. It is much more likely that conscious thought is the result of signals diffusing across a host of brain cells at the same time. Thoughts occur in the brain like waves on the sand, shifting and triggering many neurons at the same time, shaping our mind map.

Working memory, the short-term memory that we use to recall something like a telephone number, is dependent upon the level of focus we possess at the time. It is like a memory pinball machine. Someone tells you something and *ping* – you can say it right back. Generally, information such as a telephone number doesn't need to be lodged in the long-term memory bank. If you do need to remember something like that for any length of time, you are likely to want to write it down. But if you use that number a lot, eventually the memory will move from short-term memory to long-term. The neurons that fire every time you dial that number, will establish a strong link, that enables you to remember the number – possibly for ever. Similarly, if something dramatic or traumatic happens to you, the level of focus is so dramatic, that you may also remember the incident until your dying day. But that doesn't mean that the process involves only one part of the brain, or one sector of brain cells.

Over time, a replicated action, thought or piece of information will create a well-trodden neural pathway. These routes and interconnections between dendrites create the long-term memory, but it is never hard-wired. It is simply a well-used series of circuits within the brain. Other thoughts, or the passage of time, will modify it. Memories from long ago that have been retrieved many times can seem as sharp as yesterday, though that sharpness can be illusory. The trigger for memory is just as likely to be the sound of a favourite piece of music, or other sensory perceptions such as smell or a taste. It all depends on the connections you made at the time of laying down that memory and the way you have re-remembered that event in the more recent past.

The human brain is far more mutable than a computer. Every time we recall a long-term memory, perhaps a holiday taken years ago or a significant celebration, we use our imagination (another part of memory) to piece together different strands of the original experience. We then set that memory back into our mind, often in a slightly different configuration. We might conflate separate events, especially if, like childhood birthday parties, they tended to follow a pattern. We are also past masters at mixing reality with things we have seen on TV, or in photographs of our past. This means that we can be far more innovative than a computer, which simply bangs out the same old, same old. Even the sophistication of AI, isn't a patch on human thought. Humans can take short cuts, use hunches, experience, creativity and intuition to make great, sometimes life-saving decisions in milli-seconds or to suddenly see the world differently. The Eureka moment, the flash of inspiration or the tennis player's anticipation of their opponents shot are all things that AI cannot do.* That makes us less logical than a computer, but far more creative and responsive.

---

* At least AI can't do that sort of thing yet.

Habits are a form of long-term memory. Regular repetitions which are first lodged within the short-term memory can quickly turn into more permanent long-term habits. It takes conscious effort and an agile brain to kick a bad habit, or form a healthy new one. That is the way that good habits, such as regular tooth-brushing, become ingrained, but it is also how negative thinking can develop.

We all possess big brains and millions of dendrites, although they are not always stable. The more often the memory is used, the more agile the circuitry and the better the brain-function. While being able to remember lots of stuff is impressive, what really makes us seem clever is our ability to use whatever memory capacity we have to amass wisdom – the synthesis of knowledge, experience and foresight. This wisdom is called fluid ability by neurologists. The great thing about fluid ability is that it helps us to use what we already know about the world to solve novel problems, especially those where we have little experience.

Studies have shown that people of any age can improve their fluid ability by exercising short-term memory. To a computer geek the differences between short and long-term brain memories are a bit like the difference between short-term random-access memory (RAM) and the data stored on a hard disk. RAM is used to run programs in computing and solve problems in the brain. The hard disk lays down long-term memory files for future retrieval. Fluid ability uses both long-term memory (experience) and fast (short-term) decision-making abilities, enabling our minds to apply long experience to new challenges. It is the epitome of wisdom.

Over a lifetime, some aspects of cognition may decline, however many crosswords we do, or languages we learn. But decline into serious memory loss is by no means inevitable. Anyone who comes into contact with teenagers knows that mild short-term memory loss has little to do with age, and absolutely nothing to do with wisdom. Neurologists are beginning to realise that the sort of intelligence we might call wisdom keeps developing, even when our ability to remember names or long numbers wane. We don't stop learning just because we reach a certain birthday. In fact, studies have shown that vocabulary and task-based skills often continue to improve right into old age. Skills that adapt our existing knowledge to a new challenge have been demonstrated to improve with mental exercise. Every society has its sages, and they are generally the elders, the ones who have thought long and hard.[6]

Mental agility is just as positively influenced by creative, cultural and social pursuits as they are by mental exercises and puzzles. Any thinking that uses our imagination is both satisfying and healthy. Being with other people requires us to deal resourcefully with the unexpected; I have no idea what my companion will say next. It might be difficult to imagine a computer stopping to enjoy a natter with another computer, but in humans it is these social and cultural interactions that spark our creativity and fuel our spontaneity. Painting, writing, singing and dancing all have benefits for the brain as well as the body. Reading, listening to the news, watching films on TV, talking and discussing, all help our minds remain fluid. Word games, such as crosswords and scrabble or numbers games such as monopoly or poker, are all good exercises for the mind, but they are even better if practiced in a social setting. [7]

A Scottish example

On 1st June 1932, all children at school in Scotland who were born in 1921 were set a well-respected IQ test by the Scottish Mental Survey. In 2001, the Aberdeen cohort from that survey, then octogenarians, were traced. Researchers found that higher intelligence test scores from that young group of children were significantly correlated to longevity, even though many of them had risked death on active service during the

Second World War. And while social class and material wealth were also indicators of better health and longer life, it was that 1932 IQ test, when the children were only 11 years old, that gave the closest correlation and predicted their life chances for 70 years.

Why can people of higher intelligence live longer, even if they haven't had the advantages of money and education that we might expect to come to them?[8] The research team concluded that the ability to think logically, to plan and to make better decisions are all functions of an active intelligence. Perhaps the more adept had also managed to think more creatively, realising that material wealth isn't necessarily the be-all and end-all for a happy life. Perhaps they learned to think for themselves and plough their own furrow?

Dear reader, do not fret about what your own IQ score was when you were 11 years old. The fact that you are reading this and other books puts you into a literate category of people who are statistically cleverer, and thus perhaps healthier, than those who have never opened a book.[9]

It may be that of all our organs, a healthy brain is the one thing we should strive to keep in tip-top condition. We should strive to exercise our minds and enjoy the fruits of learning, memory and communication. Gottfredson and Deary, in their report *Intelligence Predicts Health and Longevity, but Why?* (American Psychological Society 2004)[10] conclude:

"The cognitive demands of preventing illness and accidents [require that we] remain vigilant for hazards and recognize them when present, we remove or evade them in a timely manner, contain incidents to prevent or limit damage, and modify behaviour and environments to prevent reoccurrence."

Look around you. There is good evidence that some of us maintain a lively mind well into old age. Pensioners going to university are no longer a novelty. Don't bother trying to enter the Guinness Book of Records with your newly-acquired degree if you are a mere stripling of 60 or 70. Unless you've reached your 100th birthday before graduating, they won't be interested. [11]

Neurodegeneration

We must guard against behaviour that might damage those precious brain dendrites, which take a lifetime to grow, but which can be damaged by brain injury, stroke, and toxins as well as some diseases. Neurodegeneration, a slow and progressive loss of brain cells in specified regions of the brain, is the main pathologic feature of diseases like Alzheimer's and Parkinson's. It has a long list of causes, including alcohol and drug abuse, poor diet, lack of exercise and pollution. The more we use a particular set of neurons (brain cells), the more we are triggering signals which travel along the dendrites to create a memory, an action or a reaction. The more they are used, the stronger and more stable the pathways become. Our neurons, with their trees of dendrites spreading outwards, are by definition as old as the memories they can induce. Neurologists are beginning to realise that the well-tempered brain exists in balance between maintaining established neuron clusters, where memories are held, while growing new dendrite links to accommodate newer skills and experiences. Protecting your head when cycling or rock-climbing is as important as nurturing new thinking through an enriching environment and a thriving sense of curiosity.[12,13]

Technically, it is incorrect to say that brain damage destroys brain cells; what is more likely is that damage interferes with brain-signalling, destroying the connections where dendrites meet and pass on impulses. This occurs at the synapses. They require a strong burst of information in order to fire, and can easily be dulled by physical or chemical damage which interferes with the signals.

The dulling of our brain signalling often presents as depression. Antidepressants, which have become the medically accepted method of dealing with depression, work on the bio-chemical processes that occur at the synapses. SSRIs (selective serotonin re-uptake inhibitors) slow the dissipation of the so-called happiness hormone serotonin, allowing a longer and stronger signal to flash between brain cells. Even in the early stages of treatment, SSRIs have been shown to support neuro-regeneration; they actually encourage repair.[14]

The treatment for depression is not just a pill. NICE advises therapy as well. NICE (the National Institute for Clinical Excellence) is the organisation that approves and advises on optimal NHS treatments. If NICE doesn't approve it, a GP won't prescribe. If NICE suggests a priority of therapies – almost always the cheapest first – then you are going to have to fight to get something different. A good therapist, and a successful therapeutic programme, will help you deal with the cause of your depression as well as the effect. Psychoanalysis can help you find the root of the problem, while cognitive behavioural therapy (CBT) provides a simpler (quicker and cheaper) training process, bringing habits into the open, finding their triggers and using conscious thoughts to modify them. Both approaches are approved by NICE, but unsurprisingly the CBT approach, which only lasts a few weeks, and tends not to delve too deeply into causes, must be tried first.

Feed the mind

No change in life comes easily, but our ability to deal with change is part of our innate ability to retain our mental acuity. When we are fully engaged in life retaining our curiosity and sociability, we are far less likely to ruminate. A full social life can influence us to drink too much or take other health risks, but becoming too solitary can have exactly the same effect. Find friends and situations that stimulate the mind and you'll find it far easier to make the lifestyle changes you desire.

We are social animals, though today we are so often caught up with work, family commitments or household chores that we sometimes forget that it is outside the home and job that we can find many new interests. Social media may help, providing a window on the world, but there is no substitute for being in the world, physically amongst people. I say this as a confirmed bookworm, a natural homebody and something of an introvert. In spite of being all these things, I know from experience that I don't do well on my own. I enjoy the company of like-minded people. I enjoy having a sense of purpose in life and part of that purpose is going out, getting about, seeing people, attending talks and exhibitions – in fact, doing all the things we need to do in order to feed the mind.

Eat! Move! Think! – The virtuous circle

The preceding three chapters have encouraged you to become a gourmet, a dancer and a thinker: to consider different ways of eating, moving and using the mind. We often talk about increasing our activity, doing a course or improving our diet, but in fact eating, moving and thinking should all be optimised in harmony. It is not necessary to diet like mad, exercise like a demon or join Mensa in order to look after yourself. If you eat *more* healthily, exercise *more* and use the mind *more*, many things will fall into place. By exercising the mind and body during the day, sleep

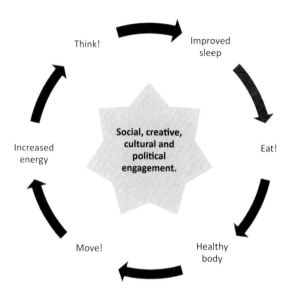

Eat! Move! Think! – important elements of a virtuous circle of health.

will come more easily. By eating healthily, you will find more capacity for exercise and more energy to resolve mental stress. It can work in both directions. A recent study showed that sleeping well could reduce calorie intake.[15] Seek balance; neither excess, nor deprivation. None of this requires you to restrict what you do. On the contrary, this is all about becoming more active, more discerning and more adventurous.

Good mental health is one of the tenets of a healthy lifestyle that complements healthy eating and activity. The virtuous circle of diet, activity and mind shows how they all interact. However, there is a focus to this virtuous circle which could well be the key to everything. In most of the last three chapters I've talked about YOU – about your diet, your exercise regimen and your mind. But just like in the aircraft, a pilot has very little to do if the plane never leaves the ground. As you age you need to schedule a flight plan for the rest of your life. That is why the focus of the virtuous circle above is engagement: getting involved. For you, that might mean a richer social life, becoming more creative or getting stuck into a cause, political party or pressure group. Life should be lived with people and for people. It's not about you – it's about us! All of this requires mental and physical energy, something that ageing tends to limit. That is why it is so important to decide where you will focus your energies.

I know that it is all too easy to put off lifestyle changes. Something more urgent and pressing always requires our immediate attention. Management consultants might say we are programmed to think about the here and now. Way back in our evolutionary past anxiety was preserved for the 'fight or flight' response. We can summon the energy to change direction when a lion crosses our path, but we have little innate resistance to a cream cake. Fortunately, in the course of modern life we rarely encounter lions. But perhaps we should go looking for the lions in our lives, in the centre of our own virtuous circle to get ourselves energised to make changes through engagement in the widest possible sense of the word. I do not think that we are all driven by instant reward and that those rewards are inevitably naughty; that would miss the point about living a full and engaged life.

Life changes are best made from a position of strength, which we attain by engaging support from friends and from practitioners. Eat with friends; move with friends; discuss with friends. This will reduce your anxieties. Take a walk in the park with a friend and suddenly you're ready to tackle that long-delayed decision.

I do not wish to underestimate the things which might hold us back. Some of us can find that we are marooned by prejudices, by poor housing, financial problems and social exclusion from the rich life we ought to be living. We can be seduced by the consumer society, laid low by a toxic environment or trapped by circumstance. Adolphe Quetelet* so eloquently described the challenge in the nineteenth century, observing that we are all subject to, *"the laws that govern life's consequences."*[16] But we are also sentient beings, named *Homo Sapiens*, or the thinking ones. Thinking leads to action; and action to thinking. As the old Esso petrol campaign encouraged us:

"Put a tiger in your tank!"

Endnotes

1   Mathisen, TF et al. (2020) *Is physical exercise and dietary therapy a feasible alternative to cognitive behaviour therapy in treatment of eating disorders? A randomized controlled trial of two group therapies.* International Journal of Eating Disorders 2020 Apr;53(4):574-585. DOI: 10.1002/eat.23228. E-published 2020 Jan 16
    Treatment effects for women with bulimia nervosa or binge eating disorder (Doctoral dissertation). Norwegian School of Sports sciences
2   Phil Stutz & Barry Michels, (2012) *The Tools, 5 life-changing techniques to unlock your potential.* Book. Publisher Random House London and New York 2012
3   Gilman, SE et al. (2017) *Depression and mortality in a longitudinal study: 1952–2011* Canadian Medical Association Journal 2017 October 23;189:E1304-10. DOI: 10.1503/cmaj.170125

*   See Chapter 2.

4   McManus S, et al. (eds.) (2016). *Mental health and wellbeing in England: Adult psychiatric morbidity survey 2014*. City University Online. Leeds Digital NHS open access files: digital.nhs.uk/pdf/q/3/mental_health_and_wellbeing_in_england_full_report.pdf [retrieved February 2024]

5   Alzheimer's Society, Dementia Statistics Hub. From dementiastatistics.org/statistics/numbers-of-people-in-the-uk/ [retrieved April 2023]

6   Borella, E et al. (2013), *Working Memory Training in Old Age: An Examination of Transfer and Maintenance Effects*, Archives of Clinical Neuropsychology, Volume 28, Issue 4, June 2013, Pages 331–347, DOI: 10.1093/arclin/act020

7   Hartshorne, JK & Germine, LT. *When does cognitive functioning peak? The asynchronous rise and fall of different cognitive abilities across the life span*. Psychological Science. 2015 Apr;26(4):433-43. DOI: 10.1177/0956797614567339. E-published 2015 Mar 13.

8   Deary IJ, Whally LJ & Starr JM. (2003) *IQ at Age 11 and Longevity: Results from a Follow-Up of the Scottish Mental Survey 1932*. In the book edited by Finch C.E., Robine JM.& Christen Y. *Brain and Longevity. Research and Perspectives in Longevity*. Publisher Springer, Berlin, Heidelberg. 2003 DOI:10.1007/978-3-642-59356-7_10

9   Billington, J. (2015) *Reading between the Lines: A study of the Benefits of Reading for Pleasure*. Report from Quick Reads, by The Centre for Reading, Literature and Society. University of Liverpool

10 Gottfredson & Deary, (2004) *Intelligence Predicts Health and Longevity, but Why?* American Psychological Society Current Directions in Psychological Science 13(1):1-4 2004 DOI: 10.1111/j.0963-7214.2004.01301001

11 Phillipson, C & Ogg J (2010) *Active ageing and universities: engaging older learners* Report Universities UK ISBN 978 1 84036 229 9 February 2010 available at universitiesuk.ac.uk

12 Meltzer LA et al. (2005) *A role for circuit homeostasis in adult neurogenesis*. Trends in Neurosciences Vol.28 No.12 December 2005

13 Shen, H. (2014) *New brain cells erase old memories* Nature News 8 May 2014

14 Santarelli, L. et al. (2003) *Requirement of hippocampal neurogenesis for the behavioural effects of antidepressants*. Science 301, pages 805–809

15 Tasali E, et al. (2022) *Effect of Sleep Extension on Objectively Assessed Energy Intake Among Adults with Overweight in Real-life Settings: A Randomized Clinical Trial*. JAMA International Medicine. Published online February 07, 2022. DOI:10.1001/jamainternmed.2021.8098

16 Van Drunen, James. (1919) Quotation from the pamphlet; *Adolphe Quetelet*, Famous Belgians Translated by Wendy Shillam 2019 Available in the London Library

8

Drugs for healthy people

We know that lifestyle changes can be the most difficult to achieve, but the most potent of medicines. Why bother, when we know that for almost every condition associated with ageing, there is a drug that might help? Today it is becoming more common to use medicines or even surgery, where a few years ago we would have been forced to take the high road and make those difficult lifestyle steps. Surely this is good news? At last, we can forego some of the struggles associated with making change. If popping a pill can lower your blood pressure, or make you slim again, why bother with anything else?

In the main we accept treatments that cure, even if they involve strong drugs. Few people would hesitate to take a pain killer when they have a bad headache, or a short course of antibiotics for an infection. Similarly, many of us will submit to challenging chemotherapy when we are faced with life-threatening cancer. But what of prophylactic drugs – pills and potions we are advised to take every day for the rest of our lives, not to cure us, but to keep us healthy?

Drugs for healthy people attract charlatans like bees to honey. In Jane

Austen's day, if the heroin was fainting, the doctor would be called, and inevitably a tonic would be prescribed, even though the cause (in fiction) was more often than not a broken heart. There is little evidence that these tonics did more than a cup of tea, a draught of brandy or a spoonful of honey. In fact, caffeine, alcohol and sugar were the major ingredients of many of these old-fashioned remedies, and before regulation, many were sometimes also laced with potentially dangerous substances, such as cocaine or morphine.

Tonics

Old-fashioned tonics almost always looked like comic book medicines. They were dark liquids, sometimes glutinous, often tasting disgusting. One of the world's most popular beverages started its rise to fame as a tonic. Until 1904 a disgustingly unhealthy cordial called Coca-Cola was sold as a patented medicine, a cure-all tonic, and distributed from the back of covered wagons by a travelling quack called John Stith Pemberton. He had concocted a mixture of sugar syrup, coca leaves (cocaine) and kola nuts (caffeine) to try and cure his own addiction to morphine. This so-called 'brain stimulant' gained immediate popularity in his home state of Atlanta, no doubt due, in part, to the fact that temperance was gaining popularity at that time. You could get seriously inebriated on the cocaine it contained, without alcohol passing your lips. Sales must have been further stimulated by the National Prohibition Act of 1920, which outlawed the sale of alcohol right across the United States.[1]

These days Coca-Cola contains neither cocaine nor kola nuts, though it still has in it prodigious quantities of sugar and caffeine. Wikipedia suggests that its nine 'secret ingredients' are, in order of magnitude, high-fructose corn syrup (HFCS), caramel colouring, caffeine citrate (a by-product of the decaffeination of coffee), phosphoric acid and

A late 19th/early 20th Century advertisement for the forerunner of Coca-Cola in the days when it contained cocaine.

small quantities of essential oils and flavourings such as citrus, vanilla, cinnamon, nutmeg and possibly lavender. According to Coca-Cola's own website, a regular 330ml can of Coca-Cola contains the equivalent of between 8 and 10 teaspoonfuls of sugar, depending on where you purchase it in the world. Diet Coca-Cola contains 42.2mg of caffeine – almost as much as a double expresso. The full-sucrose version of Coca-Cola contains less caffeine: only 32mg.[2]

However, don't for a moment assume that you are merely drinking a sugary drink. This beverage contains high-fructose corn syrup that is much higher in fructose than natural sugar and is thus absorbed differently in the gut. Neither is the caffeine hit from chemically-derived caffeine in any way similar to the taste, aroma and texture experienced when drinking a well-brewed expresso.*

We do have food regulations today – the EU is the world leader – but there is still very little control over what can be placed in foodstuffs. Apart from ingredients that are definitely dangerous, substances on the edge of pharmaceuticals that appear in ordinary foods such as fructose and caffeine are very lightly regulated. But in essence the chemical hit derived from caffeine and fructose in a modern glass of cola is just the same as taking a medicine such as a cough mixture, which is also packed full of legal chemicals such as caffeine and fructose. The difference is that we only take cough mixture for a few days at a time. Caffeinated sugary drinks are considered benign and thus drunk by some people as if they

---

* Table sugar is 45% glucose and 55% fructose, found in a chemically-bonded amalgam called sucrose. HFCS is a factory-produced mix of dry ingredients and can contain up to 90% fructose – although Coca-Cola seems to contain a lower percentage of fructose (I cannot verify this). The mix is different across the world. Aficionados in the US report that Mexican Coca-Cola that is made from natural cane sugar tastes far better than the corn syrup-derived variety. [https://americanfizz.co.uk]

are as harmless as a glass of water. Fructose is correlated with obesity and even something as innocuous as caffeine, considered to be quite benign in small doses, can pass through the placenta and give an unborn baby a high.

Drugs

You might think that anything we put in our mouths as a drug is far more closely-controlled than a foodstuff. The UK has one of the strictest prescription laws in the world. Many classes of drugs, even those that do not have major side-effects, can only be procured with a prescription. However, some pharmaceutical companies have become profitable by distributing relatively cheap prescription drugs in vast quantities and justifying them to busy GPs who have no time to treat the underlying causes of common diseases such as diabetes or high blood pressure. The older you are, the more likely you are to be offered these drugs, even though the reduction in risk may not be as large or as certain as you think. Some of these treatments are life-saving; others merely a sticking plaster. Some have proved fatal. The OxyContin scandal in the United States illustrates all too vividly the power of marketing to seduce GPs and to hook patients into taking inappropriate drugs, which they didn't realise contained high doses of opiates. Tens of thousands of people became hooked, and in the US 16,600 people died of overdoses of these type of prescription pain killers in 2010 alone[3]. Watch the Netflix docudrama *Painkiller* for a chilling account of the story.

Biguanides

Pronounced *bi·gwa·nides*, biguanides, or drugs that lower blood sugar levels, are used to treat diabetes type 2, a serious chronic metabolic disease that is on the increase in the UK, in all age groups. It occurs when the pancreas stops working efficiently, stopping or slowing down its secretion of viable insulin and consequently allowing blood sugar levels to rise. In the old days it was called age-onset diabetes. Back then people were simply advised to go carefully, reduce their sugar consumption and take a bit more exercise. But over the years we have observed that that general advice was often insufficient.

Recently, the number of people presenting with high blood sugar has risen alarmingly. The average age of onset is now not 80 or 90, but 40 or 50. Even teenagers have been diagnosed. In younger people, a disease that almost inevitably becomes progressively worse has a lot more time to cause serious illness and life-limiting disability.

In most western countries the first-line treatment for diabetes type 2 is to prescribe the drug Metformin. We know that the risk of vascular complication such as blood clots or heart attacks can be lowered by the improved metabolic control Metformin provides. But other important treatment goals, such as body weight reduction or the prevention of hypoglycaemia (high blood sugar levels) are seldom accomplished. Because of this, a review in the journal Diabetes Care in 2013 noted that many patients, even those who receive prompt anti-diabetic drug treatment, suffer an increased risk of dying from cardiovascular complications. Many people never know they have diabetes type 2, until it is too late. In the review two German medical researchers, Gallwitz and Bretzel, highlighted a 2011 study that showed that in the US, 75% of patients with type 2 diabetes die of cardiovascular causes. In addition, type 2 diabetes is the main cause of end-stage renal disease and dialysis in many countries. They concluded that Metformin does work, but far from perfectly (and recommended a whole host of other drugs including GLP1-agonists).[4]

Metformin is a very well-respected drug. First described in the 1920s, it is an artificial version of the naturally-occurring plant extract guanidine, found in French lilac and known to herbalists for centuries. For many people with diabetes, it can slow the gradual onset of serious symptoms of the disease. These symptoms become more serious as the pancreas fails, inducing progressive metabolic imbalance that in turn leads to complications that can include blindness, infections and blood vessel atrophy, which eventually can require amputations of the limbs. Diabetes UK say there are approximately 176 lower limb – leg, toe or foot – amputations carried out daily in the UK due to infections caused by diabetic complications. Metformin may slow down the progression of diabetes type 2, but it does not suppress it altogether. Eventually the effect of the drug declines and must be augmented by other drugs that have a lower success rate. The final option is insulin, self-administered daily by injection.[5]

In the UK, over a billion pounds – £1,075 million – was spent on anti-diabetic drugs such as Metformin in 2018/19.[6] It can transform lives, side effects are limited and most, such as diarrhoea and other gastrointestinal irritation, are bearable compared to the disease that it suppresses. Yet surprisingly, we do not know how Metformin works to help maintain a healthier glucose and insulin balance.

When the disease was limited to the frail elderly, a slowing down of the process was perhaps sufficient. But today we are in no doubt that lifestyle, namely poor diet, lack of exercise and being overweight, is the principal cause of diabetes type 2. We have known this for a long time. Cases of diabetes type 2 plummeted during World Wars I and II, as diets were drained of excess sugars and fats and transport dwindled, meaning we all had to walk. Ironically, in spite of the war, most British people remained healthy in WWII, perhaps helped by a *national diet*, devised by nutritionists and imposed by rationing, which ensured that nobody got too much sugar and fat, and that everybody got their fair share of protein.

Lifestyle studies hold few profitable outcomes for pharmaceutical companies; thus research into non-pharmacological solutions for diabetes have lagged behind drug research. However, recent studies in the north of England, funded by Diabetes UK, have now established that a healthy low-calorie diet can put type 2 diabetes into long-term remission, meaning sufferers can stop taking Metformin. While many people think that diabetes type 2 is caused by eating too much sugar, the facts are somewhat different. It should be noted that a low-carbohydrate diet won't help. Neither low-sugar, low-carb or low fat alone are likely to be efficient. It's a low-calorie diet that is required. That is because high calorie-density foods, which include sugary, carbohydrate rich or fatty foods, can all end up as adipose tissue in the body and even more importantly as visceral fat around the organs.

The researchers believe that it is this visceral fat that is most dangerous because it can directly clog-up insulin secreting endocrine cells situated within the pancreas. These are romantically named the Islets of Langerhans.* Simply cutting down on one food-group is unlikely to work; it may only shift reliance onto other, equally fattening, foods.

The Diabetes UK-funded Counterpoint Study showed that a short but sharp low-calorie diet, 750 calories per day over the course of six months, will result in considerable weight-loss (sometimes over 15kg) and can reverse type 2 diabetes. The diet achieves this by clearing fat in the liver and pancreas. The study discovered that a successful diet restores normal insulin secretion, particularly in the newly diagnosed.

---

* They are named after the German physician Paul Langerhans, who first described them in 1869. Incidentally, it is only the most numerous B type Islets of Langerhans that secrete insulin. The A type produce Glucagon – which switches off the secretions of B and C type islets. The C type produce somatostatin which is another crucial metabolic regulator.

What is interesting about this treatment is that it doesn't directly tackle high blood sugar, but instead treats the cause of those high levels, which are fatty deposits around the pancreatic glands that secrete insulin. Shrink the fat, and the pancreas and liver start to work again. As long as the patient gets back to an even keel of healthy eating and activity, they have the capacity to remain well, without any drug treatment, for many more years because they are using their own body to repair their metabolism, rather than relying on drugs to artificially redress the situation.

This is a relatively recent discovery, so we don't know whether we are observing a cure or simply a slowing-down of an inevitable decline. But in either case, what we observe is the reinvigoration of metabolic health, and with it the potential to slow down the process of ageing. People who have gone through this process report feeling much better, because over and above the relief of the symptoms of diabetes people also have renewed energy, better heart rates, less blood fat and lower blood sugar levels.[7]

There are two sad facts about this discovery. The first is that the UK's health service simply can't spare the time to help everyone who is diagnosed to make the necessary lifestyle changes. Even in the face of a Covid-19 pandemic, where we knew that diabetics presented a far higher risk of a poor outcome, the NHS only offered a branded version of the Diabetes Diet to a handful of people in a handful of areas. The rest of the country had to make do with online NHS diets which are, in my view as a clinical nutritionist, over-cautious, badly designed and often misleading.

There is, for example, little discussion of the need to lose fat mass, not simply weight. A loss of muscle mass in the face of metabolic disease can exacerbate the problem. In addition, the NHS diabetes diet uses branded processed foods, consisting of packeted milk shakes and powdered soups. A more wholesome home-made diet is cheaper to follow, equally successful and would surely prove better for us in the long run.

Unfortunately, the NHS just isn't set up for such close dietary support. Fortunately, the inventor of the Diabetes Diet, Professor Roy Taylor, has recently written a book, called *Life Without Diabetes,* containing sound advice in order to spread the good news.[8]

Yet before we condemn Metformin to history, it is interesting to know that some studies have observed that Metformin possesses other anti-ageing qualities, perhaps because of its impact on the metabolism. It has been studied in vivo (animal studies on microbes and crickets) for its effects on ageing. A 2017 review found that people with diabetes who were taking Metformin had lower-than-normal 'all-cause mortality' ie. they lived longer.* In another study, healthy volunteers who took the drug had reduced rates of cancer and cardiovascular disease compared with those on other therapies. This may be due to other actions by Metformin. It may be that Metformin confers protection against macrovascular complications, inhibits pro-inflammatory responses and reduces oxidative stress; three of the most damaging processes in ageing. It may simply be that Metformin reduces our appetite and thus we find it easier to lose weight. Recently Metformin has even been proposed as a potential treatment for obesity as well as neurodegenerative diseases such as Alzheimer's. But we still don't really know how it works.[9]

Statins

If you are over 50 and living in a developed region, such as Europe, the US, Japan or Australia and New Zealand, the chances are that at one time or another you will have been offered a prescription of statins. According to Dr Maryanne Demasi, writing in the British Medical Journal (BMJ)

* Lower all-cause mortality implies that Metformin can help with other non-diabetic diseases of old age. But as we don't know how this is caused, we can only note that there is a positive correlation.

in October 2018, the global sale of hyperlipidaemic drugs – cholesterol-lowering statins – was set to reach $1trillion by 2020.

Statins work by reducing cholesterol in the bloodstream. There is good evidence that cholesterol is associated with heart disease and arterial damage, blockage and encrustation. Unlike metabolic disease, where diet is very good at clearing sugars from the bloodstream, diet alone is unable to make much of an impact on cholesterol levels. Statins are more effective.

But variations between individuals are sometimes confusing. Cholesterol is linked to genetics and levels naturally increase with age. The mechanisms of cholesterol control are not clear. Some of us simply make more cholesterol than others. It is not always diet-related. However, heart disease, a consequence of cholesterol in the bloodstream, does seem to be linked to eating high levels of saturated fats, especially fatty red meat and processed meats.

The common belief is that all saturated fats are equally damaging, but recent studies suggest that some animal fats could be protective. For example, the body deals with milk fat in a different way to meat fat. Counterintuitively, milk fats seem to be able to confer protection on those who consume full fat milk – even that delicious Jersey milk where you can actually see a creamy topping at the head of the bottle. The Seven Countries Study, undertaken by Ancel Keys (see Chapter 3) concluded that Finland, a country where high levels of whole milk are consumed, had equally low levels of heart disease compared to southern countries where a classic Mediterranean diet is low in milk (but often just as high in cheese and yoghurt).[10]

Many products contain saturated fats, even if they are not animal-derived. One fifth of a portion of coconut milk consists of saturated fat. Far worse than any animal fats are trans fats, modified by cooking or processing into highly damaging elements of any diet. So dangerous are they to cardio-vascular health that artificial trans fats were eventually banned in processed foods in the US and EU, but not in the UK. We leave it up to the producers to give themselves voluntary limits – look out for labels that say hydrogenated fats or hydrogenated vegetable oils. Or simply take the easy route and cut all ultra-processed food from your diet.

If you are found to have higher than *normal* levels of cholesterol in your blood stream, your GP will show you very simple online tables that outline your risk, based on a few parameters like blood pressure, age, co-morbidity (other diseases you may have), weight and gender. I checked mine a few years ago and found one chart gave me a 10% risk of dying of cardiovascular disease within ten years. I could start taking statins today if I so wished as the NHS starting line is a 10% risk, which sounds big. But by taking statins I don't reduce my risk to zero. For me statins would reduce a 10% risk to about 6%. According to the tables, without statins I've got a 90% chance of reaching 75. With them, my chances are 94%. In the UK, on average, one in 65 women between the ages of 65-74 die of cardiovascular diseases, and one in 21 between the ages of 75 and 84. But recall that all these risk factors and statistics are based on the average person. They don't take account ethnicity and genetic pre-disposition, how much exercise I do, how healthily I eat, how carefully I monitor my health and so on. On one level, these charts are just telling me that I'm getting older, and thus statistically more likely to die, but they don't really tell me how healthy I am, or whether I should take drugs in order to remain healthy.[11]

Age is often folded up in this risk as if it confers a quantifiable impediment. But as I have explained, everybody ages differently. I would argue that if age is a major parameter of these types of estimations, we are relying on a metric that is vague in the extreme and is inextricably mixed up with other risks. In mid-life higher cholesterol levels do seem to be problematic, but there are many studies that show that once we get into our 70s, higher triglyceride and cholesterol levels confer protection rather than increase risks.[12] We have yet to discover whether some people actually require higher levels of cholesterol, and whether in this cohort, statins might be responsible for negative effects.

The body makes cholesterol because it needs it. The brain contains approximately 20% of the whole-body store of cholesterol, the highest concentration of any organ. But, while the brain appears to manufacture its own cholesterol, regardless of what we eat, there is a strong association between low blood cholesterol levels and the incidence and progression of degenerative brain diseases such as Parkinson's.[13] This has thrown a light onto statin use in the case of Parkinson's disease patients. The most recent papers are unconclusive and all simply call for further research. At present we don't know whether the associations that have been observed are cause, or effect, or merely incidental.

Cholesterol is also required in the skin to absorb and convert sunlight into vitamin D, a vitamin that everyone agrees is vital to healthy ageing. In addition, it is used to make cell membranes, hormones and bile acids (which break down other types of fats). In earlier chapters I talked about homeostasis, the delicate balance that keeps the body functioning. Any time we take a drug, even the humble paracetamol, we slightly disrupt that balance.

The National Institute for Clinical Excellence (NICE) suggest that statins should be offered to any patient who displays a greater than 10% risk of getting cardiovascular disease in the next ten years. But NICE also recommend that lifestyle changes can reduce that risk. If you are faced with the simplified risk graphs, make sure a well-versed GP is advising you.

Prevention

The busy GP cannot do much to help their patient with lifestyle changes. Instead, the most common support for high cholesterol or blood glucose levels are tablets. Even UK smoking services were reduced in 2019. Alcohol services are targeted at hardened alcoholics, not people whose alcohol consumption may be creeping up. Public health services between 2020 and 2021 were completely focused on dealing with COVID-19. Post-pandemic there is little extra money available to help people change their lifestyle, even though most clinicians agree that these moves would make an extraordinary difference to the health of the nation and our resilience to infections and pathogens. Prevention really is better than cure.

In February 2024, just before this book went to print, the King's Fund issued a new report explaining that the focus on hospital care had shifted funding away from community care. They concluded that the current system was poor value for money. The report explained that established hierarchies of care mean that urgent problems take priority over longer-term issues. For example, treatments for urgent medical problems currently take priority over services that might prevent the development of future urgent problems. [14]

But from a government point of view, while it saves money in the long run, prevention can be expensive in the short term. In my view the government's current health policy is callous. Yet, it is true that in order to be effective, preventative measures have to identify and then treat millions of moderate-risk patients, while cures, though many times more expensive, are only needed by a much smaller number of people. Is it the spreadsheet ruling the heart?

Weight loss treatments

Being overweight confers a high risk of premature death. Diseases including cancer, diabetes and heart disease are all associated with obesity. While being athletic or brainy doesn't necessarily confer sex appeal, being slim certainly seems to. It isn't surprising that Hollywood tries all these treatments first, and then they finally trickle down to us mortals.

If you are overweight you can go on a diet, take appetite-suppressing drugs, have sections of your gut removed, or undergo liposuction. But what the surgeons or the drug manufacturers won't tell you is that all of these treatments also require you to change your eating habits as well. None of them work without major dietary changes.

Appetite suppressants were not popular until recently because they tended to have rather nasty side effects, including uncontrollable sickness and diarrhoea. These days, new drugs have been formulated called semaglutides, which mimic the natural stomach hormone GLP-1 that regulates hunger and satiety. Modern appetite suppressants certainly seem to have less of the nasty side-effects, but because they are new, and have been brought to market relatively quickly, we have no idea of the long-term effects.* In spite of this, and because we face an obesity epidemic, many governments have approved the drug for treating obesity for a short period of time.

NICE (National Institute for Clinical Excellence) issued draft guidelines in 2022, suggesting that they be used for a maximum of two years alongside a specialist weight management service with

---

* By the time of editing this book, rare but dangerous side-effects were being reported. See Chapter 5 for more details.

multidisciplinary input.[15] However, that advice has been somewhat watered-down, recognising that multidisciplinary input for weight management is limited in many parts of the country.[16]

Ironically the new advice from NICE suggests that if more than 5% of weight is lost within the first six months, the GP should consider withdrawing the prescription. What these provisos highlight is that the new drugs are successful at helping people lose weight, but completely useless at changing our eating habits, or helping us introduce healthier foods. A high rate of weight loss is almost always accompanied by a loss of muscle mass, unless the patient is very carefully monitored and the diet optimised. Among middle-aged people taking these drugs, muscle mass has been found to be surprisingly resistant, but there are very few studies of the drug used in people over 60.[17] The manufacturers assume that weight gain miraculously stops after the age of 66 (NICE decided it was 68). There may be some truth in this, but there is also much evidence to show that while weight might stabilise as we grow older, the balance of muscle and fat does not. Muscle loss is something you don't want as you grow older. Once lost, muscle mass and tone is very difficult to regain.

If you do decide to take these drugs, make sure you monitor your muscle mass as well as your weight loss (the NHS are unlikely to do so on your behalf), and use the time when you are taking the drugs to change to a better long-term diet. Appetite suppressants won't give you immunity to eating high-caloric, low-nutrition foods during or after the treatment. And even the manufacturers point out that unless you change your diet, all the weight you lose while you are taking the drug will return after you've stopped.

Surgery
Bariatric surgery

This offers a last-ditch effort to help people who are risking their lives by overeating. Bariatric procedures reduce the size of the stomach by cutting out a section or diverting the route of food through the stomach (such as with the Roux-en-Y procedure). These treatments have been shown to help people who are obese or very obese. It is available on the NHS and given to approximately four to six thousand patients annually (numbers have reduced since COVID-19).[18] We think it acts in a very similar way to modern appetite suppressants, removing quite a large chunk of the stomach that secrete the hormones GLP-1 that make you feel naturally hungry. But in so doing, it also restricts or confines the capacity of the digestive system to accept food. After the surgery, attempts to over-eat will result in reflux, diarrhoea or vomiting. While it is a severe treatment, and the side effects can be rather unpleasant, it does save lives.

Before you can have the surgery, you will be put on a drastic weight loss diet for a few weeks. After the surgery you will not feel like eating very much *ever again*. In addition, because parts of the digestive tract are removed, you will be required to take nutritional supplements for life. And you are still going to have to learn to continuously eat a healthy diet. *

Liposuction

Liposuction is the surgical removal of adipose tissue from particular places, often the chin, arms, thighs and stomach. Although liposuction is not available on the NHS, it does have some benefits. Because the fat cells are completely removed, the capacity of that part of the body to store

---

* Gastric bands are reversible but rarely used these days because they can slip and cause problems.

fat again is also permanently limited. It is an invasive surgery, and can have serious side effects including numbness, infections, fluid retention and embolism. There will inevitably be a scar, though surgeons are very good at hiding them. The final effect may or may not please you. There is no going back. However badly you eat in the future, it is unlikely that you will put weight on in that position again, but you will still have to convert to a healthy diet in order to maintain a healthy, whole body and appropriate fat to muscle ratio.

Over-the-counter cures

In an effort to reduce their intake of pharmaceuticals, some people resort to over-the-counter cures. But is that wise?

A few years ago, aspirin and vitamin C were in vogue to help maintain health. Millions of people bought millions of pounds worth of these products in the belief that it might protect them from various conditions. Nowadays, anything from vitamin D to turmeric are heralded as the elixirs of life and millions of ostensibly healthy people take them. But do low-impact drugs and supplements make an appreciable difference?

Those people who don't like the sound of taking prescription drugs for life sometimes decide to use over-the-counter remedies instead. Many of these products are distillations of compounds found in various foodstuffs. Our grandmothers took cod liver oil tablets, while we take garlic tablets or curcumin, which tend to be more expensive that the old remedies.* Given we have to take them each and every day, the annual outlay can be high.

---

* Cod liver oil contains Vitamin A, D and omega 3 fatty acids. All together still quite a useful supplement.

Every week you will find one media outlet or another suggesting that by eating more of one foodstuff or another we will be protected against one disease or another. Garlic, caffeine, red wine, chocolate, or double cream may all have a small protective effect. For example, allicin is found in garlic and onions and is supposed to be good for colds and flu. Caffeine is found naturally in coffee and tea, and has been taken for years as a slimming aid. Respectable studies have shown that these substances do confer some benefit. The polyphenols found in substances such as red wine and cocoa are also said to be helpful for many conditions, though the evidence is inconclusive. There is some credible evidence that the fat globules found only in unpasteurised milk fat have protective properties for the heart. Each one of these food cures has antibacterial, antioxidative, stimulative, or other useful functions. And so, as time goes by, you will find people swearing by each and every one of these ingredients. Yet there is very little mainstream scientific evidence that any of these confer any significant benefit, taken on their own. However, as part of a healthy, well-balanced diet and taken in moderation, they certainly don't do any harm.

Turmeric

Curcumin, the active ingredient found in turmeric, is one of the fashionable supplements of the moment. Over four and a half million webpages can be found on a Google search for the term 'curcumin cure', covering pretty well any condition you care to mention. Curcumin is the substance that gives turmeric *Curcuma longa* its bright yellow colour. It is a plant phenol that endows the plant protection against certain pests or pathogens. The active ingredient is an antioxidant, like vitamin C.

Curcumin derived from turmeric is just one of hundreds of distillations, or extracts, manufactured to increase the supposed potency of the foodstuff. Is it better to eat carrots, or buy carotenoids at the local health food store? In fact, many of these potions are highly unlikely to be any better for us than the raw ingredient. We simply do not yet know whether the naturally occurring food contains other beneficial ingredients that might contribute to its effect. We don't know enough about how they work in the body, or how important the other constituents of the plant or foodstuff might be.

At first glance, curcumin is not a good candidate as a supplement. It is chemically unstable, and its lack of solubility means that when ingested, little of the substance can escape the gastric tract. Most is simply excreted, undigested in faeces. If any curcumin is able to enter the blood stream, its inherent toxicity means that interaction with bioactive proteins is unpredictable, and in large quantities could be potentially harmful.

Curcumin is said to inhibit cancer, having antimutagenic effects. This means it reduces mutations of DNA. However, despite the US government investing $150 million in research, no medical benefit has so far been discovered.[19] This has led to the U.S. Food and Drug Administration to describe curcumin as a 'fake cancer cure'.[20] In spite of this announcement, there seems no let-up in the social media storm. People seem to have decided that it might do them some significant good. The global curcumin market size was valued at $58.4 million in 2019 by Grand View Research and is predicted to rise.[21]

Supplements

Vitamin or mineral supplements are big business. They are easy to purchase, relatively cheap, and even nutritionists tend to use a scattergun approach. That is because even though we can't tell whether they do any good, we are pretty sure that most of them do no harm in small doses. A surfeit of most vitamins will simply be flushed out in your urine. I certainly would not advise going the way of billionaire Bryan Johnson, who having sold out his tech company to PayPal for $800 million while still in his 30s, now devotes his entire time to self-medication, hoping to live forever. Reports suggest he is spending $2 million a year on a phalanx of doctors, tests and pills. In an interview with the BBC in July 2023 he admitted to taking over 100 different supplements – every day! It looks like he's found the most direct route to throwing money straight down the drain.

Whole grains

Whole grain foods were only available in health-food stores until a few years ago. Now they have escaped from the shelves of elixirs and curatives to find their way into the mainstream. We were turned on to whole grains in the 1970s, about the time that scientists were discovering that a lack of fibre in the diet is a cause of common cancers such as bowel cancer. People started to supplement their meals with bran, the fibrous husk of the wheat berry. Today in the UK most of us still do not eat adequate fibre. It would seem supremely sensible to simply sprinkle a little bran onto your cornflakes every morning. But recent studies have shown that eating refined bran on its own isn't as useful as eating the whole food, such as wholemeal bread or brown rice.

Dr Anthony Fardet, a research nutritionist based at Clermont-Ferrand University in France has collected much evidence that wheat fibre (the bran) can help reduce the risk of obesity, diabetes, cardiovascular disease and cancer. But he is convinced that it is an orchestra of ingredients found in the whole wheat cereal that achieves this, not simply the sole action of wheat bran. He pointed out in a recent paper that the magnesium in whole wheat contributes to better blood sugar balance and that the antioxidant and anti-carcinogenic properties found in the bran *and* the germ, including other minerals, trace elements, vitamins, carotenoids, polyphenols and alkylresorcinols (plant lipids), all add to its potency. Whole-grain wheat contains an impressive list of ingredients that Dr Fardet suggests are far more bio-actively available when eaten together. He concludes that the polyphenols assist cell signalling and gene regulation and that tiny quantities of various sulphur compounds, lignin and phytic acid confer antioxidant protection. In addition, whole-grain wheat is also a rich source of substances that naturally break down fats. This mix of substances may all have their role in protection of the heart and liver by being able to regulate metabolic processes and to switch genes on and off. Fardet also points out that whole-grains (not just the bran) provide a host of benefits that require more analysis. In 2010 he suggested that we should also consider the:

"...potential protective effects of bound phenolic acids within the colon, of the B-complex vitamins on the nervous system and mental health, of oligosaccharides as prebiotics, of compounds associated with skeleton health, and of other compounds such as a-linolenic acid, policosanol, melatonin, phytosterols and para-aminobenzoic acid."

It is perhaps unsurprising that there is a rich mix of beneficial ingredients in whole wheat flour. It has been a staple of human diets for tens of thousands of years. There may be complex effects that have allowed healthy grain varieties and healthy humans to evolve in symbiosis, to the point that eating just one part of the grain – the bran – cannot match.[22]

So why, in a world where we know so much about the benefits of a simple wholemeal loaf, does the bread industry try so hard to persuade us to buy very different 'bread' products? It is almost impossible to find a 100% wholemeal loaf anywhere in Britain. Since 1998, wholemeal flour must consist of unadulterated whole-grain flour and contain at least as many vitamins, minerals and fibre as the white refined variety does by virtue of supplements (usually it naturally contains much more). Since 2022, wholemeal bread sold in Britain should contain, by law, 100% wholemeal flour, though supermarket wholemeal breads often contain 'rising or conditioning' agents which are in fact refined grain flour or gluten and soy flour, which they maintain is a legume and not a flour at all. Beware weasel wording such as seeded, brown, wheatmeal or whole-grain, when bread is concerned. They generally mean white bread – always well below 100% wholemeal.

Modern consumers get hung up on sourdough or ciabatta as an alternative to the sliced white bread we were all given in our youth. Supermarkets pander to this trend. Now modern fancy breads are more interesting, more flavourful and probably more nutritious than the white sliced loaf, which – make no mistake about it – is a processed, factory-made product, far too high in yeast and sugar (to make it rise quickly) and containing 100% white processed flour. Sourdough, if it is authentic, will contain smaller quantities of yeast and will have been left to rise slowly overnight. This creates a crusty, well-risen loaf, but if the dough is made with white flour, it won't increase nutritional content. In fact, some loaves like *ciabatta* contain a lot of fat, an ingredient that is not found at all in a traditional loaf, and which decreases its food value. Neither ciabatta nor sourdough will be likely to possess any wholemeal flour. Such loaves, however expensive, simply don't contain the same amount of fibre that is contained in wholemeal bread. It is the fibre which is the missing ingredient in most adult diets. *

---

* The RDI for fibre is 30g/day for 16+.

Ironically, during the war, when rationing was in place, people were offered just one bread option. The National Loaf was a 75% wholemeal-flour bread, sometimes with added oatmeal or rye. People may have found it heavy compared to the white fluffy cottage loaves they were used to. This brown bread was designed to keep for a week, and to be sliced thinly. Forget weaning yourself off gluten (which is a protein and actually a pretty important part of the loaf's nutrition). The thing that causes flatulence, bloating and discomfort is the white flour, the sugar and the over-yeasted baking processes! Forget trying to lose weight by giving up bread; instead try a small slice of a real wholemeal loaf, and you'll find it low in calories, fats and sugars and deliciously filling.

Vitamin C

Vitamin C has gone slightly out of fashion as a supplement. Professor Linus Paulin (1901-1994), the only person to have won two individual Nobel prizes*, was a chemist who spent the last 20 years of his life studying the benefits of Vitamin C. He observed that that the bioactive ingredient in Vitamin C was a strong antioxidant. It is derived from citric acid, a compound that is found in lemons, cabbages and vinegar. The vitamin works by binding with reactive oxygen atoms in the body, to neutralise them before they can do damage by disrupting important metabolic processes. Paulin's hypothesis was that far higher doses than are usually recommended might deliver far greater benefits.

After years of careful study, we now know that vitamin C forms part of a group of vitamins that help to clear out what are called 'free radicals' in the cell. These free radicals, either oxygen or nitrogen molecules that

---

* In 1954 Linus Paulin won the Nobel Prize for Chemistry. Eight years later he was awarded the Nobel Peace Prize for his opposition to weapons of mass destruction.

possess free electrons, can easily damage and thus disrupt the normal activity of the cell. Vitamin C is an acid, containing hydrogen, that naturally binds itself to free-radicals and neutralises them. People who eat a diet high in fruit and vegetables are naturally consuming a healthy proportion of antioxidants that give them essential protection.

Paulin thought that we should consume doses of vitamin C that were far higher than those provided even by the most generous plant diet. He recommended really high doses, up to 10 or 12 g/day. The current UK recommended dose is 0.04 g/day.[23] What Paulin failed to consider was that antioxidants form part of the sensitive balancing act of homeostasis; more is not necessarily better.

In the 1980s, studies by the Mayo Clinic revealed that very high doses of vitamin C do not confer any benefit. While a small dose of antioxidants can help reduce the wear and tear on normal DNA and cell membranes, protecting every cell in the body is not universally beneficial. We need the binding powers of some free radicals in order to kill bacteria in the body and eliminate fast-replicating cancer cells. Taking very large doses of vitamins, such as vitamin C, can tip the balance too much in another direction, causing an unnatural state in which the immune system is less able to neutralise harmful invaders.

Supposedly, Paulin was never convinced, even after his own wife died of cancer, untreated, except by a daily dose of ten grammes of vitamin C, which is over 250 times the current recommended dose.[24]

Personally, I enjoy eating a casserole spiced with turmeric, a fresh orange, a splash of cream, a small glass of red wine or a chunk of wholemeal bread and wild horses would not encourage me to swop those delights for anything I might find in a medicine bottle. The philosophy of food first is not only prudent, but much more fun.

The complexity of the bioactive ingredients in all foods is an argument for making sure we eat a large variety of fresh and high-quality foods. The suggestion that we mix different colours of food on our plates is not simple gastronomic decoration. The different colours are a crude representation of the different bioactive ingredients, in particular signifying different varieties of vitamins and polyphenols in fruit and vegetables.

Crutches

If an ankle is broken, some people will try and get away from using crutches as quickly as possible. Yet they are a very useful tool, allowing us to get about more than we otherwise can. There's nothing wrong with using them, particularly if it is a means to an end and that end is regaining mobility. Even when we are old, it is better to make use of tools that help us get about rather than to remain stationary.

Declining ability is not limited to our ability to move about. Some conditions may not be so noticeable, but all of them can be limiting. For example, even quite mild impairments to hearing or vision can make living alone seem frightening. For those that have a hearing problem, things that were easy before, such as ringing for a taxi, can quickly become too difficult to contemplate. What we might consider today to be a simple process can become tricky when hearing, sight or dexterity start to fail. Hearing aids, cataract surgery and a good pair of varifocals should be considered as important as hip surgery. Keeping the senses sharp ensures we hear and see what's going on; we get the joke, we admire the view, we enjoy the concert. There is no excuse for bashfulness about wearing glasses, or a hearing aid. It is misplaced vanity.

Lifestyle, hard drugs or supplements?

In August 2019 Age UK called for a more considered approach to prescribing medicines for older people. Their report, *More Harm than Good*, expressed concerns that drugs were being prescribed unnecessarily, and as a substitute for better therapies and closer care. In England, more than one in 10 people aged over 65 take at least eight different prescribed medications weekly, and this increases to one in four among people who are aged over 85.[25]

There is a justifiable concern that people are taking drugs in excessive numbers, in unsafe combinations and without any real understanding of what these drugs do, or why they are being asked to take them. But the bigger question is whether people actually need those drugs at all, or whether other treatments might prove equally effective. We are beginning to learn that for every common drug taken in older age, there may be a non-chemical therapy that works just as well, if not better.

While we might decide that a supplement will be useful, or that it is worth taking long-term prescriptions of blood thinners, statins or biguanides, the jury is still out on many treatments. For example, there is scant evidence that supplements work as well as a healthy diet. And while prescribed drugs, once we have been diagnosed with an ailment, can mediate the symptoms, even the rather staid and cautious National Institute for Clinical Excellence (NICE) recommends that better results can be obtained by making lifestyle changes, as well or instead of using prophylactic prescription drugs. The list is a familiar one:

- Stopping smoking
- Eating a healthy diet
- Getting enough exercise
- Becoming a healthy weight

- Reducing alcohol
- Enjoying moderate sunshine

The advice must surely be 'lifestyle first'. By all means use a drug for a limited period of time if you need one, but think twice before taking a drug that you will need for the rest of your life. Check the need with your GP, find out if there are lifestyle alternatives, and scrutinise the risk data.

Non-communicable diseases, such as diabetes and heart disease, could be said to be the diseases of civilisation. The really dreadful thing about the non-communicable diseases that are caused by lifestyle is that they are far more prevalent that they should be. Levels of many of these diseases, such as type 2 diabetes, have been increasing, not decreasing. It is unlikely to be the individual effect of any one lifestyle habit or toxin that can cause the problem, just as it is unlikely to be the effect of any one food or drug that can safeguard us. Unhealthy ageing is far more likely to be the cumulative effect of a lifetime of many different events, including environmental factors and incautious lifestyle choices. When we do get ill, the doctor is more likely to reach for their prescription pad than anything else, even though changes in diet, a short course of supplements or exercise could have been equally beneficial and less chemically disruptive. However, it must be stressed that the only thing that has kept many of us out of an early grave has been advances in medicine that can now repair a dodgy heart, or drugs such as statins and Metformin that keep high levels of blood cholesterol or blood sugars under control. Thank science that these all help to extend life, but they do not stave off disease forever. The root causes, and thus the root cure, of many of these ills are in our own hands.

Endnotes

1   Kat Eschner (2017) *Coca-Cola's Creator Said the Drink Would Make You Smarter.* Article Smithsonian Magazine March 29, 2017. smithsonianmag.com [retrieved March 2021]

2   The caffeine content of expresso is very variable. In making a good expresso, Illy suggests that it is good practice to cut off the stream of coffee once the black liquor has turned pale, to reduce the pure (white) caffeine content and to maximise the flavourful (dark) liquid. Your expresso should have a rim of the pale caffeine mousse, not a layer of it. Chemically-derived caffeine is a white powder and does not contain any of the coffee flavour or aroma

3   US Centre for Disease Control Website cdc.gov/vitalsigns/prescriptionpainkilleroverdoses [retrieved February 2023]

4   Gallwitz, B & Bretzel, R (2013) *How Do We Continue Treatment in Patients With Type 2 Diabetes When Therapeutic Goals Are Not Reached With Oral Anti-diabetes Agents and Lifestyle?* Diabetes Care, Volume 36, Supplement 2, August 2013

5   Mike Watts, (2020) *Rising number of diabetes-related amputations in England, Press Release.* 27th February 2020 Diabetes UK; diabetes.co.uk [retrieved August 2023]

6   NHS Digital (2019) *Prescribing for diabetes in England 2008/9 – 2018/19* digital.nhs.uk/data-and-information/publications/statistical/prescribing-for-diabetes/2008-09---2018-19/results-and-charts [retrieved August 2023]

7   Lean MEJ, et al. (2019) *Durability of a primary care-led weight-management intervention for remission of type 2 diabetes: 2-year results of the DiRECT open-label, cluster-randomised trial.* Lancet 2019; 7: 344–55

8   Taylor, R. Prof. (2020) *Life Without Diabetes: The Definitive Guide to Understanding and Reversing Type 2 Diabetes* Book. Publisher Harper One London 2020

9   Rojas, LBA & Gomes, MB. (2013) *Metformin: an old but still the best treatment for type 2 diabetes.* Diabetology & Metabolic Syndrome 05,06,2013. DOI 10.1186/1758-5996-5-6

10 Ancel Keys (ed), (1980) *Seven Countries: A multivariate analysis of death and coronary heart disease.* Book, Publisher Cambridge, Mass.: Harvard University Press. 1980 ISBN 0-674-80237-3

11 Office of National Statistics (ONS) (2005) *Mortality statistics 2005.* National Statistics Series DH2 no.32 available from statistics.gov.uk

12 Tuikkala, Päivi et al. (2010) *Serum total cholesterol levels and all-cause mortality in a home-dwelling elderly population: a six-year follow-up.* Scandinavian journal

of primary health care vol. 28,02,2010: pages 121-7. DOI:10.3109/02813432.2010.
487371

13 Jin U, et al. (2019) *Cholesterol Metabolism in the Brain and Its Association with Parkinsons Disease.* Experimental Neurobiology 2019; Issue 28: pages 554-567. DOI:10.5607/en.2019.28.5.554

14 Baird B, et al. King's Fund (2024) *Health and care services. Making care closer to home a reality; Refocusing the system to primary and community care; Report* 13 February 2024 kingsfund.org.uk/insight-and-analysis/reports/making-care-closer-home-reality [retrieved February 2024]

15 NICE (2023) *Semaglutide for managing overweight and obesity. Technology appraisal: Guidance* [TA875] Published: 08 March 2023 From https://www.nice.org.uk/guidance/TA875/chapter/1-Recommendations

16 Under normal circumstances BMI should be 35kg/m^2 i.e. the patient will be obese. Though lower cut-offs apply to people with co-morbidities such as diabetes type 2 and for people from South Asian, Chinese, other Asian, Middle Eastern, Black African or African-Caribbean family backgrounds

17 Ozeki Y, et al. (2022) *The Effectiveness of GLP-1 Receptor Agonist Semaglutide on Body Composition in Elderly Obese Diabetic Patients: A Pilot Study.* Medicines (Basel). 2022 Sep 16; 9(9):47. DOI: 10.3390/medicines9090047

18 NHS Digital (2022) *National Obesity Audit*; digital.nhs.uk/data-and-information/publications/statistical/national-obesity-audit/bariatric-surgical-procedures-2021-22-provisional/content [retrieved August 2023]

19 Nelson KM, et al. (2017). *The Essential Medicinal Chemistry of Curcumin.* Journal of Medicinal Chemistry. 60 (5): 1620–1637. March 2017 DOI:10.1021/acs.jmedchem.6b00975.

20 Metzler M, et al. (2013). *Curcumin uptake and metabolism.* BioFactors. 39 (1): 14–20. DOI:10.1002/biof.1042

21 Grand View Research (2020) *Curcumin Market Size, Share & Trends Analysis Report by Application* (Pharmaceutical, Food, Cosmetics), By Region (North America, Europe, Asia Pacific, Central & South America, Middle East & Africa), And Segment Forecasts, 2020 – 2027. From grandviewresearch.com/industry-analysis/turmeric-extract-curcumin-market [retrieved March 2021]

22 Fardet, A. (2010) *New hypotheses for the health-protective mechanisms of whole-grain cereals: what is beyond fibre?* Nutrition Research Reviews 2010, Volume 23, pages 65–134 DOI:10.1017/S0954422410000041

23 GOV UK (2016) *Government Dietary Recommendations: Government recommendations for energy and nutrients for males and females aged 1 – 18 years and 19+ years.* Public Health England

24 Oregon State University Libraries Special Collections & Archives Research Centre, Paulin Collection (2015) *Vitamin C and Cancer Raising the Stakes;* The Paulin Blog, Article; paulingblog.wordpress.com/2015/12/02/vitamin-c-and-cancer-raising-the-stakes [retrieved March 2021]

25 Petchey, L & Gentry, T (2017) *More Harm than Good.* Report, Age UK available at ageuk.org.uk [retrieved March 2021]

9

Making change

If you want to live a happier and healthier life, then it follows that you will want to make changes for the better. Doctors talk blithely about making lifestyle changes, as if it were as easy as swapping winter coats; but we all know that it isn't.

There is a tendency to think that it is all our fault – we lack willpower. And the average self-help book will suggest that all you have to do is to change something within yourself and your 'lifestyle' will miraculously improve. But anyone who has tried to pass an exam, lose weight, or get a good job knows that feeling of not being good enough. We can blame ourselves too much. We can feel held back by our genetics, our lack of self-control or where we went to school. But the evidence tells a slightly different story.

Changes happen to us throughout our lives, whether we like it or not. We move house, we make new friends, we fall in love, we follow new pursuits. When those big changes happen, we can find smaller changes creeping in. We rent somewhere next to a park and we walk more; we move close to a cafe and we get into the habit of meeting friends there.

Some of us fight change, some of us fear it. But we should embrace it and most of all – we should plan for it.

Making positive change isn't solely an internalised process; it isn't only about 'me'. Of course, making changes like giving up swearing, or remembering to wear a seat belt, are down to our own actions. But those actions are inextricably linked to our social environment: who is supporting us, or helping us, what the majority think, what prejudices they may possess and what law and social pressures tell us.

For example, in the case of something like wearing a seatbelt, the proposed law changes were at first met with derision. Then, when the law was passed, many people acquiesced grudgingly. But after a very few years most of society recognising the sense of it. It is 40 years since seatbelt laws were brought into the UK.* In the first year 90% of the population were to be observed buckling up. During that first year, seatbelts saved the lives of an estimated 400 people. Since their introduction, seat belts have saved thousands of lives in the UK and are now ubiquitous across the world. It's a classic example of how a good law, combined with advertising and publicity can nudge us into doing the right thing.

Personal change

Agency is the term we use to signify how much independence we have; that we are in charge of our own destiny. It is an important capacity to hang onto as we age, but even youngsters have less than they think. We are all subject to influence, sadly much of it malign. Even our nearest and dearest, our friends and family, can hinder us. We receive good and bad advice from all quarters; our doctors, therapists and the whole of the media in all its messiness and madness. There is now a section of society

* January 1983.

called influencers – but they take no exams, they take no responsibility for their advice, you can't sue them if they tell you something wrong. It is difficult to judge when any advice is sage, and often even more difficult to heed it. Economic pressures may weigh us down, commercial pressures seduce us and we can feel abandoned by a government that puts healthy and happy ageing low on its list of priorities. On a larger scale, our concerns can feel insignificant in the face of world events, natural disasters and the galloping onset of a climate emergency.

Empowerment keeps us young

The best way to feel supported as we age is to support others. When you fight for your own rights, you fight for other people as well. It empowers us all. Almost every person on the planet will experience ageism to some degree in their lifetime. After all, ageing commences at gestation. A good proportion of our fellow men and women will get old, and some of them will grow to be very old. When we stand up for the rights of older people, we are supporting a very large cohort. The comparative rights and duties of young and old, rich and poor, men and women are discourses we should all join, to ensure a brighter and fairer future for everyone.

Campaigning by taking up a political cause, joining a pressure group or volunteering for a charity will reward you a thousand-fold. It may sound hackneyed, but joining a group or simply taking up a hobby is a good thing to do at any age. If you look around in vain for a suitable local group – then start one up yourself. You will find that your gathering age will open doors and unlock coffers. Don't let anyone tell you that you can't do something because of your age and don't let anyone tell anybody else that age should bar them. A number of candles on a cake should never hold anyone back.

I believe that lifestyle change is inextricably linked to taking a more assertive stance regarding the political and societal situation. When you decide to eat more healthily, or walk instead of taking the car, you are contributing to a better future for all of us. It isn't hard to imagine a world where the norm has shifted a bit, where cars give way to bicycles and pedestrians, where local farm produce and homemade goods at affordable prices are available in every food store, and where every town has community restaurants where well cooked, wholesome food is available at a reasonable price for hungry residents.

Perhaps there will be a time when each neighbourhood and village will possess a hub: a pub, post office and/or cafe selling local produce, offering health services, banking facilities, classes and social opportunities, and somewhere where you can be sure of a warm welcome. Since Covid, we know that we can adapt to change overnight. We can all turn on a sixpence if we recognise the need to. Surely the message of 'build back better' will eventually get through to policy-makers, to food manufacturers, to GPs and to the general public. We can and should all take part in that promised re-think.

Making changes for the better is rarely a one-day process. We can feel ourselves mired in inertia or hobbled by laziness. Our New Year's resolutions often pale by the time we reach February. If you feel you are stuck in a rut, don't beat yourself up. Personal agency does not preclude asking others to help you achieve your goals. In fact, change requires outside support.

Gradual change often feels more comfortable than sudden change. The positive aspect of gradual change is termed continuous improvement. Making incremental improvements in this gentle way should be catnip to those of us who are fast achieving the wisdom of longevity. Making big changes, such as moving to a different region or de-cluttering the house, can seem very drastic. Approaching life-changes gradually can really help by, for example, renting first, or clearing a cupboard at a time.

Instant change often requires us to let go of something, without really knowing whether we will be strong enough to withstand breaking the old ties. Planning ahead is the best method of avoiding painful, enforced changes.

However, there are times when it is a really good idea to turn over a new leaf. For example, many practitioners recommend that simply giving up smoking is faster, cheaper and easier than cutting down, or migrating to patches and vapes that can prolong and even increase nicotine addiction. Allen Carr's book *The Easy Way to Quit Smoking Without Willpower* is strong stuff.[1] Carr smoked like a chimney from the age of 18 until he saw the light 38 years later. In the end, in order to quit, he found he had to understand the psychology and physiology of smoking and addiction for himself. He wrote a book about his experiences and founded a successful business helping others to give up. Sadly, it was too late for him, as he eventually died of lung cancer, but not before his books had become best-sellers and by his reckoning his method had helped 25 million people.

It takes a lifetime of dedication to become wise, but only the action of a moment to decide to follow a different path. And while throughout life we need to be mindful of a healthy lifestyle, those lifestyle changes can be even more important as we age. Never think that you are already too old to make changes. Modifying your diet, becoming more active, giving up smoking and moderating alcohol can all be easier as we get older. Sometimes physical change is on our side – but always the wisdom that comes with old age can help us.

How ageing helps us make changes

Several studies have shown that losing weight becomes easier as we get older and keeping it off becomes less taxing. That is partly because weight tends to reduce quite naturally after the age of 60.[2] But finding help to reduce weight if you are over 60 can be difficult. The usual adult diets do not apply. Embarking on a new gastronomic regimen after that age requires far more careful monitoring. All in all, properly designed and supervised over-60s diets do work extremely well and certainly result in health improvements.[3] Many diet advisors have no experience of older people and don't know what to suggest. They either refuse to treat, using age as a discriminatory limit, or they recommend a diet designed for a thirty-year-old and wonder why it doesn't work.* If your diet isn't working, change tack; don't give up. It is probably the diet, not you (see Chapter 5).

One of the very best things you can do at any age to make immediate improvements to health is to give up smoking. Studies have shown that older smokers have very good success rates. Many older people tend to be less dependent on nicotine and smoke fewer cigarettes anyway, having managed to cut down earlier in life. These characteristics are both really strong indicators that smoking cessation support will succeed. It is never too late to kick the habit. The evidence shows that the resulting health improvements do not diminish with age. It is just as important for a 70-year-old to give up as a 30-year-old. Large-scale prospective cohort studies have found that smokers who quit after the age of 65 years enjoy longer and healthier life, as well as reducing the severity of chronic illness they may encounter on the way. [4]

Yet GPs and other advisors have a tendency to give up on people once they reach older age. A study of smoking support services in England reported that all forms of support fell away after the age of 69. The

---

* Women past menopause and men over about 50 should be very cautious of 'magazine' diets – they could do more harm than good. See Chapter 5.

evidence showed that the chances the patient would even be advised to quit went down with age. This was particularly observable in older men.[5]

Many people are finally persuaded to give up because they receive a health scare. At any age, this can be highly motivating, but as a GP advised a very healthy friend of mine who still smokes:

"Today you are fine, so why wait until you get cancer to give up? Do it now, before it is too late."

The US National Institute of Ageing [6] advises older smokers that:

"It doesn't matter how old you are or how long you've been smoking, quitting smoking at any time improves your health. When you quit, you are likely to add years to your life, breathe more easily, have more energy, and save money. You will also:

- Lower your risk of cancer, heart attack, stroke, and lung disease
- Have better blood circulation
- Improve your sense of taste and smell
- Stop smelling like smoke
- Set a healthy example for your children and grandchildren"

Alcohol use disorders often become more severe with age, and sadly the lower muscle mass and higher levels of fat mass that are symptoms of both ageing and drinking too much will increase sensitivity to alcohol. This can make it more difficult to moderate ones drinking. Social reasons can make giving up, or cutting down more difficult. Isolation and lack of mobility can have an impact. Alcohol can very easily become a useful crutch and compensate for loneliness or insomnia. Many older people might have been functioning alcoholics for a long time, but once they retire, those functional aspects of life can wither, making their drinking more destructive. However, unlike smoking and over eating the evidence, set out in Chapter 2, shows that continuing moderate alcohol use in old age may have beneficial effects for some people. That may be because of the social aspects of drinking. That daily trip to the pub for a half of bitter, may actually be helping.

I don't think it is really true to say that old people become set in their ways. That may be a cliché. There is a lot of evidence to show that changing our habits can in fact be easier the older we become. Yet often family and medics will fail to address the problem, even if it is evidently affecting someone's health. Even at the risk of offence, I think we should raise the issue with someone we love. That conversation should always start with the phrase; 'I love you, and because I love you, I feel you might be ...'

Sometimes we don't notice what's happening to our nearest and dearest, or even to ourselves. Falls, confusion or forgetfulness due to abuse of medication or alcohol can be misdiagnosed as the inevitable consequence of age-related frailty, dementia or infections. They all present with similar symptoms. Only medical tests, or observant and trusted family and friends, will be able to diagnose the true cause.

Get help

If you decide to make a big change, the next challenge is to seek help. Tell your friends and family what you are doing and engage their support – it is gold dust. If someone is less than helpful, address it. Ask them straight out why they feel they can't support you, listen carefully to their response, but be assertive. In the end, even if they don't approve of your decision, this is your life.*

If you decide to go cycling more, to learn to cook, or attend dance classes, joining a group can be an effective way to get support for whatever new activity you decide to pursue. You will immediately meet a new set of people who are as motivated as you are. Being positive about change is an important part of the process. Ageing is change. It isn't inherently good or bad – it's just different.

Professional support comes in many guises. You will find a myriad of coaches, teachers or advisors willing to help you on whatever route you choose. There exists a confusing array of experts, many of whom are no such thing. You can go private, which can be expensive and is no insurance against charlatans, or you can make use of NHS services, which are best described as 'patchy'.

Always check the credentials of the advisor, whichever route you take. Personal recommendations can be helpful, as can the recommendations of reputable organisations. Whatever the discipline, the organisations you should respect are those that demand professional standards. If you go to a private practitioner, look at their academic qualifications, enquire whether they have professional insurance, a code of ethics and continual professional development. More information listing the most relevant organisations can be found at the end of Chapter 11.

---

* The nay-sayers are often un-supportive because of their own hang-ups. They may also wish to make lifestyle changes, but feel they don't have the capacities to do so. Such people will often under estimate the value of making changes, being aware of their own difficulties. If a friend seems to treat your problem as insignificant, it is probably because they know, deep down, that it is their problem too. Respect their views, but you don't need to follow them down what could be a dark pathway.

NHS therapies for weight loss, smoking or alcohol consumption can be formulaic, designed to be delivered by non-clinical trainers – but you may be lucky. Local intelligence is important. Before you sign up to a programme, check what other people have said about it. And if you go along and it doesn't feel right, ask your GP to suggest another course of action. If it is a GP service, and you are not satisfied, make a reasoned complaint in writing.

A good GP can also prescribe drugs that help with eating disorders, reduce nicotine cravings and support alcoholics, but none of these pharmaceutical supports are recommended in isolation. Making change requires most of us to engage the support of a professional expert, a counsellor or a therapist. There is no lifestyle change you can make by simply taking a pill. Your GP should be able to prescribe a course of therapy that will help you, or they may suggest what is called a social prescription. Social prescriptions, for anything from walking groups to cooking classes, are now available and often subsidised across the country. Some are excellent.

The willpower has to come from you, but it does not all emanate from within you. Support, a positive environment and a good social milieu will all help. Remember, the sooner you start, the sooner you'll feel better. *You know you're worth it!*

Continuity of care becomes more difficult as we get older. In March 2022 Dr Jennifer Burns, president of the British Geriatrics Society, warned of a nationwide shortage of geriatricians, when figures published by the Royal College of Physicians (RCP) showed there was an equivalent of just one full-time geriatrician per 8,031 people over the age of 65 in the UK. Unsurprisingly, the shortages reveal a north-south divide. She warned that the situation is only likely to get worse as the number of old people rises, because nearly half (48%) of consultant geriatricians are set to retire by 2032. The RCP warned that we are 'sleepwalking into an avoidable crisis of care for older people'.[7]

If you find someone good, hang onto them!

Medical resilience

One of the biggest changes to our lives occurs, often unexpectedly, when we are diagnosed with a new condition, or when we are faced with a hospital procedure. Think of the pilot making a detour to avoid a heavy storm. In flying, it just makes sense; in life, it makes even more sense. That will inevitably mean that urgent changes need to be made. You might also be triggered into making changes that you have been putting off.

Don't believe the old chestnut that says an old dog can't learn new tricks. This particular myth originates from the sixteenth century and needs to be updated.* In fact, both dogs and men can make changes at any stage of life.

Writing recently for VCA, a US veterinary group, Weir and Buzhardt dispels this old myth: [8]

"Teaching and learning new tricks can be a fun pastime for you and your dog, no matter what your respective ages are. Time shared while learning new tricks will deepen the bond you already have with your canine friend. Plus, tricks provide mental stimulation for older dogs who may be suffering from dementia. Keeping the brain active is always a good thing.

---

* In 1523 an English gentleman called Fitzherbert wrote one of the first dog training manuals. In it he stated: The dogge must lerne when he is a whelpe, or els it wyl not be; for it is harde to make an old dogge to stoupe.

> Just use your experiences and common sense to pick tricks
> that are on par with your dog's physical abilities. And rewrite
> that old adage. You CAN teach an old dog new tricks!"

Older dogs are wiser and calmer dogs, just like their human owners. We can all learn new skills as we age. We can all make changes. And these changes are almost always worth it.

Without question, medical treatments should always be seriously considered, whatever your age. It is too easy to write oneself off at the age of 40 or 60 or even at the age of 110. But whatever age you are, it is important to remember that scientists have not found one cell in the body that is life-limited. All cells, in all lifeforms, are designed to endure, not designed to die (unless or until they are replaced by a new cell). If confronted by someone of say, 85 years old, one might conclude that their age deems them too old to undergo surgery. But these days 85-year-olds receive hip replacements every day of the week. It is now routine in the over-90s. Given that modern artificial hip joints only last for about 15-25 years, then it would seem imprudent to start replacing them in an otherwise healthy adult much before those sorts of ages.

However, the corollary is also valid. It is never a good idea to delay simple procedures. My dentist told me just the other day that it was really time to finally get my two remaining wisdom teeth removed. Over time wisdom teeth can become impacted, can crowd the mouth and make cleaning more difficult. If it needs doing, get it done before the whole process becomes too stressful.

Similarly, opticians advise that cataract surgery should be undertaken sooner rather than later. After surgery, a cataract cannot grow back and the lens, should last a lifetime, although it may need laser corrections at a later date. If you get a cataract, don't delay. Not being able to see properly inhibits our vision as well as clouding our minds.

It may be relatively easy to make decisions when considering minor surgery. However, we sometimes confront more difficult decisions when diagnosed with conditions that require major surgery. Every day of the week quite elderly people go through chemotherapy, heart bypass surgeries or other major interventions and come out smiling. The secret, if you decide to take that course, is to prepare for the surgery and learn how to recuperate successfully. For example, women suffering from breast cancer are advised that they can undergo a lumpectomy, or even a breast removal at pretty well any age. Our UK figures are not exemplary, but in Finland the average five-year survival rate in patients diagnosed with *any* cancer at 75 years of age or older, is 61% in men and 53% in women. That's impressive compared to the prognosis just a few years ago. New techniques are coming along all the time. If you have to undergo serious surgery or complex treatment, you can do a lot to help yourself get through it. But if you are older, you may sometimes have to be prepared to fight to get that treatment.

Frailty assessment

Assessments of frailty are sensible measures to ensure that we don't give seriously frail people invasive treatments that might not help them. There is always a risk in surgery and a good surgeon will help the patient understand that risk. Whether the decision is the patient's or the physicians' is a moot point. Most surgeons will respect a patient's right to refuse treatment, but it is difficult to get a doctor to change their minds about treatments they consider futile.

Sometimes you have to assert yourself in order to be told the risks and understand the assessment made. The doctor is duty-bound to make an assessment of frailty, which increases the danger of an intervention going wrong, during the op, or during recovery. Make sure that you or a trusted friend goes through the questions with the doctors treating you. Sometimes a history can be incorrect, at other times home situations can be misunderstood. Diagnoses of dementia will place you lower down the list. Being independent and having a role in life, such as being the bread-winner, or caring responsibilities, will place you higher up the list. Demonstrating that you have made good preparation and that you are willing to taking care of yourself in recuperation are also important. Being prepared to do your bit, before and after the operation, may swing things in your favour – if you elect to go through with the procedure.

Once again, consider yourself to be like the airline pilot. You have set a life course and something has come along to force a change of direction. You've had years of training; you might have thought about this type of eventuality; you may even have rehearsed your response. Once in the air, the pilot will get advice from his co-pilot and air traffic control. We all need help and support, but in the final analysis it is the pilot who makes the decision – no one else. There is only one hand on the joystick. In terms of your health, that decision is yours. The best advisors may ask you to follow a new regimen and for a while, they will seem to be in control, just as the co-pilot supports the pilot. But those same advisors will complete their advice by handing all control back to you. Take advice, weigh up that advice carefully and then take full responsibility for yourself.

Preparation and recuperation

Preparation and recuperation are the self-help aspects of a medical procedure. Little is mentioned in the NHS about preparation for a procedure, or about recuperating from illness or surgery. That may be because the NHS is not tasked to help patients before entering or after leaving hospital. It sits in that grey area between hospital care and general practice/community care where a GP or the local authority are responsible. But a good surgeon will not operate until they are satisfied that the patient is strong enough to withstand the treatment as well as being able to manage their recovery when they get home. Any discharge procedure will include checking on home support, providing medicines, nursing care if need be and as some advice about diet, exercise and support.

Preparation for some operations, particularly bariatric procedures, where stomach or intestinal surgery is performed in order to induce weight loss, require an overweight patient to follow a very strict *liver diet* for four to six weeks prior to the operation. For this diet, they are admitted to the hospital. It is very important to get it right. Prior to other types of operations, there may be less advice available, and certainly no close supervision, even though time and again studies show that good food, exercise and a good mental state will help prepare for and aid recovery after any surgery.

In illnesses such as cancer, we often observe a dramatic muscle-wasting. This *cancer cachexia* is caused by dietary protein being re-directed to the immuno-metabolic system, in order that precious amino acids can be called into use to counter tumour growth. We know that simply eating more doesn't necessarily help. Early intervention is vital, including targeted diets, nutritional supplementation and physical exercise. In addition, because appetite is often dulled by chemotherapies and treatments, appetite-inducing drugs and supplements can also help.

An army would be ill-advised to enter a fight without training and a good meal. It is just the same with any procedure. Before surgery the patient is often fasted, and may have been eating sparingly for quite some time due to their illness. These days, assessments for malnutrition are taken on admission to hospital as a matter of routine. Elderly patients, or those who live alone, may have faced many barriers to good nutrition during the previous weeks and days. It is better to build you up a bit before the onslaught of surgery, rather than afterwards. The European Society for Clinical Nutrition and Metabolism (ESPEN) recommends that in cases of severe malnutrition, it is better to delay treatment by one or two weeks, rather than subject an unfit patient to major surgery. Also, unless there are special risks, most patients are now encouraged to take clear liquids, including tea and coffee before an operation, to reduce the risk of post-operative dehydration and sickness. Some medication, for example semaglutides, may be withheld for a few days to reduce the risk of delayed reflux during the operation. The old routines of nil-by-mouth are outdated.[9]

Recuperation from a bone fracture will almost always include physiotherapy. The therapist will be well-practiced in getting someone with a broken leg or hip back on their feet. This can be achieved at pretty well any age. But recuperation diets are far more difficult to access, in spite of the importance of eating a highly nutritious diet after surgery to help with healing.

Different types of recovery protocols, at different life stages, dictate different emphases. However, in general, a high lean protein diet, with plenty of fruit and vegetables, would be a good start. The classic sickbed food of chicken soup would be excellent. The old remedy of fresh air and sunshine will be wonderful. As we age, we become less able to metabolise vitamin D from sunshine. Thus, vitamin D supplements can also help re-build muscle loss after injury and during periods of bed-rest, or inactivity. Rebuilding muscle strength is important, whatever the injury, because they drive metabolism and support bone restructuring.

After surgery, the entire digestive system can become sluggish, degrading the microbes that shelter in our digestive system and have important jobs to do. The microbiota helps to extract every last bit of nutrition from our food, easing elimination and supporting the immune system. After an operation, after chemotherapy, or simply during bed-rest, foods that were once well-tolerated might become problematic.

We often hear older people complaining that cheese is difficult to digest, or onions too gassy or that high fibre produces discomfort. After any treatment it will take time to re-balance gut flora. Protective microbes that have an important health role may have been completely washed away during the course of pre-operation purgative cleansing, bowel irrigation or intestinal decontamination. In addition, post-operative antibiotic treatment can reduce the danger of infection, but will completely kill off even more of our delicate gut flora. That is why antibiotics or purgatives post-operation should be targeted and limited to essential treatment only.

Gut muscle strength, the transporters that convey nutrients from the gut into the bloodstream, and the delicate flora of the microbiota, can take time to re-establish themselves. The cure is simple: good, wholesome, fresh food, in all its infinite variety. Any post-operative diet should include lean protein, fruit, vegetables, wholemeal grains, cereals and dairy, but not too many extra cream buns.

'Eat what you feel like,' is often the advice given by the nurse who discharges you. It isn't particularly helpful advice. Temporary physical changes caused by an operation can be augmented by changes in taste and smell as well as changes in energy consumption. If you have recently had an operation, then energy is being expended in order to repair the wound. Internal resects (joins in the tissue) are repaired by the body, not by the surgeon. A few dissolvable staples are often all that the surgeon needs to implant in order to start the bodily process of repair. Once you are home, you will be responsible for making sure your body has enough nutrients to make a long-lasting repair.

Recuperation diets are often higher in calories than the diet you might have had before your treatment. In fact, after major surgery, ESPEN, the European Society for Parenteral and Enteral Nutrition, advises that the anabolic phase of rehabilitation, during which the body is rebuilding itself, requires a caloric intake of 1.2 to 1.5 times the normal resting energy expenditure – or the diet you would have required just to sit at home in an armchair. A requirement for extra nutritious food may last for up to 12 months post-surgery. And once the 12 months is over, you will find that you have picked up some new and hopefully healthier eating habits along the way. Taking care of yourself, pre- and post-treatment, can be as important as the treatment itself. [10]

Yes, we can!

Once you are aware that the body is designed to live, not programmed to die, then recovering from any setback should be the expected outcome at any age. That means that older people, if they decide to make changes, should be encouraged to do so.

Being able to change one's mind isn't the sole domain of the young. Our minds remain flexible for life. Argye Hillis M.D., director of the cerebrovascular division at Johns Hopkins Medicine, observed in an interview that there is surprisingly little difference between an 18-year-old brain and a 100-year-old brain.[11] In a Johns Hopkins-led study of *atherosclerosis* – hardening of the arteries – the researchers tracked more than 6,000 people aged 44 to 84 for seven years. They found that those who had made healthy lifestyle changes such as quitting smoking, following a healthy diet, exercising regularly and maintaining a healthy weight decreased their risk of death in the time period by 80 per cent. But only two per cent of the study cohort achieved this high lifestyle score. Smoking seemed to have had the most negative effect.[12] Professor Hillis advises that you are never too old to adopt new healthy habits.

Governance – how the uk compares

In some countries more effort is put into helping people maintain a healthy lifestyle and enjoy their old age. It is not a matter of chance that in countries such as Finland, Japan, or Iceland, overall life-expectancy is consistently higher than in the UK. Concerted effort, analysis, money and thought have gone into creating public health systems that are much better than we have in the UK today. When in 2023 the NHS celebrated its 75th anniversary, opinion polls cited lack of funding, staff shortages and government policy as threats to a system that most British people are proud of – even now, when we know it isn't working as well as it should. At the time the government didn't mention the other aspects of national governance that directly impact our health, such as care systems, dietary recommendations, health education or the state of community services. These aren't managed by the NHS, but by a motley selection of government agencies, charities and local authorities, struggling on meagre grants from central government. Often the services themselves are farmed out to private firms of questionable quality*. Standards are inconsistent. Joined-up working is the exception rather than the rule. Strategies barely exist.

But it is not simply a matter of money. In the US, healthcare is a billion-

---

* Government procurement procedures, designed to eliminate corruption and foster fairness, can have the effect of favouring large companies over small, measuring hoop-jumping and process rather than assessing quality and outcome.

pound industry. There is no shortage of cash, but the system is not equable and excludes many ordinary citizens. In addition, the insurance-led approach has tended to favour treatment over prevention. Healthy living is nowhere on the radar. A successful healthcare system is about how that money is spent and about the policies surrounding those budgets. Policy-making is as important at a national level as thinking and planning is to the individual.

Britain does not do well in the international league tables. Some countries spend a far greater proportion of their wealth on caring for their populations and their citizens benefit from it. Our nearest neighbours, France and Germany, similar in size and economic power to the UK, can boast far better health care systems these days; that is due to better management but also higher funding.

For example, in 2023 a potential treatment for Alzheimer's hit the headlines. The drug company Lilly published a study of the drug Donanemab, showing excellent results and in the USA a similar drug called Leqembi was already receiving a license for accelerated approval. The successful trials offered real hope of an imminent treatment for the disease, but only if patients were diagnosed and treated early enough. At the time, The Guardian reported that in the UK there are not enough PET scanners compared to other comparable countries, so even if Donanemab were to be licensed, many people could not be able to access it in time; they simply wouldn't get a diagnosis until it was too late.[13] Lately that complaint has been taken up by the Alzheimer's Society, who have pushed for an experimental blood test for Alzheimer's to be licenced.[14]

Political change

We should all be prepared to press for improvements, by speaking out or at least by making sure we cast our vote. In the final analysis, particularly when we are frail and vulnerable, we will all require strong and resilient national systems to help us through. Campaigners are portrayed as young and rebellious, though I am not sure this stereotype actually holds true. In fact, it must surely be a combination of youth and experience, rebellion and wisdom that will make the world healthier for all of us in the future. Involvement is strength. Maintaining engagement with the world around us is, in my view, a vital part of life – at any age.

The north-south divide is not mythical. Where you live and how much you earn can have an extraordinary influence over your life-prospects. People in Cumbria live on average five years less than those of a similar income and background in London. Even within the county of Cumbria the difference in life expectancy between the poorest and wealthiest wards is now almost 20 years.[15] That is very much a result of government policy, and while health policy definitely plays its part, other local and national government decisions regarding economic development, planning, housing, transportation and education have all had an impact.

It is not simply the people of Cumbria who are hard done by. In any city across the land, including southern cities such as London, we can find pockets of social and economic deprivation that impact people's incomes, but also the quality of their housing, the food they eat and the facilities available to them. These are the factors outside of our control that impact healthy ageing. It is a false assumption that we all have free will and can decide how we live. As we get older, the challenge increases as we have less ability to move about and possess less energy to make the choices we would like to make. Age can deprive us, even more than poverty can. Start campaigning now.

Food legislation, saving us from ourselves, it difficult to get past governments of any hue, who are timid to legislate for healthy food. The assumption is that fresh and healthy foods cost more money, and thus further restrict poorer people's options. This is a bit of a fallacy. Small-scale interventions, such as lunch clubs, offer older people a healthy well-cooked meal, within their budget and without resorting to packaged and processed foods. Yet when we visit a supermarket, we cannot influence the amount of sugar in our deserts and soft drinks, let alone our bread! And we certainly have little influence over the prices. We cannot control the price of fresh produce over processed foods. If you live in a small community with only one accessible shop you will be forced to buy what they have on offer, take it or leave it. Consumers can pressurise, and elderly consumers are a large voice – but only legislation can really turn the tide.

It wasn't a national newspaper, or a political party, but campaigning by the Alliance for Better Food and Farming (called Sustain) that finally saw legislation introduced in the UK to limit the amount of sugar in soft drinks. It was called the sugar tax and widely lampooned by some politicians and the right-wing press. The tax imposed a cap on the amount of sugar in drinks. It didn't transform soft drinks into healthy drinks, but it paved the way for less unhealthy formulations. This tiny change was vehemently opposed by the soft drinks industry, but within a year of its introduction, most manufacturers found that they could reduce the amount of sugar to below taxable levels without ruining the appeal of the product. In 2018 the industry magazine, Beverage reported that a third of sugary drinks manufacturers had reduced their sugar content by almost half, in order to bring the drink below the highest sugar tax level of 24p/litre. Ironically full sugar Coca-Cola did not reduce the sugar content of their drink, instead putting up the price by more than the levy, possibly in order to fund bigger and more luscious advertising campaigns. But we can decide to ignore the Coca-Cola ads. We can teach the world to sing without an expensive bottle of fizzy, over-sweetened, over-caffeinated, dung-coloured water in our hands.

When I used to work as an advisor to the Commission for Architecture and the Built Environment, our teams would regularly visit new developments where basic facilities such as a pharmacy, a GP or a bus service had not yet been provided. I once visited a housing estate, billed as a new sustainable suburb, where hundreds of homes had been handed over, many of them to people from the council's waiting list. Very poor people suddenly found themselves stranded in new homes with no jobs, little support and without the means to buy basic furniture or floor coverings. Some people were living out of boxes and plastic bags on bare, hard concrete. They didn't know their neighbours. They were forced to walk miles to find facilities. The shops hadn't been built and the promised fast rail link was behind schedule. We were shocked to discover that the only way of accessing the local GP surgery – in the next village – was to walk along a narrow footpath for a mile or so, alongside the busy main road. The route was inaccessible for prams or wheelchairs and there was no bus. These are the barriers that ordinary people face day in, day out. Can we blame them if their health isn't optimal?

The UK is the fifth wealthiest nation in the world. According to GDP rankings from 2023, we come behind the United States, China, Germany and Japan and slightly ahead of India, France, Italy, Canada and South Korea. But when it comes to health and longevity, the UK is nowhere near the top. The official world longevity data for 2021 put the UK at number 26.[16,*]

---

* You might recall Boris Johnson arguing mortality figures at The Covid Enquiry, trying to convince the judge that the UK wasn't the worst in Europe; while barristers argued that UK figures were pretty dreadful compared to other *comparably wealthy* Western European nations. See Jon Henley, *Is Boris Johnson right that UK had fewer Covid deaths than much of Europe?* The Guardian 6 December 2023.

We have always been proud of our NHS, but in 2018 the Euro Health Consumer Index, ranked the UK 18 out of 35 European nations. This organisation analyses national healthcare using 46 indicators including, patient rights and information, accessibility, treatment outcomes, range and reach of services, prevention, use of pharmaceuticals. The UK ranked behind most Western European nations and even several Eastern European nations.[17] We live in a democracy; don't people vote for things like better healthcare?

Does willpower really matter?

I would say that the quality of old age and healthy life expectancy has less to do with willpower than many self-help pundits suggest. Happy and healthy old age is a political issue. It is highly unlikely to be your fault as much as it is the fault of society and of government.

As individuals we cannot control the amount of pollution we are exposed to, or the amount of sugar in a supermarket cake, or how long the waiting list might be for a lifesaving operation. Our individual lives are inextricably linked to the success or failure of public institutions like the NHS and the myriad of public policies that affect (or ignore) our daily lives. Our personal finances are influenced by the taxes we pay when we are in work, and the corresponding support we receive when we need help. As individuals, we do have some leverage to change things, either by modifying our own behaviour and setting a good example, or by campaigning with others to effect wider change. These days it seems that government policy is not prioritised by need, and instead politicians listen most attentively to those who shout the loudest.

Older people make up a high proportion of the voting population. About one in five voters in the UK are over the age of 65 and most of them are considered to be diligent voters. This voting power is often seen as regressive, but I don't think it is as homogenous as pollsters believe it to be. Older voters are sadly familiar with bombardments of unsubstantiated promises, supported by half-truths and inaccuracies that, in the absence of first-hand experience, or reliable information, have led to some pretty regrettable governance over the years. Perhaps older people are not as gullible as their government thinks?

Corporate change

Corporate law is based on the principle that the function of business is to make money for its shareholders. Anything else that a company can get away with is fine (as long as it isn't against the law). In Britain there are people who would say that freedom to make money shouldn't be fettered by regulation at all. But do we as individuals really have the energy to counter the commercial heft of Big Tobacco, Big Pharma, Big Food and Big Alcohol? Our voting powers should be able to lever government policies to limit the self-interest and indifference of some commercial players. Yet in the mainstream media such issues are rarely tackled head-on. Do some media outlets fear the displeasure of big business or the loss of advertising revenue? All ethical corporations should be brave enough to concede that the spreadsheet should not be read without the engagement of heart *and* head.

Many businesses, especially the larger corporations, feel that they have a duty to ensure that legislation is minimised. However, it has been enshrined in law for a long time that all companies have a legal duty of care to third parties, especially their employees and their customers. It's called the law of tort. Since 2007 that duty of care has extended even to the gravity of corporate manslaughter. Lack of corporate care that causes death, does not have to name an individual within the company, but can be levelled at the company itself, as a legal entity. The redress, if an individual cannot be identified as the perpetrator, is a hefty fine, though never imprisonment of directors.

Those who hate regulation call it red tape, and maintain that it is merely a nuisance. Yet it is part of the process of democratic checks and balances to legislate for companies to be more ethical in their approach to products and services. So why is the time-lag so great between establishing a harm and legislating to minimise it? Time and again we see that it is the companies themselves, using well-financed lobbying powers to delay legislation, even if they know themselves the dangers the products they sell are posing.

Back in the seventies, the father of a friend of mine died of lung cancer. He was only in his late forties and had never smoked – but everyone else smoked in his office. In those days we could only mourn what seemed like dreadfully bad luck; nowadays we'd recognise the dangers of secondary smoking. In fact, his death was due less to the malice of his fellow workers (who knew no better) than to the idleness of the tobacco companies, the real culprits, who we now know used every trick in the book to discredit the mounting evidence that passive smoking was killing men, women and children in shocking numbers.[18]

It wasn't until a good twenty years after my friend's father died, that governments started to legislate. In 2004 Ireland became the first country in the world to institute a comprehensive national smoke-free law covering all indoor workplaces. Since then, the world has increasingly embraced the idea that people should not be exposed to the risks of cancer because someone else wants to light up; and that everyone should be supported to give up. The results have been staggering. A 2003 experimental smoke-free law in the town of Pueblo, Colorado found that hospital admissions for heart attacks dropped 27 per cent within 18 months; in neighbouring towns without such by-laws, there was no change.

I would question why so many government interventions take so long. The reason must be that even ethical and responsible governments are hide-bound by corporate intervention. It is corporate money that funds political parties and it is advertising revenue that drives the media. Similarly, the corporate lobby will always threaten job loss and tax loss within the industries concerned.

Just one example; in the UK today about £25billion pounds in fuel duty is received by the Government each year.[19] No wonder they don't want to wean us off oil.

Pollution

Big business sells it, gas guzzlers ooze it, smokers inflict it and uncaring employers expose us to it. Even governments wage war with highly toxic pollutants that leave acrid smoke, dust, asbestos and heavy metal, not to mention deadly nuclear or toxic chemical particles. And we are complicit in this pollution every time we dispose of something incorrectly, burn the wrong fuel in our fireplace, use inappropriate cleaning agents or leap in the car.

Pollution is a hidden killer that is rarely mentioned on death certificates, though since the Ella Kissi Debrah case, it is now recognised as a serious threat to health. Yet somehow many parts of our cities *and* countryside still suffer its scourge. If you smoke or work in a dirty industry, then the effects of environmental pollution can multiply the risk manyfold. The impacts of accidental exposure can last a lifetime, or shorten a lifespan. There are hundreds of cases from coalminers to alarm clock makers, whose lives have been cut short by industrial exposure. Pollution attacks the young, the weak and the old. This is an issue for self-control, but also for concerted pubic campaigning.

Health education

Our entire knowledge of the world, including our understanding of what constitutes a desirable lifestyle, is coloured by the sort of education we received when we were at school and the continuing public information we receive as adults. Today, the three 'Rs' are considered all-important. But surely a good education is about learning how to be curious, how to find things out, how to judge the quality of information we are given and how to use what we know to make better decisions – in our work, for our families and for ourselves?

We've forgotten that education should be teaching us how to live well, not simply to earn more. Really important lessons have been neglected for so long that it will take an earthquake to get issues like healthy eating back into the curriculum – not to mention teaching by example and ensuring that school meals are nutritious. The Japanese do this brilliantly, teaching children healthy eating, alongside learning about traditional Japanese cuisine and how to recycle. And, as you might expect, a Japanese school dinner is a gastronomic delight! They even have a special word for food education – *shokuiku.*

In Britain, we've even taken sports off the agenda for primary school children. And with all this focus on the three Rs, levels of literacy and numeracy haven't risen that much. What has risen, while we've been looking the other way, is levels of childhood obesity. That rise is alarming.

The untrumpeted scandal of poor, or nonexistent, food education means that almost one quarter (22.3%) of reception age pupils in 2021/22 were obese or overweight. That proportion rises to more than a third (37.7%) of aged 10 to 11 years-olds. All the education we give these young kids is doing nothing to stem the tide of childhood obesity. They are simply getting more and more over-weight. Childhood obesity, while children are still developing, sets a predisposition to being overweight in adulthood. Perhaps that is why almost two thirds (64%) of adults are currently overweight or obese.[20]

Social change

Changes in the way our friends and neighbours see things can make personal change easier or harder. In different countries all over the world people live longer or shorter, happier or unhappier lives depending on the social mores that exist in those countries. Society as a whole can make a difference and could make much more of a difference if encouraged to do so.

Don't beat yourself up if you feel your resolve is weak. It is not your weakness; part of the issue is social and peer pressure that can lead us astray. No wonder we don't always do 'the right thing' while so many powerful forces exist to encourage, cajole and trick our friends to thinking that there is no jeopardy in doing the wrong thing.

World change

Sometimes we need an extra impetus to do the right thing. If you've been reading up to now and wonder about how consistently virtuous you can be, faced with an uncaring government, greedy businesses and social prejudice, let this section convince you in a different way. It is a fantastic coincidence that most of the lifestyle changes science recommends for a long and happy life are also marvellously beneficial for life on earth.

The climate emergency will require us to end our reliance on fossil fuels, but eating healthy, fresh, local, organic and natural foods and avoiding toxins also makes a positive environmental impact. Cycling or walking instead of driving reduces harmful emissions. We all know that personal changes in consumption may not change our world immediately, but if we start, others will follow. The choices we make today will influence the world we bequeath to the next generation, as well as ensuring that we will be there to enjoy the implications of a greener, more equitable world. The UK target for emissions remains net zero by 2050, 77% of 1990 emissions by 2035, and a 68% reduction by 2030.[21]

We sometimes forget, and I would argue our shortsighted political leaders often forget, how closely these deadlines loom. If the world succeeds, both old and young will reap the benefit. This will affect the younger generation. But if you are 60 today, chances are that you'll see all these changes in your own lifetime. And if we reach those challenging deadlines, then chances are that more older people will still be around, reaping the benefits of fresher food, better transport and a less consumerist society.

"The Earth is more than just a home, it's a living system and we are part of it."*

The Climate Emergency has crept up on us over the last 30 or 40 years, but back-to-nature environmentalism has been a thread running through many philosophies for centuries. That thread links Saint Francis of Assisi, Luther and William Morris via the National Trust, the Ramblers Association and Greenpeace, to 21st century luminaries such as David Attenborough and Greta Thunberg.

Ideas we consider modern are not always so new. It was Edmond Becquere who discovered the photovoltaic effect in France in 1839, the fore-runner to the solar panel. Charles Fritts installed the first solar

---

* James Lovelock describing the Gaia hypothesis

panels on a New York rooftop in 1884. Solar-powered units, often hand-made using recycled elements, became popular during the hippy era in southern California in the 1960s and were given further impetus by the oil crises of the 1970s.[22]

The slow movement that was born in Italy in the 1990s echoes much of what EF Schumacher said in his 1973 polemic, *Small is Beautiful*.[23] Schumacher believed in the Buddhist view of human activity, that the function of life (and thus work) is:

- To utilise and develop our unique faculties
- To overcome ego-centredness by joining with others in a common task
- To bring forth goods and services needed for a becoming existence

It can be revelatory to realise that following a healthy regimen in pursuit of a long and active life is not an egocentric occupation. It is simply making the most of our unique skills and energies for the common good.

There are many examples of studies that claim to accurately predict the behaviour of large numbers of people. That might imply that only a small minority of people exercise their freedoms, escape from the madding crowd and find their own path. You would imagine that those few are unlikely to significantly affect the overall outcome. But history teaches us that a trickle of people changing their minds about something often becomes a flood.

In recent years we can see the popularity of the cotton tote bag, electric vehicles and glamping, all starting small and becoming mainstream. Eventually we can change the world. And while we are doing it, we change ourselves as well. By swapping a luxury hotel in Thailand for a yurt in Somerset we reduce our carbon footprint, but we also change our sense of ourselves. I might even venture to suggest that a bracing holiday in the countryside might be much better for our longevity that a sun-soaked beach fest. Schumacher would contend that important innovations and changes normally start from a tiny minority of people who make use of their creative freedom to influence others. It is a lesson well-learned.

By looking outwards, and refusing to take a self-centred view of longevity, we can benefit our own wellbeing by continuing to contribute to the world, long after our last pay-check has been spent. Each one of us must decide what is for us the common task that Schumacher refers to.

For me the synchronicity of living healthily, whilst doing my bit for climate change, seem too good to ignore. By looking at what is healthy for the planet, we see self-care a little differently.

Sustainability is defined in all sorts of different ways, but whether you look at the Intergovernmental Panel for Climate Change (IPCC) or your local campaigning group, you will find a checklist which is remarkably similar to the prescription I have suggested for long life:

- Health and happiness
- Equity and local economy
- Culture and community
- Land use and wildlife
- Sustainable water
- Local and sustainable food
- Using sustainable materials
- Sustainable transport
- Zero waste
- Zero carbon

The checklist above is from the The One Planet Living® Framework by Bioregional. It is one of many systems that seek to encompass a holistic approach to the climate emergency. It could be considered the grandchild of Schumacher's idea that *Small is Beautiful,* espousing a sustainable economics based on localism, equity, culture and community. Their inclusion, alongside de-carbonisation and energy conservation, widens opportunities and enriches consequences. It allows us to frame answers to how we should live in the future and contemplate new kinds of lifestyles to bequeath to those that follow. These very fundamental questions are informed by the very thing that older people possess in spades – experience.

I like the fact that right at the top of the One Planet Living Framework we find health and happiness. Our food consumption choices take up almost a quarter (23%) of the energy we use, while transport uses up a further 13%. Thus, changes in the way we eat and shop as well as the way we move around are significant contributors to reducing climate change as well as maintaining health.[24]

If you find it difficult to make changes for your own benefit, then you might find changing your outlook will help. If you embrace a sustainable lifestyle, you will quite naturally be living a pretty healthy life. It will do you good and will do the planet good.

Reduce, reuse, recycle

When we wish to take care of the environment, we will often use the phrase reduce, reuse, recycle. We know that by reducing our consumption and not being extravagant means benefits will accrue to our planet and to the ecosystem. These days those three Rs are often extended to six or more, each focused on saving our most precious resource – energy.

- Reduce
- Reuse
- Recycle
- Repair
- Repurpose
- Renew

Mother Nature learned that energy is precious eons ago. A major motivator for evolution has always been the limited availability of energy. In our daily lives, conservation of energy is about turning down the central heating, switching to walking and cycling and getting what energy we do use from renewable resources. Exactly the same happens in the body.

In human biology the imperative to reduce, reuse and recycle is highly evolved. Our bodies are primed to run on the minimum of fuel – to *reduce*. We are super-efficient machines; nothing is wasted. Every cell in our body can break down and the resulting cargo of amino acids and other molecules is efficiently *reused* in other new cells. Very little is wasted. Elements of tissue are *recycled* over and over again in order to conserve resources and re-use energy. For example, charged and uncharged hydrogen atoms bounce back and forth, producing the tiny electrical potential that exists in every cell. That energy, multiplied a trillion-fold by the sheer number of active cells within our bodies, is used to power anything in us that moves, grows and responds, from a pumping heart muscle to firing brain cells. Stem cells are always on hand to provide the raw material for the *repair* of tissue and organs. Even more amazing is the body's ability to *repurpose* critical infrastructure if the original is lost or damaged. For example, we can even recover from serious head injuries. Undamaged areas of the brain are repurposed to perform the critical functions lost to damaged cells and thus we can learn to speak again and to walk again.

We should also learn from the body in the way that it performs *renewal*. This efficient use of energy accepts imperfection. Maintaining the same old brain cells for decades means that we have long memories, leading to wisdom and experience. Even if that memory isn't perfect, it doesn't benefit from being swept away. Every scar we carry is documentary evidence of a long life well-lived, and a cell renewed to just the right level to do the job. The body doesn't waste energy on unnecessary newness.

A balanced diet is an example of *reducing* energy consumption to a minimum. It is no coincidence that we talk about the need to *reduce* when we go on a diet. A calorie is a measure of energy. What we are *reducing* is energy input – principally in the form of glucose and fat, which form the highest concentration of calories in our diet. When we exercise, we use up energy calories. In human terms, conservation of energy is about achieving balance between energy in and energy out. In medical terms we call that homeostasis. In planetary terms we call it Gaia.

Nature is scrupulous in *reusing* every atom of matter. Plants are eaten by animals, that are in turn consumed by creatures higher up the food chain. One of the reasons why humans are so ubiquitous in the world is because we are omnivorous. We have evolved to eat a variety of different types of food, depending on where we live and what is available. Our digestive systems can grow different nutrient-absorbing cells in a matter of days, in response to new diets, or atrophy outmoded nutrient transporters. Our bodies can make do with many different diets and many different environments; to be omnivorous is to be strong. Our bodies can *reuse* whatever comes our way and our cells can adapt and reform themselves in response to the current situation.

Life is not bashful about *repairs*. When we cut our skin, we don't expect a perfect job. Stem cells gather to 'darn' the gash, sometimes with the aid of a few stitches from a nurse's needle or even the surgeon's staple gun.

Many of us carry the marks of an injury through life. Sometimes these imperfections can become hugely meaningful for us.

Imperfection is fashionable

In our everyday lives we are now all intensely aware that we should not squander resources. Cars are being designed so that if a section is damaged, a new piece of bodywork can simply be clicked into place. Even if our clothing is worn, we shouldn't throw it away.

The Japanese have been doing this for centuries, creating beautiful objects from worn clothing and potter. Recently the Brunei Gallery at SOAS in London exhibited a collection of exquisite *Boro* and *Sakiori* textiles and lovingly restored *Washi* and *Kin-tsugi* pottery.[25]

I now refuse to throw away any loved clothes, just because they are damaged. These days darning is trendy. The London artist Celia Pym started to darn old clothes when she inherited a well-loved jumper from her uncle Roly. It was quite simply a labour of remembrance to repair the elbow that was rubbed bare by a repetitive movement – drawing – while he was sitting in a particular armchair. Since then, she has gone on to develop an artistic practice by repairing moth holes, relics from museum archives and fire damage. She makes no attempt to disguise the damage, instead drawing attention to it using colourful, contrasting materials.* She says:

"The holes in our clothes are a visible sign of the life lived."

---

* celiapym.com

Prejudice

Ageism is illegal in the UK. The Equality Act protects us against:

- Direct discrimination – age-related limits and bars to access
- Indirect discrimination – services that indirectly limit access or use due to age
- Harassment – behaviour that makes you feel intimidated, humiliated, degraded, or that creates a hostile environment (this is generally only pursued in the workplace or where services are being offered. For example, if a bank clerk makes offensive jokes about your age)
- Victimisation – unfair treatment as a result of a complaint about discrimination

Age prejudice can be overt, or it can be insidious. As we get older, we are encouraged to take it easy. Yet stopping doing the things that make life worth living, even giving up the basic chores of life, can divorce us from the pleasure and satisfaction of achievement. Taking-it-easy can actually remove us from controlling how we really want to live. In countries such as the Netherlands, care homes have been re-imagined to allow residents to retain their independence. In spite of medical or mental disabilities, people are encouraged to do their own cooking or shopping, and to take part in the day-to-day running of the household.*

While we may need more help as we grow older, we should still fight to retain the good things of life, which in my view includes doing normal activities for as long as we can do them. But doing our own chores is not a raison d'être. For me it is much more important to remain engaged

---

* See Chapter 10.

with society; caring about how we live in the world and caring about the world we live in.

In modern life we are so often divided by generations. It is quite possible that you can live your whole life without intimate knowledge of what it is like to grow old, until you confront it yourself. We receive no education about the natural process of ageing; young health practitioners are given scant instruction in order to help or support their older patients. Doctors and clinicians are taught about the body in great detail, but often conditions of ageing don't get the airing they should. I noticed in my own clinical lectures that many of the sessions would run chronologically. More often than not, the information relating to older people would come at the end of the lecture, leaving little time for questions or discussion. Sometimes the lecturer would run out of time all together, so aspects of ageing were left for us to mug-up on at home. How many of my (younger) fellows didn't bother?

No wonder that the medical profession often underestimates older patients. During the course of my professional relationship with carers, rookie house-doctors and community nurses, I have become aware that many of them fundamentally misunderstand what it is like to age. They see a date of birth – not a person. The scant information a doctor is given about their patient invites them to make age, class *and* gender judgements, as well as making sweeping assumptions on the relative values to society of different people. Perhaps none of us really 'get it' until we reach that level of maturity ourselves.

You may already have discovered that ageism continues to be a very powerful prejudice. Don't collude with it. Correct the young doctor who is too quick to condemn you as past it. Enlighten the ageist employer. We need to make our voices heard, to take the initiative, to make plans and demand new legislation even when government is passive.

Perhaps by our actions, older people can remind policy makers that they can still be useful members of society. Leaving older people to languish is a waste of resources.

Should ageism matter?

Ageism is one of those nasty isms that infiltrates and insinuates itself, like a miasma, into every part of society and, even more frightfully, into our own minds. Ageism can cost us our independence as well as leaching our finances. While I'm willing to bet that my readers rarely condemn themselves as too old, how many of you have altered your appearance to try to look younger for a job interview or been persuaded to purchase an expensive wrinkle-defying skin cream? There is no reason why fighting the good fight should not include fighting to look young for as long as possible. But are we fighting the fear of ageing, rather than trying to preserve our wellbeing?

The market value of non-medicated facial skincare in Great Britain can be counted in millions (£800 million in 2019).[26] We scrutinise film-star facelifts with a mixture of envy and horror. Neither is it just women who are subjected to this pressure. We laughed when ex-mayor Rudy Giuliani's hair dye ran down his sweating face during the 2021 US presidential shenanigans. But Giuliani is not alone among the growing number of men and women who try to hide their grey hair. In the UK we spend £7.2 billion each year at the hairdressers, and over £300 million on home hair-dye kits. The beauty industry gets fat on the back of our anxieties.

Attempts to look younger are not mere vanity. If you have grey hair and wrinkled skin you are less likely to get the good job or find a new life partner. A study commissioned by the Equality and Human Rights Commission found that a higher proportion (26%) of adults reported experiencing prejudice based on their age compared to any other characteristic. If you go for a job, you might very well be written off because you are too old, but also because you are too young. And if you are a woman, you may suffer the double whammy of age and gender discrimination. In the same study 22% of respondents had suffered gender bias.[27] The worst of it is you might have made a decision not to apply for a job or not to start dating because of your own self-prejudice. You might be writing yourself off, even before others do. Fear of rejection is a very powerful emotion.

Ageism can affect our lives and close down our options. We can suffer direct age discrimination (such as being excluded from a shortlist due to age); negative stereotypes can pigeonhole us; and negative self-perceptions can limit us. Not only can these three components influence our self-respect and our earnings ability, they can also damage our health. Doctors make a lot of clinical decisions based on age, even though that type of health rationing is illegal and discriminatory. We all have an equal right to treatment. The constant drip-drip of age discrimination that we are all subjected to can result in our not feeling good enough about ourselves. We stop bothering.[28]

Some age campaigners might condemn anybody who dyes their hair or invests in Botox treatment. But until ageism is conquered, there is plenty of justification in hiding one's age. In California's Silicon Valley young men in their 30s are advised to improve their appearance by investing in hair dye and face-lifts before going to a job interview.[29] But as with any other form of prejudice, society is the poorer because of its existence. If we judge by hair-tone alone, we are dismissing the person underneath the fringe, who in spite of their chronological age may have far greater wisdom and experience. Missing the good candidate is detrimental to the employer most of all.

If we judge by looks alone, we are in danger of condemning most of the adult population to expend money and time on completely unnecessary cosmetic treatments. We ought instead to be able to embrace the fact that we do change with age and encourage those around us that looking old doesn't mean we are past it. Conversely, healthy ageing doesn't mean staying forever young. Thank goodness! Who would want the stress of school exams again, or to re-live the horror of that first teenage party?

The dynamic Ashton Applewhite, author of *This Chair Rocks: A Manifesto Against Ageism* – Macmillan 2019, gives a thought-provoking TED talk where she delivers a spirited anti-ageist rhetoric. Her strategy is to make adjustments, as and when required. We won't be able to do or be everything we used to do, but we shouldn't fight it. And whether we are talking about deciding to use a walking stick, or dying our hair, the same logic applies. We should learn to adapt to a different type of life and not allow ourselves to be penalised or marginalised for requiring those adaptations.[30] Applewhite is unconcerned that she doesn't look 20 anymore. What you look like is far less important than what you are doing and saying. Only by us older people getting out there and being in the world will younger people learn that age is not a disability. In a podcast interview with Bruce Devereux, she said:

"... a metaphor I use is that it's like letting a genie out of a bottle. Once you see it in yourself, you see it everywhere. But I find that comforting. It's like, 'Oh, it's not my bad. It's not something I did wrong'. It's in the culture; there's these massive social and economic forces that want me to think this way. And I'm going to try bit by bit to reject that dogma and try to learn to see differently".[31]

Unfortunately, politicians and policy-makers rarely see older people as individuals, and society has conditioned them to think we have no purpose. Discussions about living a long and happy life are never called that. For example, the ageing problem, the ageing crisis or even the age tsunami are all used to preface discussions about long life. Most articles we read, in even the most progressive of broadsheets, commence with a litany of statistics revealing the rising number of older people. These data are presented as bad news!

Surely, shouldn't we welcome the fact that there are so many older people around these days, celebrating their experience and their fortitude? According to the Office for National Statistics (ONS), there were 1.6 million people aged 85 years and over in England in 2018; by mid-2043, this is projected to nearly double to three million. If the pension age sticks at 67 then today's 12.3 million pensioners will become 15.9 million by 2043. During the same time period, the working-age population is only set to rise by two or three percent.[32] That isn't a reason to be gloomy; that's a reason to consider how at least some of those 16 million over-67s might be encouraged to contribute to the society, to our economy and to our collective wisdom. These statistics present an opportunity, and maybe a challenge, but not a disaster.

Making valuable contributions to the economy does not mean low-paid, part-time jobs stacking shelves or working behind a bar. It means re-structuring the workplace by bringing in experienced staff for a specific project or program, by recognising the value of advisors and mentors and by changing the way we arrange the working week for everyone. The pandemic has changed work patterns already, illustrating the ability of business to make immediate change if it really needs to. Full employment, limited immigration and a lack of skilled workers will require firms to think differently about their recruitment policies. And while homeworking can be useful, I would not like to see it as the only solution to escaping the hard grind of commuting. I'd really like to be able to visit a convenient work-hub a few days each week in order to earn a bit, but also to contribute a lot. Organisations such as banks and estate agents that already possess branches would do well to reconsider some of their head office jobs as satellite roles. This would benefit not just the ageing cohort, but students, carers and parents as well.

Fortunately, demographics gives us a lot of time to plan for future age-group changes. Most babies born today will live to see the 22nd century. This is wonderful news. Pundits will often highlight the stress that older people will exert on our health system and the economy. However, this may be an over-played concern. There is very little evidence to show that older people put more strain on hospitals than sick younger people. A study of English hospitals in 2004 concluded that neither total hospital days, nor the number of admissions in the three years before death, showed a positive correlation to age at death. In fact, it is sick children who spend the longest time in hospital, before death. Fortunately, there are not too many of them. On average, those who have lived longer are less of a burden on the NHS at the end of life (and they have certainly paid into the system for long enough!). In one study the average number of hospital admissions during the last three years of life peaked at 10.4 admissions in the five-to-nine years age group and then decreased with age to 2.2 admissions in patients aged 85 and over.[33] These figures would imply that the longer we live, the more we contribute and the less of a drain on NHS resources we become.

Tax specialists will worry about loss of revenue from an older population. The received wisdom is that older people have more wealth and pay less tax. Some people think that you stop paying tax when you retire. That is far from the case; pensions are taxed in just the same way as earned income, though National Insurance contributions are not required. It is a well-vaunted myth that the young are paying tax to support the old. And while it really shouldn't become a tournament between age-groups, I feel I should point out that the old have already paid their fair share, in a lifetime of taxes and hard work.

I would like to see older people valued for their current and historic contribution to society, just as many older people value youngsters for their potential and their vigour in campaigning to change the world. All of us hope to be able to rely on the kindness and strength of the young at some time.

Please do not allow yourself to be side-lined because of other people's prejudices. If you decide that in order to continue to be taken seriously you ought to dye your hair, or Botox your forehead, then I would be the first to defend your right to do so. But I regret that you have to do such things, especially as both hair dye and Botox are toxins.*

Just like the women's movement of the 1970s, when the burning of bras and the abandonment of the married prefix Mrs. became symbols of defiance, so now the signs of ageing could become symbols of 'age assertiveness'.

---

* Botox is a derivative of the pathogen that causes the disease botulism. Permanent hair dyes (the sort you have to use in order to hide the grey) contain strong cleaning agents, colour-stripping agents and toxins such as ammonia, paraphenylenediamine (PPD), para-toluenediamine (PTD), allergens such as quaternium-15, and known hormonal disruptors such as resorcinol, alkylphenol ethoxylates (APEs) and phthalates. I can make no claim to telling you whether the small and legal proportions that these substances will harm you.

The status quo is not a given. Studies commissioned by the World Health Organisation, show that small-scale, low-cost interventions and programs can have lasting positive effects on the health of older people and on the understanding of younger people. In particular programs that combine both educational elements and inter-generational contact seem to work well.[34]

In Caerphilly in Wales, the Over-50s Group make weekly visits to a lunch club, located in a local school. Mike Oliver, the assistant head teacher, explains the success of the project:[35]

"At Lewis School, Pengam we have embraced the Community School concept and have placed it at the heart of our school ethos. We run a series of activities and events both during and after school. In order to run these, we work in partnership with statutory and voluntary groups. Our recent ESTYN Inspection called our inter-generational work exemplary; the work consists of monthly sequence dancing, run by Eileen and Brian Swithens and a weekly lunch club which sees 50 – 60 over 50s coming into school on Wednesdays. The benefits to the school have been enormous with our pupils engaging on a regular basis with a generation they sometimes don't mix with. At the same time, it has been wonderful for our over 50s to have the opportunity to socialise with our youngsters. Without doubt this is, as Head teacher Chris Parry described it, the 'Jewel in the Crown' of the activities at Lewis School."

Inter-generational activities echo what normal daily social life should be, although I might advise that it would be better to join Extinction Rebellion than the local over-60s club. Ageism can only be addressed by destroying the stereotypes it creates. It is better to be in the world than sit on the boundary observing. Perhaps it is better for each of us to highlight some of the important ageing issues we have today, than to bother with highlights in our hair? We all need to stop thinking of older people as a separate species. They can be cantankerous, mudded and obtuse. But so can teenagers, so can middle-aged 'jobsworths'. That bloody-mindedness may well be a protective blanket against the insults and omissions that we all suffer at different stages of life.

Endnotes

1 Allen Carr, (2020) *The Easy Way to Stop Smoking Without Willpower*, Book; Publisher Penguin Books 2020

2 Erens, B., Primatesta, P. (1999) *Health Survey for England. Cardiovascular Disease* The Stationery Office London UK

3 Gill LE, et al. *Weight Management in Older Adults.* Current Obesity Reports. 2015 Sep;4(3):379-88. DOI: 10.1007/s13679-015-0161-z

4 Taylor DH, et al. (2002) *Benefits of smoking cessation for longevity.* American Journal of Public Health 2002; Volume 92: pages 990–6

5 Jordan H, et al. (2017) *What are older smokers' attitudes to quitting and how are they managed in primary care? An analysis of the cross-sectional English Smoking Toolkit Study.* British Medical Journal; Open. 2017 Nov 15; 7(11) Epub. e018150. DOI: 10.1136/bmjopen-2017-018150

6 Webpage: *Quitting Smoking for Older Adults from:* nia.nih.gov/health/smoking/quitting-smoking-older-adults [retrieved February 2024]

7   Royal College of Physicians (RCP) Press Release. *RCP warns the UK is Facing a Crisis in Care for Older People* RCP london.ac.uk/news/rcp-warns-uk-facing-crisis-care-older-people [retrieved February 2023]

8   Weir, M & Buzhart, L *Can Old Dogs Learn New Tricks?* VCA Hospital Blog vcahospitals.com/know-your-pet/can-old-dogs-learn-new-tricks [retrieved February 2024]

9   Weimann, A et al. (2021) ESPEN *Practical Guideline: Clinical Nutrition in Surgery* Journal of Clinical Nutrition 40(2021)4745e4761 31 Mar 2021/DOI:10.1016//j.clnu.2021.03.031

10 Weimann, A et al. (2021) ESPEN IBID

11 Hillis, A. Blog: *It's Never too Late.* Johns Hopkins Medicine Website; hopkinsmedicine.org/health/wellness-and-prevention/its-never-too-late-five-healthy-steps-at-any-age [retrieved February 2024]

12 Diane E Bild et al. (2002) *Multi-Ethnic Study of Atherosclerosis: Objectives and Design*, American Journal of Epidemiology, Volume 156, Issue 9, 1 November 2002, Pages 871–881, DOI:10.1093/aje/kwf113

13 Pharmaceuticals (2023) *Lilly's Donanemab Significantly Slowed Cognitive and Functional Decline in Phase 3 Study of Early Alzheimer's Disease.* Press Release. May 3, 2023 investor.lilly.com/news-releases/news-release-details/lillys-donanemab-significantly-slowed-cognitive-and-functional

14 Gregory, A. (2023) *Experts urge health regulators to approve 'turning point' dementia drugs.* Article; Guardian 17th July 2023

15 Cumbrian Community Foundation, (2017) *Cumbria Revealed. A county of Contrast.* Available from: cumbriafoundation.org/cumbria-revealed [retrieved February 2024]

16 Worlddata (2021) *Life expectancy for men and women, by country.* worlddata.info/life-expectancy [retrieved February 2024]

17 Bjornberg, et al. (2019) *Euro Health Consumer Index* Health Consumer Powerhouse 2019-02-25 Report by Health Consumer Powerhouse Ltd., 2019. ISBN 978-91-980687-5-7 from healthpowerhouse.com/publications [retrieved February 2024]

18 World Health Organisation (WHO) *Tobacco Industry Interference; A Global Brief.* Website; who.int/tobacco [retrieved 2023]

19 From website: statista.com/statistics/284323/united-kingdom-hmrc-tax-receipts-fuel-duty [retrieved 2024]

20 Baker, C (2023) *Obesity statistics, House of Commons Research Briefing* Published Thursday, 12 January, 2023 available at commonslibrary.parliament.uk/research-briefings [retrieved February 2024]

21 UK Government (2023) Press Release; *PM-Recommits UK to Net-Zero by 2050 and Pledges a Fairer-Path to Achieving Target to ease the Financial Burden on British Families.* available at: gov.uk/government/news/pm-recommits-uk-to-net-zero-by-2050-and-pledges-a-fairer-path-to-achieving-target-to-ease-the-financial-burden-on-british-families [retrieved February 2024]

22 Chu, E & Tarazano, EL (2019), *A brief history of solar panels.* USPTO, for Smithsonian Magazine By, U.S. Patent and Trademark Office smithsonianmag.com April 22, 2019 [retrieved March 2021]

23 Schumacher EF (1973) *Small is beautiful, A study of economics as if people mattered.* First published by Blond and Briggs Ltd Great Britain.

24 For further information, there is an extensive website at bioregional.com and a useful webinar to be found here; oneplanetnetwork.org/webinar-discover-one-planet-living [retrieved March 2021]

25 Exhibition SOAS London website archive at soas.ac.uk/about/event/japanese-aesthetics-recycling [retrieved December 2023]

26 From website: Statista 2021 statistica.com [retrieved March 2021]

27 Abrams, D et al. (2018) *Developing a National Barometer of Prejudice and Discrimination in Britain.* Report Equality and Human Rights Commission. Published October 2018

28 Shien Chang, et al. (2020) *Global reach of ageism on older persons' health: A systematic review* PLOS 1, Published: January 15, 2020 DOI:10.1371/journal.pone.0220857

29 Ashton Applewhite (2018) *Let's end Ageism.* TED talk, September 14 2018 youtu.be/WfjzkO6_DEI

30 Applewhite A. (2018) *Lets end Ageism* TED talk, IBID

31 Applewhite A. (2021) Interview with Bruce Devereux January 27, 2021 *The Creatively Engaging* thecreativelyengaging.com/the-creatively-engaging-ashton/

32 ONS *National population projections:* 2018-based website data Available from https://www.ons.gov.uk/peoplepopulationandcommunity/populationandmigration/populationprojections/bulletins/nationalpopulationprojections/2018based [retrieved March 2021]

33 Dixon, Tracy et al. (2004) *Hospital admissions, age, and death: retrospective cohort study.* British Medical Journal (Clinical research ed.) vol. 328,7451 (2004): 1288. DOI:10.1136/bmj.38072.481933.EE

34 Burnes, David et al. (2019) *Interventions to Reduce Ageism Against Older Adults: A Systematic Review and Meta-Analysis.* American Journal of Public Health vol. 109,8 (2019): e1-e9. DOI:10.2105/AJPH.2019.305123

35 From website caerphillyover50.co.uk [retrieved 2023]

10

Looking forward

"Look forward, and make that as beautiful as you can."
Ruth Slenczynska: the pupil of Rachmaninov still releasing music at 97.*

Most of us are capable of looking forward to an easier life, to a pension that we've worked and saved for all our lives, and perhaps to trading down and releasing some of the rent or value of our home for whatever takes our fancy. But in the back of our minds, putting a signature on the cheque book can be hard. It commits us to consider a financial and existential future that some of us would prefer to ignore.

What happens when we get really old? What happens when we need looking after? Who will do it and who pays? That we should be plagued by these sorts of worries is an indictment on society and our political masters. For most of us, looking forward to our old age will be tinged by some trepidation. How can we sit down and contemplate the gradual loss of all the capacities and autonomies that we treasure, especially if we don't even know what will come, or when? How can we set aside money and time for something that might last 10 years or two months,

---

* The Guardian, 30 January.

or might never happen? At the end of the long path of life, many of us fear the care home.

Avoiding the care home

Let's get a bit of perspective here. The likelihood that you will ever need to go into a home is quite limited. According to a market survey in 2016, only one in seven of the over-85s were living in a care home at that time. In 2019, an Age UK survey reported that the vast majority of over-65s (93%) were living in their own homes.[1,2] Even if you are not destined to be one of the six out of seven elderly people still living at home after 85, you may receive some comfort from reports from the charity, Independent Age. They suggest that it is rare for people to require care home care for very long. Before the pandemic they reported the average stay at 30 months.

Please don't save up for some mythical form of end-of-life care. Even a tiny bungalow would pay for such care in most cases*. And if you don't own your own home or hold considerable savings, the Local Authority has a duty to step in. You are highly likely to find yourself living alongside

---

* According to Statista.com, the average cost of a bungalow in the UK in 2022 was £340,000. That value, invested, would cover livings costs in quite a fancy home for three years or more in the south east ie. for longer than the average stay. Once the money runs out the local authority have a duty to house you, and if you are frail, chances are they will let you stay put. Local Authorities pay far less than private renters in the same homes. If your property is worth a lot less than this, or you rent, then the Local Authority will house you once your needs increase. The moral is, aim to adapt your home, or move to a more convenient place before it is required, and to stay there as long as possible. This strategy is born-out by predictions of care home market analyses such as the Laing and Buisson market survey 2016, which despite the rise in elderly population, suggests that fewer and fewer of us will be living in them for very long. Better options are coming available including co-housing and ageing in place; discussed later in this chapter.

people who are paying far more than the Local Authority is being charged, for the same service.

There is no doubt that for people who own their own homes, or have savings, care home care can be cripplingly expensive, and the cost will come from your own assets, one way or another. Inevitably people put it off, and perhaps that's not always such a bad thing. Others scrimp and save in order to cover the eventuality of a care home, forgetting that statistically their money might be much better spent making their own home safer and easier to use.

The forever home

What we can and should plan for in some detail is the step before the care home. Making what you might call the 'forever home' as comfortable and adaptable as possible, so we can enjoy living there as long as possible. That may mean moving house sooner rather than later, making adaptions if necessary and planning the home-help we may need, even if it is as simple as advertising for a cleaner. There is no reason why that forever home should not be a *Shangri-La*. If by moving, you also release some money from a larger family home or reduce your rent, you could provide yourself with a nest-egg to be spent on looking after yourself and having fun.

Living in a care home should not be your greatest fear. Instead, anticipate what you might need and make those changes to your own home, sooner rather than later. If your home isn't well-located or not very flexible, then making a move to a new adaptable home, well before you need to, might be a good option.

Ageing in place, means remaining in your own home and adapting it. Some homes, and some locations, are better than others. If your home doesn't seem to be very amenable for old-age living, then I think it is better to move house while you are younger and still energetic, than to cling onto your old home for too long. Moving house becomes very difficult as we get older and is one of those activities that can impose unexpectedly hard physical and mental stresses.

Planning the home you wish to occupy in your very old age should be an important part of the life-plan. A 'forever home' is a place where you could live even if you couldn't do a lot of the things that you now do.

The main reason for moving into care is that the family home itself is not suitable. Make it suitable and you may never need to go elsewhere. Almost a third of old people who were asked in a recent Age UK survey, said they would like to move to more suitable accommodation if practical, financial and emotional factors could be overcome. Don't leave it until it is too late!

The other big barrier to living at home is the cost of receiving home care. Two-thirds of old people receive some sort of care in their own homes, with over half of that care being provided by family and friends. Many couples manage a home together, but once one of them dies, the remaining partner is suddenly presented with a whole series of immediate problems which can tip the scales. Yet almost a third of the over-65s do live alone, many of them very contentedly.

Some people fear dementia, but in fact the number of people who have to go into a home because they have cognitive impairment is thankfully very small – less than 2% of the elderly community, although they represent 40% of the entire care home population.[3]

Rather than dwell on the very end of life, when there is also more care available from NHS and the local authority, in the form of hospices and palliative care homes*, it might be better to consider those 20 or 30 years of old age that can be spent largely independently.

---

* Both of which are free

Let your imagination run riot. If you want to spend the glorious summer of your life playing chess, sitting in an Adirondack chair, overlooking a Caribbean beach – then now is the time to plan for it. A cottage with roses around the door will require a quite different set of plans. If you have a partner, try this exercise alone and then repeat it with the partner. Listen to any constructive criticism and questions and, consider your response. Make modifications if you need to. Back-of-envelope modifications are far easier to make than any changes once the die is cast. Take professional advice if you need to, but do not let the professional try to dissuade you from achieving your own dream; their role is to help you make it a reality.

Making plans

The most difficult question of all, and the most difficult discussion to have within the family, is what you will do if your partner leaves home, dies, or is seriously incapacitated. It is a hard discussion to have, and I recommend doing it in small chunks, as early as possible. Considering the marriage vows specifically mention *in sickness and in health*, as well as *till death us do part*, I am astonished that more couples don't ask each other searching questions early on. The result of such a discussion raises all sorts of questions, from 'what's the joint account password?' to 'shall we make living wills?'

Talking about these things when the pressure isn't there can generate a wonderful feeling of being loved and valued. In most relationships one person will take on certain tasks and the other will pick up the slack elsewhere. But in reality, it is far more sensible to make sure that both parties in a relationship know a little about everything. That means where things are, how to cook basic meals, where the money comes from and how to get about. Make changes right away if you need to. While discussing practicalities, you might feel able to tackle a few of the more challenging subjects, such as end-of-life care and funeral wishes. A couple I know keep what they cheerfully refer to as a 'death book', where all the important information about household and financial management is written down.

Maintaining the ability to live independently can certainly help us live longer, but even the most independent person can become dependent by virtue of disability, or simply because they suffer from loneliness. The people you discuss these things with should be asked to take on the role of a critical friend, having your best interests at heart, but curious enough to ensure that your dreams have a foundation of practicality.

Flexibility should be an important aspect of your forward plan. Ageing is not linear. Approach the issue with enjoyment top of the list, followed by practicality and spiced with a little originality. No one is judging you. There is no right or wrong way to approach the issues. However, there are some fundamentals that should be considered.

Making lists

There are hundreds of pretty standard needs checklists on the internet. If the local authority gets involved, a needs assessment will be required. But their assessment of your needs and desires may be very different to your own.

Think about these sorts of things:

- Emotional and social preferences: Who are my nearest and dearest? How will we care for each other? What about friends, neighbours, supporters and paid carers?
- Skills and abilities: What are my interests? How will I continue to enjoy them? Do they have value to others? Look for companionship in following whatever interests you have.

- Religious views and cultural background: What establishments will be important? Churches? Bingo halls? Libraries? Opera houses? Or all of the above?
- Physical abilities: Access to swimming pools, dance classes, shopping, parks or gardens? Can they cope with reduced mobility issues?
- Access to health and wellness services: Is the access easy? Don't forget to consider opticians, dentists, pharmacies and mental health support.

Do not let yourself be shoe-horned into a model of old age that really doesn't suit you!

Integrated neighbourhoods

Finding a friendly and welcoming neighbourhood can be a boon as we grow older and enlightened local authorities are finding ways that older people can remain part of the community within integrated neighbourhoods. Even living entirely alone and independently can be perfectly pleasant in the right location, especially when friends, family and neighbours can provide some support. It is not always ideal to live among old people when you are old yourself. In fact, the research on ageism suggests that cross-generational social structures are far more robust than uni-generational ones. Some really inventive programs have combined nursery schools with old person's day centres and found that both generations benefit. If you are an opera buff, or a football nut, then you might consider relocating somewhere where your passion can be exercised with people of very differing ages. All cultural and sporting organisations have neighbourhood outreach programs and some are aimed particularly at older people who enjoy their sport or activities, making it easy and comfortable to watch the spectacle.

The wider opportunities offered by cities suggest that retiring to the centre of a city might be better than the middle of the countryside. My London ballet classes take place at a community centre almost next door to Sadler's Wells Ballet School. Developers, who are never slow to capitalise on opportunities, are now making bids for redundant city centre department stores and shopping centres.

The Buurtzorg approach

Buurtzorg in the Netherlands is a pilot project investigating how older people can continue to be socially integrated into the community while remaining in their own homes. In 2017 The Guardian reported that the 'Buurtzorg approach' was being seized on by policy-makers as a means of enabling people with care needs to live independently with much less formal support. Since then, this experimental project has been very thoroughly evaluated and in 2021 a blueprint was published.[4]

In one of the pilot experiments, a nurse coordinator was employed to establish the needs of almost 200 frail elderly people living within one district. The coordinator then worked to link their needs with volunteers who were already working in the community. This approach provided a far more individualised form of support. It proved popular with residents and enjoyable for carers and volunteers. The community nurse was freed up by the number of volunteers, so they were able to act more as a health coach than a first responder, emphasising preventive health measures. When the need arose, they had more time to deliver any necessary care or call on others to do so.

The project found that this pilot model enabled the community nurse to spend far more time with their clients. Cost savings of up to 40% were calculated, compared to the cost of normal district care services where no volunteers were available to support the professionals.

In the UK, such approaches are still at very early stages. However, some Local Authorities have commenced using 'integrated health neighbourhoods' (the term is defined rather narrowly in the UK) to simply cover the integration of primary NHS and community (public health) care agencies. But watch this space, any incoming government is likely to consider expanding such services – they are such good value for money.

Mixed communities

The concept of intergenerational care has been knocked back by the pandemic, when generational mixing was seen as positively dangerous. However, the Social Care Institute for Excellence has a few modest suggestions:[5]

- Support people to continue pursuing their own interests outside the home wherever possible, and maintain their membership of clubs or organisations.
- Individuals or groups of residents can go out to entertainments (cinema, concerts, theatre, sport), learning opportunities, talks, political meetings or library gatherings rather than sit in a common room. Staffing levels should support this.
- People who have had their own gardens or allotments will miss them and the health benefits they bring. Is there gardening to do at the home or are there gardens to visit?*

---

* You can read between the lines that the writer is still considering an institution rather than a community.

If there isn't a program in your area, and you see yourself growing old there, then perhaps you could get together with some neighbours and local organisations and start an intergenerational care initiative in your area?

Getting about

You may own a car right now, and driving may seem the best way of getting about, but one day your ability to drive may leave you, or be taken from you. At the relatively young age of 70, all driving licenses expire and from then on require renewal every three years. In general, we have to self-certify our state of health. But if you have lied, an accident may find you uninsured, and if you have an impairment, even something that seems quite trivial such as sleep apnoea, your GP is legally required to inform the licensing authority immediately. Your license can then be summarily revoked.

Even if you recover it can take months to get the licence back. According to the Department of Transport, older drivers tend to start reducing their mileage at the age of about 60.[6] By the age of 80, very few people are driving very far at all, although their accident rate per mile (on average) will have soared. The Royal Society for the Prevention of Accidents (ROSPA) organises safe driving courses via The Older Drivers Forum,* offering several simple things we can do to help us continue to drive, safely, for as long as possible, such as recognising new limitations, taking regular driving assessments and undergoing refresher training.

I am astonished by the number of my friends who haven't considered how they might get about if they can't drive. Health experts will tell you that it might be better to give up the car sooner rather than later.

---

* https://www.olderdrivers.org.uk/

Living somewhere where you can get about by walking or cycling can be more pleasant and offers better exercise. Even a 10-minute daily walk is remarkably healthful. Try to keep that in your routine for as long as possible. And tricycles, or electric cycles and scooters, are a bit more fun (and cheaper) than mobility vehicles.

Public transport is a boon at all times of life, but with frailty comes the inability to walk to the bus stop, strap-hang on a tube, or step up into a train. And journeys of any kind become a bit more trying as the fear of being caught short renders cramped or dirty WC facilities even less attractive. Londoners are lucky, as we have excellent black cabs and disabled and elderly residents can apply for a taxi-card which gives really good discounts. But deciding to live in the Outer Hebrides, 10 miles from the nearest shop, might not be the greatest idea, unless you're prepared to employ a chauffeur, or a tractor driver!

Jump before you are pushed

When we get older, our choice of home becomes an increasingly emotive issue. If we all had a crystal ball and could predict the circumstances of our old age, we might have a better chance of making the inevitable transitions a little easier. We tend to anticipate that it will be disability or illness that will force our final move. But many other things can influence us. Family circumstances can change; finances can come unstuck or suddenly improve; even social norms come into play.

Many people assume they will wish to remain in their own home, the family home, for as long as possible. We may have to move in the end, but people shouldn't have to move because they are forced to. The change is easy to put off, and in the end might be reluctantly precipitated by well-meaning friends or relatives. If a partner dies, the dynamics of living independently will change overnight. Yet a sane decision to move at that time may be overwhelmed by nostalgia. It can be hard to have the conversations, but if a serious illness is diagnosed, a sibling or offspring can (and should) help facilitate such a discussion.

A lot of people advise that after a bereavement the widow or widower should stay put for a while, to find their feet. But I'm not sure that is always the best advice. Sometimes after a few months of reflection we may want to embrace change, and planning a move can be a very enervating way of starting to looking forward.

It is human nature to put off changes until it is too late, but the later decisions are taken, the more restricted (and expensive) the choices become. In the UK, where we have a very weak social care sector, the options can be limited and some solutions can be eye-wateringly expensive. What matters, especially in the context of a loving relationship with a spouse or partner, sibling or children is that the prospect of being left alone, or suffering from a disability, should not become taboo. Just as it is a good idea to prepare for old age by investing in a pension and maintaining a healthy lifestyle, so it is a good idea to maintain a plan of action for the key stages of growing old that might occur.

Choosing a new place

Planning a move to a new 'forever neighbourhood' should be fun. If you are considering moving into a new area, take a look around first. How many elderly people do you see on the streets? Draw some timed walking lines onto a local map. Where might you go to sit in the sun, or to watch the world go by? Is there decent public transport? Are there street cafes, convenient shops and a reliable taxi service? Do friends or family already live nearby, or will you be faced with making new friends? What social facilities exist? What services are available from the local authority or local charities? Try to look at it through the eyes of an older you.

I have found immense differences in services for older people between different local authority areas. Before you decide to move to your dream retirement cottage, it is worth checking on the local situation. Don't limit your search to activities aimed specifically at older people. For example, most wool shops hold knitting bees once a week – and even if arthritis makes the act of knitting slower – the knitting chat may be just what you crave, even if you are outnumbered by trendy 20-somethings!

Don't imagine that your dream retirement pad already exists. You may need to make changes once you move in. And like everything else, that should be done sooner rather than later. Installing a domestic lift which is far cheaper these days, or alternatively installing a downstairs bathroom, is always a wise plan.

We need a bit of imagination to foresee the future. Gradually even very local facilities may become difficult to use. The increase in internet shopping and the resurgence of delivery services are helping, but as we all found during lockdown, staring at a computer screen is far less pleasant than sauntering round a food market, or meeting friends for a cuppa. Location, location, location is as important in old age as it is in youth.

Kinship and companionship

The solution to keeping safe and well into very old age is inevitably linked to making sure there are people around who can help and support you. There is no need to demand complete independence – although agency, our control over the process of living – remains vitally important. The contrast between paid help, personal care and familial or friendly support is often overlooked and makes the biggest difference.

Across the global north, family structures are breaking down. Women are having fewer children, and monogamous relationships are under more stress. Longevity is not always a recipe for a long and happy relationship.

This has resulted in a decrease in kinship among older people, a lack of close relatives or family ties. The assumptions have been that kinless ageing implies ageing alone. Yet recent research in Europe suggests there is a marked variation in the potential effects of *kinlessness* for older adults.[7] It seems that those people who do not have close relatives may actively construct wider networks of friends and may in fact have a greater and stronger support system than peers who rely upon family ties. We can choose our friends, but cannot choose our families!

All the studies report that living with someone extends life. A big hurdle for many people comes when they find themselves forced to live alone, perhaps for the first time in their life. This may be occasioned by a number of circumstances. In England around 2 million people aged over 75 live alone. Three-quarters of women over 85 are widowed. Even if you've lived alone for many years, that choice becomes gradually more difficult and potentially dangerous over time.

Notwithstanding the emotional difficulties of living alone, there are financial penalties to be considered. The adage that two can live as cheaply as one still holds true. According to the Office for National Statistics (ONS), people between 25 and 64 who live alone spend an average of 92% of their disposable income on living expenses*, compared with two-adult households who spend only 83% of theirs.

A better solution might be to live with a housemate, invite a relative to live with you, or team up with a trusted friend. This can happen well before you get to the stage of *needing* a lot of extra help, endowing the relationship with more of a family feel.

To live in is cheaper than to live out. When I was a child, my father's well-heeled 'maiden' aunt enjoyed the company of live-in companions for

---

* Disposable income is total personal income minus current income taxes.

years. The best arrangements are like my aunt's – self-organised. Perhaps there is someone who might want to swap some light caring duties for a room in a home near to their job or university?

Refuse to retire

I hate the word 'retirement' because I don't believe older people should retire, in many senses of the word. There is no law that demands you retire from your job until you wish to leave. Even if you happily retire from the day job there are still plenty of other things you could do. And these days public opinion is coming round to realising how valuable an older workforce can be.

Despite our assumption that old age will inevitably bring retirement, many older people have no option but to remain in work in order to pay the bills. In 2016 in the UK almost 1.2 million people aged over 65 were in work. Many of those jobs were part time or self-employed.

Since that study, the state pension age has risen and is currently under further review. The government's rationale is that we are all living longer. But of course, if you've been reading this book closely, you will be aware that that is not quite true. The Department of Work and Pensions website jauntily states: "When the State Pension was introduced in 1948, a 65-year-old could expect to spend 13.5 years in receipt of it – around 23 per cent of their adult life. This has been increasing ever since. In 2017, a 65-year-old can now expect to live for another 22.8 years, or 33.6% of their adult life."

But these statistics say little about the capacity or enthusiasm of people over 65 to do a full-time job, or of the willingness employers have to engage them. The government assumes that we are all healthier at 65 than we might have been 20 years ago, but in fact the opposite is true. While social norms have certainly changed, a lifetime of hard graft still takes its toll. At the time of writing (August 2023) the UK State Pension age is 66 and is due to increase to 67 by 2028 and possibly to 68 by 2037/39. Ironically, both state-generated statistics and scientific reviews still use the age of 65 as a cut-off. It may well be that the only people who noticed that we don't stop work at 65 were those who were surprised when their state pension didn't start coming in when they reached their 65th birthday.

As the formal retirement age increases, it will be interesting to discover whether people will have the ability or the enthusiasm to continue working for more years than their parents. At the moment, life expectancy isn't increasing in the UK and the number of years we might spend in illness or disability is going up, particularly in areas of high deprivation, where more than the average number of people rely on state pensions. While continuing to work can be good for us, the daily nine-to-five will become harder and more tedious if we haven't got the same strength or if there is no career recognition.

However, the psychologist Martin Seligman* says that finding meaning in our existence is an important aspect of happiness. For many of us our job is a vocation, we can feel bereft when we hand in our notice. But a job which has become too easy by dint of repetition, and dead-ended by virtue of an uncaring employer, does not make for happiness. The Centre for Ageing Better reports that the 2022 National Statistics data counted over 306,000 more workers aged 50-64 years old as economically inactive than the numbers before the first outbreak of COVID-19.[8]

The pleasure of giving up the day job, often masks the imperative to make decisions about a new direction. But investing time and some money into a new career can be a very positive decision. If you are short of ideas The Guardian runs the series *A New Start After 60*, which I always

---

* See Chapter 11

read with glee! It contains loads of good examples of looking forward post-retirement.

If you need care

If you decide to live in your own home for as long as possible, then the cost of care may need to be factored in. There are now many companies that will provide home-based carers, although choosing and setting up care can take some time and effort. These companies charge between £20 and £30 per hour for modestly-trained staff, who can help with housework and shopping, provide personal care such as washing and dressing, or accompany you to the park. Such companies also provide night staff, or part-time staff. This can very quickly become a far more expensive option than a care home and their service does not necessarily guard against loneliness. A carer may not be on your wave length at all. If you do the maths, £30 x 24 hours x seven days a week comes to £5,040 per week, or over £262,080 annually, on top of household bills and food costs. Care costs are not tax- deductible. 24/7 care for any long period of time can bankrupt even the wealthiest people.

Going it alone, directly employing people can be cheaper, but UK law requires the employer to set up contracts, manage tax and National Insurance payments, holiday pay and so on. Selection and experience can be difficult to judge. A few tenners rolled up at the end of the week is no longer an option, even for part-time staff. Generally, the employer, not the employee, is liable for unpaid taxes and for following all employment laws. Though many private carers may work for several people and thus are legitimately self-employed.

Local authorities are duty-bound to provide care in some circumstances, but the extent and quality of this care is limited and will continue to be so, even when the new social care regulations of 2023 kick in. Social services hardly ever provide a full-time home carer, except in exceptional circumstances. On the other hand, it is a very measly local authority that cannot arrange helpers to come in during the morning to wash and dress someone who suddenly finds themselves unable to cope. Hospitals will not allow discharge until the home care-package, as it is called, has been set up. Whatever your financial circumstances, there are grants and payments that everyone is entitled to receive. Age UK run an advisory service, but the GP will be a first port of call, followed by social services.

Approximate adult wages you can expect to pay for different types of home care.

| | Hourly Adult Wages | |
	Min (outside London/SE)	Max (inside London /SE)
Living wage*	£12.00	£13.50
Care agencies	£20.00	£35.00
Direct employment	£12.00 (advisory living wage)	£25.00
Nursing care	Generally covered by NHS or district nursing services	
Palliative care	Generally covered by NHS or charitable hospices	

*Living wages are taken from the Living Wage Foundation recommendations, October 2023. Statutory minimum wages, now also called living wages are slightly lower.[9]

Any care beyond the minimum is means-tested. If you are lucky enough to be eligible for supported care, you will find the quality of carers to be variable. If you own your own home, have an income or any savings, then you are likely to have to pay for most of it yourself, or see the bill deducted by a charge on your home.

Taking advantage of family or friends can be a good option, but if you are expecting a child or sibling or even just a friend to help you, what will you be willing to pay them? What will happen if they are unable to help when the time comes? Becoming a carer, especially being the only person available, can be a thankless role, putting a strain onto even the strongest relationships. This is probably one of the most important things to discuss with loved ones, well before the time comes.

Many services exist to help us remain at home. Meals on Wheels do still exist, but in spite of the questionable quality of mass-produced chilled ready-meals, that is what you'll be given. The food I've sampled is at best uninspiring, and in the view of this nutritionist, inadequate for long-term health. Local lunch clubs often offer better food as well as the opportunity of social interaction. But if you've spent your life making your own decisions about friends and food, you may find these lunch clubs uninviting. In some local authorities the opportunities are excellent. For example, in Islington the local authority supports charitable organisations such as the Claremont Project at the Angle and St Luke's Centre in South Islington which are both exemplary. It's a post-code lottery and, however carefully you make plans, local authority services are patchy and can sometimes disappear overnight.

Live-in care

While you might opt for a companion or sharing with a friend, more formal arrangements generally have the advantage of independent oversight. The paid-for version of live-in support is not cheap, starting at about £850/week and rising to £6,000 or £7,000 a week if you require complex care, cooked meals or a driver. It is thus a lot more expensive than living in a care home. Hundreds of agencies will exist in your area, but advisors are thin on the ground. The GP or Age UK can't make recommendations. You are on your own – another reason to make plans for such an arrangement well before you absolutely need them. In my experience few care firms offer a good service, especially if there is an element of emergency in setting up the arrangement. If you see this sort of need looming, then arrange it well before it becomes a necessity and be prepared for several false starts. A friend of mine interviewed over 70 women before she selected a small team to care for her ailing mother.

Think once, twice and three times if the live-in companion will be caring for you on their own. You should certainly ensure that some safeguards are available, whether you opt for a formal or informal approach. Organisations tend to offer two carers, two weeks on and two weeks off, or a night and day carer, which goes some way to limit the danger. You will have to provide the carer with some time off each day. They will only be formally working for a maximum of ten hours each day, and do require rest periods, sick leave and holidays – as any staff would. Most carers require a separate bedroom, preferably en-suite, a TV and internet connection.

A full-time housekeeper will require self-contained facilities and will command a salary of at least £40,000 per year, plus employment on-costs. If you wanted a Jeeves, you'd be paying upwards of £50,000 and would have to allow him use of the vintage Aston Martin as well!

A good home care company will send a supervisor regularly, to ensure that the relationship is working well on both sides. But the contracts are somewhat flimsy and it is not unusual for a firm to withdraw care if the subject becomes too difficult to manage, or staff suddenly disappear (which often happens). Post-Covid, withdrawal of care has become very common. As of 2023, (the time of writing) a shortage of care staff means that it is often impossible to find good long-term home care. Reputable care firms are regularly discontinuing services for established clients, simply because they cannot get the staff.

The granny flat

Living with relatives has many benefits, not least the presence of family support. And to feel part of a larger family can be far more pleasant. However, before embarking on such arrangements, all parties should give it careful thought. Age UK recommend that a set of ground rules are written down and agreed upon. Consider the following:

- What sort of care will you need and who will be able to provide this for you?
- Will the home need to be adapted?
- Will you pay rent or help towards bills?
- If your family members are claiming benefits, will these be affected?
- How might the living arrangement affect your council tax?
- If you live with a couple, what would happen if they split up?
- What would happen if the arrangement was no longer working? For example, would you need to move into sheltered accommodation or a care home?

Don't underestimate the pressure on both generations that such a situation might generate. In particular, it is worth thinking carefully about who is going to provide and pay for daily care, heating, cleaning, maintenance and shopping etc. Take advantage of Local Authority assessments to ensure that the accommodation is suitable for now and can be modified later, if necessary. When you are planning your forever home, consider where a full-time carer, or a night nurse, might stay, if that were required and who would pay their wages.

Taking someone from their own home and accommodating them somewhere else will tear them from whatever social circle they may already have. Once ensconced, it may become increasingly difficult to make new friends. That in itself can put extra pressures onto the family, especially if it is difficult for someone to get out and about under their own steam. It is highly desirable that either paid carers, volunteers or friends are encouraged to visit or phone on a regular basis to continue to widen the individual's horizons.

Sometimes it might be possible to trial the arrangement for a few months before setting the whole thing in stone. Eventually the disposal of your own home and possessions will be traumatic, unless it is seen as a positive step forward towards something new, enjoyable and desirable. That new phase could involve living closer to loved ones and feeling that we can be helpful to them by looking after children, walking the dog or helping with household duties. Now that working at home is well-established, I have encountered grannies and grandpas minding the shop, answering the phone and sending out invoices!

Retirement villages and sheltered housing

One option is to move early to a home that can be modified later, or where support is available, if and when it is required. Retirement villages are more popular and more progressive outside the British Isles. In the UK they tend to be pricey, a bit flashy and modelled on a country club. Cheaper versions are available in some Local Authority areas, but may be means-tested or only open to people who do not have savings.

While you may or may not wish to be surrounded by old people, even if you are one yourself, the advantage of this type of arrangement is that you will still have the opportunity to do quite a bit for yourself. That not only offers cost savings, but it also provides a sense of independence, adds to activity levels and fills the day with meaningful tasks. The simple activities of daily life, such as preparing meals, caring for the home, shopping and entertaining are so important to maintaining health.

Sheltered housing works well for many people. You can move in and make friends while you are still hale and hearty, allowing support systems of different kinds to be introduced gradually. However, scrutinise the conditions carefully. Some villages have the right to evict you if your needs change. Because you have bought some type of lease, you may be faced with spiralling service charges. Some of these leases have proved impossible to sell on, leaving residents or their families tied to a white elephant. Good legal advice is therefore essential.

The almshouse model can be charming, where it still exists, but these days most of them have been converted into bijou homes for young professionals. However, if you are lucky enough to qualify, recent studies have found that the format can extend life by two or more years, raising working class people up to a lifespan more often associated with much higher socio-economic groups. Researchers associated this improvement with the stronger sense of community that such housing provides and the extra support built into the arrangement, such as post-hospital care, communal dining and events.[10] There must be something else going on, making this type of arrangement more beneficial than a *normal* care home. What seems to me to be different is that people elect willingly to move into an almshouse, often at the relatively young age of about 70, giving them plenty of time to make new friends and local connections before really old age makes such activity difficult. In addition, almshouses are generally well-designed, located in sought after areas, often delightfully pretty and are often clustered around generous and socially engaging gardens.

There are psychological benefits too. Almshouses are a step up, not a step back. One of the most charming examples is Blaise Hamlet, a group of nine picturesque cottages designed by John Nash around a green in the suburb of Henbury. It was built in 1811 to house retired employees of the

Quaker banker and philanthropist, John Scandrett Harford, who owned the nearby Blaise Castle. The revered architectural commentator Nikolaus Pevsner described Blaise Hamlet as 'the ne plus ultra of picturesque layout and design'.[11]

Such schemes carry none of the negative implications of the care home. If you look around you may find some mainstream, modern developments such as well-designed city-centre flats, which may lend themselves to being appropriate for older people. You may decide to move to a more convenient dwelling in your own area, to reduce the risk of losing your social network. The inimitable Joan Bakewell has recently downsized to a smaller house in her old neighbourhood, Primrose Hill. The new home has a ground floor bedroom that she can use if she needs it, and she's made plans for a full-time carer to take the upper bedroom, if necessary, later. She has chosen to remain close to her existing network and her work. When she took this decision, at the age of 86, she was still broadcasting.

Bakewell chose an urban location, but many people decide to make their money go further by moving to a rural or coastal location. At the moment ONS records report that retired people tend to migrate to the coast, away from cities and towards areas of natural beauty. The South Coast, Norfolk, Lincolnshire and the Malvern Hills have the oldest populations, with cities, especially central London, Bristol, Coventry, south Gloucestershire and Salford attracting a younger population.

I am not sure that it is a brilliant idea to retire or downsize to places already overpopulated with older people. For example, the South West has the lowest number of critical hospital beds per head of population in the country, but an equivalent, if not greater need. London has the best provision. In addition, GP services can be very variable. A smaller, scattered population also implies fewer facilities, inconvenient public transport, longer ambulance waiting times and less local support.

Novel solutions

Hotels are often overlooked, as potential refuges, but before retirement homes became commonplace, people used to retire to genteel boarding houses on the coast. It is still possible to spend some years living in hotels, but sadly very few hotels accept long-term guests any more, due to planning restrictions or tenancy laws. Many of those that do tend to be at the very bottom of the hotel hierarchy. You could find yourself living out your final days alongside social security claimants or refugees, who are often housed in the cheaper chain hotels.

If money is no object, you may find the fancier hotels can accommodate you. Baroness Thatcher died on 8 April 2013 at the Ritz Hotel in Piccadilly after suffering a stroke. She had been staying there, in a suite, since December 2012, after finding difficulty using the stairs at her house in Chester Square. You've probably never thought that a four-month stay at a posh hotel might be a way of ending your days. I'm guessing in today's money such an arrangement might cost £150,000.* Hotel companies such as the international brand Accor, who allow pets, can *rent* you a serviced suite (with restaurant and cleaning facilities available) in all the major European cities. It is never going to be a cheap option, but compared with the average UK house price of £300,000 you may decide releasing money to allow you to live in some luxury right at the end of your life might be a good solution. By law, modern hotels, must provide disabled facilities. Many have lifts and most will allow carers or live-in companions. Some Local Authorities are forced to place elderly or infirm residents into three- and four-star hotels because of the shortage of suitable care homes. You may be lucky.

---

* Posh hotels don't publish their rates.

Fancy a cruise?

Some people will happily spend almost their entire dotage on ocean liners. Mario Salcedo, at the sprightly age of 45 years, discovered he enjoyed cruising so much that he got into the habit of booking back-to-back tickets for round the world cruises, lasting two years at a time. He chose the cheapest inside cabin, but took full advantage of onboard facilities, including running a financial management business from one of the lounges. His vessel of choice was the Royal Caribbean Line's mega-vessel *Voyager of the Sea*. Even booking the cheapest cabin, he still racked up bills of £60-70,000 each year. Apart from a 15-month hiatus during the covid pandemic, he has now been cruising for over twenty years. He was apparently still to be found in 2023 on the MS *Freedom of the Seas*, working from a deckchair with a sea view, swimming in the pool and scuba diving. My own limited experience of cruises confirmed that these large liners do cater very well for older or disabled travellers. They all have on-board doctors, but medical services are costly and nursing or care services would be limited, should they be required.

Co-housing

Co-housing might be a good solution, especially if you would like more control over your future home, but recognise that financial and support difficulties do not allow you to completely go it alone. There is nothing to stop you getting involved in something right now, which could help support you as well as your friends and neighbours. Look at the co-housing movement, and the more recently inaugurated eco-housing movement.

Co-housing started in Denmark in the 1960s. Typically, a development consists of a group of single-family homes clustered around shared spaces such as a communal kitchen and dining area, laundry, gardens or recreational spaces. Sometimes neighbours also share resources like tools and lawnmowers, or swap skills such as baby-sitting or DIY. These communities take a while to set up. Neighbours collaboratively plan and manage community activities and shared spaces. The legal structure is typically a homeowner's association or housing cooperative.

This can be a very social, not to say idealistic, way of living. Community activities may include shared meals, clubs or events. Schemes make it far easier to organize child and elder care, and carpools. The website *Diggers and Dreamers* provides links to national and local schemes, but you could set one up with like-minded friends. It could be very exciting and ultimately very pleasant.

Senior co-housing groups have sprung up as people have become more and more disenchanted with what traditional residential care offers. Charities and groups of individuals are taking it upon themselves to make better arrangements. The Older Women's Co-Housing Group have built a scheme for over 50 women in north London as an alternative to living alone. The Vivarium Trust in Scotland and the North London Housing Partnership have also set up some groups with a view to developing schemes. Outside London, communes of various types regularly advertise for new residents. It is reported that vacancies are quickly snapped up.*

A village called Hogeweyk

Care homes sink to the bottom of everyone's lists. But they don't need to be so dispiriting. It is not impossible to provide more enlightened care, even for very frail people. For example, a little sheltered village just

---

* See further information at the end of this chapter.

outside Amsterdam, called Hogeweyk (pronounced *hoog-away*) caters for 152 people, all of whom have advanced dementia.

On the face of it, this is simply a quiet village, with a pedestrianised main street, a few shops, a hairdresser and a coffee bar. It has the look of a rather stylish model village, with modern lines and picture windows. The flower beds and pathways are studded with benches and meeting places. But this village is in fact a safe and a wholly-protected enclave. The philosophy is that residents follow as normal a life as possible. They live in eight-strong households dedicated to different lifestyles, such as crafts, religious, cultural or homey. Residents are encouraged to continue to buy and prepare their own food, attend the hairdressers or simply join one of the 25 activity clubs that have sprung up. Because the homes are arranged like shared houses, the day-to-day social aspects of home-life can continue. Each apartment provides space for eight residents as well as the eight full-time carers who look after them 24/7.

The most amazing thing for an English observer is that this style of living is funded exactly the same way as every other high-dependency care home in the Netherlands. Fees are about £5,000 per month, and funded by state-sponsored insurance premiums. Proof of the success of this type of active care home is shown in the general health of the residents. They are encouraged to think for themselves and have more independence (within safe boundaries). They still have some agency in their lives, they are encouraged to go out, wander in the gardens and exercise. The results are encouraging. Residents remain healthier and happier and their dementia does not progress as quickly. TV pales into the background as social functions and creative activities, as well as the day-to-day responsibility of caring for oneself, take the foreground. It feels more like living in a college hall of residence than a care home!

Forward-planning

I know it's a cliché, but forward planning for what you might like to think of as your forever home involves a bit of blue-sky thinking. Making positive plans for the future and contemplating contingencies should not be a dreary task. I think the secret is to start by imagining the perfect solution, then hold onto that vision while you mould the plans to suit practicalities such as budget restrictions and family responsibilities.

The vision might not be written, but instead take the form of a picture or even a song. But you will need to be quite rigorous about this. For example, many of my clients tell me that they can remain living in a tiny village even if they lose the ability to drive, because there is always someone around who would give them a lift. I'm sceptical about this, knowing from personal experience how difficult it is to regularly ask for help, and how the odd helping hand, offered generously, does not always translate into a reliable 'service'.

Translating a vision into something practical requires some stress-testing. Assess each aspect of your new life to see how adaptable it might be to some of the common challenges you may have to face. This is your future. Many people can offer advice, but this author, your friends, advisors and family should all recognise that the decision is yours alone. What feels right for one person may seem completely mad to someone else. By all means listen to critical friends, but make your decisions yourself. This should help you make practical, imaginative and enjoyable plans for your future life and your forever home. You might be pleasantly surprised with what you come up with.

Do not expect to get it right first-time. It is an iterative process.

Most people who summon the courage to discuss with friends and family find the process positive, involving a lot of laughter. At least the topic has been broached. Old age should be comfortable, enjoyable, satisfying, engaging, social and rewarding. I'm not describing an ideal – it is a right.

On the whole, planning for the future provides the best chance of realising your dreams and your right to maintain your agency and your independence for as long as possible. As that old advert for the mobile company Orange used to say:

_____

"The future's bright ..."

_____

Endnotes

1 Laing and Buisson, (2016) *Market Survey 2016.* Note this is an expensive market report. The report below published by a government body provides a lot of the same data. The Competitions and Markets Authority (2017) *Care Homes Market Study final report, 30 Nov 2017* from website: assets.publishing.service.gov.uk/ media/5a1fdf30e5274a750b82533a/care-homes-market-study-final-report.pdf [retrieved February 2024]

2 Age UK (2019) *Later Life in the UK*, Report from website ageuk.org.uk/ globalassets/age-uk/documents/reports-and-publications/later_life_uk_ factsheet.pdf [retrieved February 2024]

3 dementiastatistics.org

4 Lumillo-Gutiérrez I, Salto GE. (2021) *Buurtzorg Nederland, a proposal for nurse-led home care.* Enfermería Clínica (English Edition). 2021 Sep-Oct;31(5):323-327. DOI: 10.1016/j.enfcle.2020.08.004. E-published 2021 Feb 10

5 Social Care Institute for Excellence (SCIE) (2024) *Personalised and Person-centred Care;* Resources, information and guidance on providing personalised and person-centred care for care providers, managers and practitioners. Website from scie.org.uk/person-centred-care/older-people-care-homes/in-the-community [retrieved February 2024]

6 Department of Transport (2016) *Older Car Drivers Road Safety Factsheet 2016:* Published May 2018 at website assets.publishing.service.gov.uk/government/ uploads/system/uploads/attachment_data/file/706517/older-car-drivers-factsheet.pdf [retrieved February 2024]

7 Mair CA. (2019) *Alternatives to Ageing Alone? "Kinlessness" and the Importance of Friends Across European Contexts.* The Journals of Gerontology. Series B, Psychological Sciences and Social Sciences. 2019 Oct;74(8):1416-1428. DOI: 10.1093/geronb/gbz029

8 Centre for Ageing Better (2022) *Work: The State of Ageing* Report from ageing-better.org.uk/work-state-ageing-2022 [retrieved February 2024]

9 Living wages: *What are Real Living Wages*: Website from livingwage.org.uk/what-real-living-wage [retrieved October 2023]

10 Benzimra et al., (2023) *Almshouse Longevity Study*, Report Bayes Business School, City of London University May 2023 Website: bayes.city.ac.uk/__data/assets/ pdf_file/0011/731297/Almshouse-Longevity-Study-Report.pdf

11 Historic England. *Blaise Castle and Hamlet Listing No.* (1001426). National Heritage List for England. [retrieved 8 August 2016]

Planning a bright future

How to use the chart

Down the side of the Bright Future Planning Chart opposite are some headings to help you think about potential needs at each stage, including physical, financial and social requirements. Along the top there is a progression from active to frail. Consider physical as well as intellectual frailties.

Please note that there is nothing to say that a progression from active to inactive is inevitable, nor that it is going to be a one-way street. We change every day and need to plan for the ebb and flow of abilities that is a feature of the whole of our lives.

The outcome should be a more distinct image of your future, underpinned by knowing where you will live, who will be nearby, and what facilities and support you might need. It should reduce any worries about the challenges and disabilities that might face any one of us – even tomorrow.

Start with your vision, keep the image firmly in your brain, (if it is an image pin it up somewhere), and work from there.

Bright Future Planning Chart

	Active	Slowing	Sedentary	Frail
Social	Activities: Preferences Location: Cafes, bars, clubs, churches			
Skills	Professional expertise: New skills: Classes, education			
Access	Within the home: Kitchen, bathroom, stairs, garden Outside: Travel options including public transport and walking			
Facilities	Shops: Food and non-food, pharmacies, specialist shops Pastimes and entertainment: Stimulation for mind and body			
Support	Friends and family, GPs, nursing, night-time help, holidays LA and charitable services Paid services			
Activity	Exercise: Sports, walking, swimming, classes, physiotherapy Location: Pools, garden, parks, trails etc.			
Money	Capital: How much to invest and how much to save Disposable income: Now and in the future Cost of future care: Where would the money come from?			
Location	Where will the forever home be? Cost, making adaptations Contingencies: Do I need to move now? What might trigger a move?			

Useful co-housing organisations

Community-Led Housing Group; People-Powered Housing
communityledhomes.org.uk

Community-Led Housing London
Includes the Older Women's Co-Housing Group, North London
communityledhousing.london

Threshold Centre
An international association of co-housing groups, including the Vivarium Trust in Scotland
thresholdcentre.org.uk

General advice and interest groups

Age UK Charity: Information and Advice
Focuses on older people who need it most, but don't expect too much support if you have savings
ageuk.org.uk

Centre for Ageing Better
A think-tank and pressure group. They challenge ageism and seek to build an age-friendly movement, particularly in the spheres of employment and housing
ageing-better.org.uk

Independent Age
Publish advice on paying for care and care homes. Can provide you and your family with clear, free and impartial advice on issues of income, costs, community, and housing
independentage.org

Social Care Institute for Excellence
A spin-off of from government. Now independent and self-funding. They support the care sector
scie.org.uk

Care Quality Commission
The independent regulator of health and social care in England. They publish assessments and regulate improvements
cqc.org.uk

Housekeepers
The magazine *The Lady*, now also online, is still a good source of staff, especially if you can offer pleasant surroundings and a good salary

Further reading

Valliant, George (2002). *Ageing Well Surprising guideposts for a happier life from the Harvard Study of Adult Development.* Little; Brown Spark Books, New York, Boston, London.

Levy, Deborah (2021). *Real Estate – a Living Autobiography;* Hamish Hamilton, London

11

Glorious Summer

Getting the best from life

Regardless of how carefully – or disgracefully – we care to age, the prescription to 'take care of ourselves' has some flaws. Living well, eating healthily, maintaining exercise, agency and purpose are no-doubt important. But it is too easy to ignore the pleasures of life that make it worthwhile.

The French call it, *joie de vivre*. Literally translated, it means 'joy of life.' As is so often the case, a translation does not do the phrase justice. The French think of *joie de vivre* in terms of pure emotion – a passion for life. It cannot be measured and thus need not decline in the face of diminishing strength or capacity. It is something to be lived up to rather than simply lived by.

The idea of simple happiness goes back to Greek philosophy. Aristotle conceived of the notion of *eudaimonia*, which is generally translated as *the good life*; as human flourishing, prosperity and blessedness.[1] In more prosaic terms it means health, wealth and happiness. But in Greek philosophy it was a description of one's ethics as well as one's actions. It is about doing things to the best of one's abilities, whatever those abilities happen to be. The idea of following a life *as good as it can be* gives us an important clue to the way we should view the future.

Many of us know the phrase, 'the good life' because it was the title of an amusing TV comedy starring Felicity Kendal and Richard Briers. Perhaps that comedy, conceived during the oil crisis, a time of soaring inflation and political unrest, still has a lot to say to us about what is important in life today. The series is still available on the internet and definitely worth a second viewing.

After you've enjoyed an episode or two of *The Good Life*, it might be time to ask yourself what happiness, contentment and fulfillment really mean to you. Having a positive vision of the future is a really good way of climbing out of depression, recovering from set-backs and finding new strength to face the world. But optimism should never become complacency. There are many instances where we might want to change the world, in order to realise our perfect futures. We need to be both clear-eyed and hopeful if we are to find the capacity to plan for an old age in spite of external forces, such as ageism, that might work against us.

Finding our 'Glorious Summer' of old age should not become a trial. Admittedly, there might be effort involved in thinking ahead to make the changes that need to be made. Whether you are naturally a pessimist or naturally an optimist will influence your thinking. There is room in this world for the Eeyores as well as happy bears like Pooh.* Finding happiness in old age is sometimes about letting go, accepting change and adjusting to it. Like Sisyphus, the mythical Greek, rolling a rock up a hill can sometimes feel like a struggle, especially if some interfering

---

* If you need a little cheering, I highly recommend re-reading AA Milne's enchanting Winnie the Poo books.

deity comes along in the night and rolls it back downhill again. Even the greatest efforts can go unrewarded, but the *Myth of Sisyphus*, scrutinised by Camus in his philosophical text of the same name, teaches us in the modern world that it is pointless to dwell on what cannot be achieved. Instead, we should focus on the things we can achieve and take pleasure in them. We should always look forward. Tomorrow holds a fresh opportunity to achieve something more or something new. [2]

Seeing old age as a happy period of our lives is not new. Traditionally old age has been viewed as a reward for hard work, a well-earned rest, and a chance to do things we never had time for. But before you get too comfortable in those slippers, it is important to point out that modern psychologists don't recognise happiness as a solitary game. It isn't about retiring, opting out, or keeping out of the way. There is always plenty to do in the world.

In the West, happiness has more or less been taken out of the hands of priests and religions and dropped into the laps of philosophers and psychiatrists. The Hungarian psychologist and academic, Mihaly Csikszentmihalyi, wrote in the 1990s about the concept of *flow*. He suggested that civilisation had not made us happier by one iota. On the contrary, Csikszentmihalyi's theories revolve around the notion that wealth, better education and thriving commerce has, in many ways, simply made us more competitive, more hedonistic and greedier. He thought that we had forgotten the positive aspects of human experience like joy, creativity and that feeling of being totally involved with life. In an article in the New York Times in 2021, Clay Risen reported that Mihaly Csikszentmihalyi blamed television above all for the decline in 'productive' pastimes, or activities that blend aspects of work and play, which he felt offered the best opportunity for the creative concentration he called *flow* and that he advised would lead to happiness.[3] I call it *joie de vivre.* But whatever you call it, the important revelation is that Csikszentmihalyi doesn't believe that joy bears any relationship to wealth or state of health alone.[4]

More recently the seeds of optimism have taken root in the practice of positive psychology promoted by the psychologist and prolific author Martin Seligman. He has spent his career trying to understand the good life and helping people achieve it. He believes that in order to say we are happy we need the right frame of mind (that positivity I mentioned before). For him happiness is about engaging with life and finding meaning from that engagement. His approach is certainly optimistic and positive. And it seems to have worked for him. Last time I checked, at the age of 82 he was still teaching at Pennsylvania University, the place where he received his PhD in 1967.[5] Deciding to be happy is difficult enough. Deciding to make lifestyle changes so that you get a good chance of being happy right up until the moment of your death is harder still. But surely it is worth a try?

The hardest thing to do is to start thinking about how you will respond in really old age before it happens. For example, it is wise to make important lifestyle changes early. Every year we put it off, the more difficult it becomes. Good early decisions will have real and lasting effects upon your mental and physical health. But how can we anticipate how we will feel?

Whether it is starting a new evening class, getting out and about or deciding to move house, the task ahead will sometimes feel as impossible as Sysiphus' rock. Doing exactly what you did yesterday is often the easier option. Most self-help, live-longer books will pressure you into being the best person you can be. They will try hard to make you change bad habits. But for me that is putting the cart before the horse. Of course, all *bad* habits can be superseded by better, more enjoyable or more expedient actions. Of course, taking care of yourself is important. However, I recommend trying to get into the habit of enjoying life first.

Enjoy

Achieving *joie de vivre* will be different for each of us, and will be different at different stages of our lives. But in terms of long life, this concept possesses one unique attribute. It is simply a process of mind – it doesn't require physical strength, and it doesn't even require logical thinking. Many people with advanced dementia enjoy *joie de vivre*. Many people in hospices and cancer wards can still find pleasure in life. *Joie de vivre* does not seem to be confined by physical and cognitive limitations. It is an ideal. As Deborah Levy points out in her excellent autobiography *Real Estate*;[6]

> "After all, to think and feel and live and love more freely is the point of life..."

I think that the skill of *joie de vivre* probably has to be practiced before we are faced with serious challenges. Positive emotions, according to the inventor of positive psychology Martin Seligman, are awe, love, compassion, gratitude, forgiveness, joy, hope and trust (or faith). He advises us to;[7]

> "try happiness, you'll like it a lot more than misery."

Part of looking forward is realising that old-age can still bring enjoyment. Listening to Chopin's Mazurka No 25 the other day, I noticed that the piece combines loud and lyrical stanzas, echoes of the same passages, played at completely different pitches. I was surprised to discover that the quiet sections were more enjoyable than the loud ones. I listened intensely to try and work out why this was. Surely the sheer barrage of louder sounds would be more moving? But no. Having heard the tune played at high volume (perhaps the equivalent of experiencing the drama of youth), I found the reprise of those same sections, played very quietly, to be far more enjoyable. Memory plays a part, being an important aspect of comprehension. Our memories become richer with age; they add another dimension to a life that is only accessible after the benefit of experience.

My response to the quiet sections intrigued me. The quietness made me focus. I needed to put down my work, to stop and really listen. The 2nd, or 3rd or 43rd rendition of a piece of music will inevitably be different to the first. And there seems to be something that concentrates the mind when music is played just that bit too quietly to hear without stopping in our tracks and focusing. To me, it was a revelation to realise that there can be greater enjoyment in the *pianissimo* of reprise than ever there was in the loudness of the first performance.

Cultivating joie de vivre

Surely the key to *joie de vivre* is in cultivating a full life, enjoying what can be enjoyed, while it can be enjoyed. A social life, independent living, mental stimulation, play, curiosity, travel and memory are all positives. Self-actualisation, finding meaning and being able to express ourselves as individuals can be found in an enduring ability to pursue novelties as well as reprise old pleasures and old memories. As Heintzelman says, 'we can still explore, learn, develop, and grow.'[8]

Ageing can be messy; life is not perfect. But perhaps that doesn't matter if we can hold onto the things we value. Longevity is a medical issue, but ageing well is a social, financial and political as well as a health issue.

One of the interesting phenomena surrounding ageing is the different ways we treat old men and old women. There are more older women than men, but the gender gap is narrowing year by year. Like many things that happen to women more than men, growing old is often side-lined. The disaster in our care homes during 2020 occurred more often to women than to men. And it has been predominantly female carers, daughters, mothers and sisters that have had to pick up the pieces. That needs to change. Building back better means re-configuring everything we think we know about getting old. Ageing and age prejudice may very well be a feminist issue as well.

Agism is rife in families, in politics, in the job market and in medicine. Older people can be subjected to all the same prejudices that women, the mentally ill, LGBTQ+ or BAME people suffer, and like them, we can tend to limit ourselves by heeding those prejudices. For far too long people with even a strand of grey hair have been lampooned, belittled or simply ignored. And perhaps we've accepted too much of it. Yet given what we now know about life, how to achieve a more satisfying and healthy long life should be knowledge that is freely available. Science has many of the answers, but politicians and pundits are not listening. Perhaps they are far too influenced by the myths and traditions that surround ageing.

- **Fact 1**
  People are not living longer *these days*; we've had that capacity for thousands of years.

- **Fact 2**

  People are not genetically engineered to die; we have evolved to survive.

- **Fact 3**

  We don't wear out like old bangers; our bodies self-repair.

- **Fact 4**

  Old age is not depressing; people are often happier at 80 than they were at 20.

- **Fact 5**

  At any age humans possess the potential to improve their wellbeing, to heal and to enjoy life.

At what other stage of life does the government provide a modest salary on which to live? Pensions aren't generous – but they are better than a student loan.

Some things have to change before we can look forward to old age. We need to change our viewpoint about what ageing is; we need to think about it and make plans. The world around us must change. Certainly, we all need to campaign for it. But most of all, we need to ensure that we live it. I encourage each and every one of you to seek out that place where you can enjoy every second of life's long and glorious summer.

Endnotes

1 Woolfolk, RL & Wasserman RH (2005) *Count No One Happy: Eudaimonia and Positive Psychology* Count No One Happy: Eudaimonia and Positive Psychology Journal of Theoretical and Philosophical Psychology April 2005 25(1):81-90 DOI:10.1037/h0091252

2 Camus, A. (1942) *The Myth of Sisyphus* Translated by Justin O'Brien. Book. Published by Hamish Hamilton 1955 London

3 Risen, C. (2021) New York Times obituary. 27 October 2021

4 Csikszentmihalyi, Mihaly (2008) *Flow: The Psychology of Optimal Experience* Book Published by Harper Perennial Modern Classics USA Paperback 30 June 2008

5 Seligman, MEP. (2003) *Authentic Happiness: Using the New Positive Psychology to Realise Your Potential for Lasting Fulfilment* Book. Published by Nicholas Brealey Publishing New York Paperback 6 March 2003

6 Levy, D. (2021) *Real Estate – a Living Autobiography* Published by Hamish Hamilton London 2021

7 Seligman, MEP. (2003) IBID

8 Heintzelman, SJ. (2018). *Eudaimonia in the contemporary science of subjective well-being: Psychological well-being, self-determination, and meaning in life* In E. Diener, S. Oishi, & L. Tay (Eds.), *Handbook of well-being.* Salt Lake City, Book. Published by DEF Publishers. Available at nobascholar.com/chapters/18/download.pdf

Action list

Start today

If you are fired up with enthusiasm for your future life, these are the things you can start with right away. All the evidence points to the fact that it is not one aspect of life that is important, but a cornucopia of different actions and strategies that will give you the best chance of the best old age.

I've broken the advice in this book into seven action topics. Under each topic, I provide more ideas and links to providers. Many of the services I recommend are free or modestly priced, but they don't necessarily exist in all areas of the country.

I have received no endorsements or financial benefit from any of these recommendations.

1 Become a gourmet (Chapter 5)

Review how you eat – does it correspond to a healthy diet?

Make a list of positive diet changes that will benefit you – in the long term.

These might include:

- Increasing protein in your diet
- Learning to cook
- Finding a good local grocer or farmer's market
- Eating more whole foods
- Drinking more still water
- Buying fresh, not ultra-processed, food
- Asking your GP about vitamin D supplements

Cookery classes are a great way of pepping up your diet. There are hundreds of classes to choose from. Try to establish their policy on healthy eating before you embark on a sugar or fat-fest. Your local authority or local community centre may provide subsidised classes. Avoid professional cookery classes, which are quite different to home cooking.

Jamie Oliver Cookery School

Includes bread-baking, easy (and healthy) suppers and Japanese cookery. Online across the country and in-person in London
jamieolivercookeryschool.com

Monitor

While you are making changes to your diet, observe and take a record of the way your body reacts. Purchase a good-quality body composition analyser and record:*

- Muscle mass
- Bone mass

---

* Those made by Tanita or Omron offer a four-point measuring method, where you step onto a plinth, but also lift or hold a handle, which provides a more accurate reading. Some link by Bluetooth to a smart phone app for easy recording.

- Hydration
- Weight
- Visceral fat
- Mood (on a separate chart)

Seek professional advice if you feel you need to lose weight or gain muscle mass.

Nutritionists should be registered with the Association for Nutrition, the body that regulates the qualification and practice of nutritionists throughout the UK. Nutritionists help people improve their diet and thus their long and short-term health. For example, they can help with special diets, weight loss, frailty, recuperation diets, food intolerance or allergies, high blood sugars, high cholesterol and irritable bowel syndrome.

Clinical nutritionists, such as me, are trained in research and practice covering nutrition in the sick, people with eating disorders, as well as the healthy.
associationfornutrition.org

Warning – the term nutritionist is not protected by law, so you will find a lot of unqualified individuals passing themselves off as nutritionists. In particular beware the term nutritional therapist – the practitioner is likely to be neither!

Say Tomato! is a social enterprise that I set up some years ago. Their mission is to provide free and trusted weight loss advice for women over 40. They are also the publishers of this book.
saytomato.org

For more serious dietary issues, the Association of UK Dieticians (formerly the British Dietetic Association) regulates qualified health professionals that assess, diagnose and treat dietary and nutritional conditions such as irritable bowel disease, short bowel syndrome, Crohn's disease and food allergies. They principally deal with sick people in hospital and with chronic conditions. Their general advice pages are usually very good.
bda.uk.com

Further reading

Elizabeth David: Any of her books are marvellous to read, and I particularly recommend *Summer Cooking, Mediterranean Cookery* and *An Omelette and a Glass of Wine.*

Roy Andries de Groot, 1966, *Feasts for All Seasons:* out of print but second-hand copies still available online.

Prof Roy Taylor, 2020, *Life Without Diabetes: The Definitive Guide to Understanding and Reversing Type 2 Diabetes,* published by Harper 1, 17 March, 2020.

Chris van Tulleken, 2023, *Ultra-processed People,* Penguin Books.

Bee Wilson, 2023, *The Secret of Cooking: Recipes for an Easier Life in the Kitchen.*

2 Get moving (Chapter 6)

Dance

Any dance class will do you good, but if you want to learn ballet then the Royal Ballet School sponsors free online and local classes for older learners – no age bar *royalacademyofdance.org/dance-with-us/silverswans*

Walk

The Ramblers Association sponsors group walks in cities and hikes across the countryside ramblers.org.uk

Many places provide free walking tours. Search online for *free walking tours* and the location in question

Enjoy nature

The National Trust have guided nature walks at most of their nature reserves *nationaltrust.org.uk/visit/countryside-woodland/visit-our-nature-reserves*

Or try the Woodland Trust, who offer a range of guided walks and events *woodlandtrust.org.uk*

Your local nature reserve or wild area may have a friend's group or a volunteer group that welcomes new members.

GYO

Gardening ticks many boxes, but organic vegetable-growing ticks even more. To apply for an allotment, go first to the government's allotment hub, which provides a link to all local authority allotments in England and Wales – or search for local providers. You will be surprised to find vacancies in many locations

gov.uk/apply-allotment

Shared gardens

If you can't find an allotment, but would like to participate in vegetable culture, many parks and smaller gardens have projects. One of the best is Brockwell Park in Lambeth where volunteers look after greenhouses and a beautiful and productive walled garden brockwellgreenhouses.org.uk

Join a sports club

Most mainstream clubs have veteran groups. And there are some special games, more suitable for less active individuals. For example, have you thought of walking football, *padel* tennis, and swimming pool water-workouts, some of which are aimed specifically at people who are getting back into fitness after surgery?

Go to a shed

If you'd simply prefer chatter and none of the gardening – try Mensheds, an organisation for men (and sometimes women) to get together and chat

The sheds are kitted out community spaces where people can enjoy practical hobbies. They're about making friends, learning and sharing skills. Many men visit for the tea and banter, and everyone is welcome. They're run by volunteers, so if there isn't one in your area you could always start one

menssheds.org.uk

Get a dog

Or walk a friend's dog. The RSPCA runs a volunteer program from each of their local centres

rspca.org.uk

Volunteer

Possibly the most satisfying way to get moving. You may have to search or ask around for the type of volunteering that will suit you. Organisations are crying out for volunteers and there may be some perks to the job. For example, if you volunteer at a National Museum, you are likely to be offered the much-coveted Museum Card. Neighbourhood and local authority websites may also be helpful. Volunteer Match covers the whole UK – simply type in your postcode.

volunteermatch.org

Monitor

Buy yourself a step-counter. Any cheap one will do; they don't have to be fancy. There's one on every smart phone, but it can only count the steps you take when it's in your pocket or handbag! Wristwatch-style step-counters often monitor your sleep as well as your activity.

3 Think (Chapter 7)

Feed the mind by attending events, concerts and lectures, preferably in person. Consider inviting a friend to go with you.

Book clubs

Adult education

Information can generally be found for these types of activities at your local library or bookshop.

Go back to university

Mainstream universities will consider applications from older students; you can also contact the University of the Third Age (U3A). This is a national organisation, but they offer regional websites and local events. For example, the one near me in London advertises that they run 140+ classes a week for £45 a year, covering anything from Arabic to yarn-based skills

u3a.org.uk/regional-u3a-websites

Concerts and plays
Do not dismiss local school or college events which are often highly enjoyable and free, or low cost. Most theatres and concert halls offer pre-performance talks, classes and backstage tours

Shop talks
Book shops offer author talks – seek out your local independent book shop – and are always a good source of social interaction as well as mental stimulation

Music
Learn to play a musical instrument, or join a band or choir

Games
Join a chess, bridge or poker club

Take up a hobby
Honestly, this is an endless list. Any activity that gets you out and into a social setting where you can discuss something with fellow enthusiasts will be beneficial

Cinema
Almost all cinemas have afternoon screenings at low cost. Some even allow you to bring the dog!

Societies
There's a society for everything!

Be kind to the mind

Sleep
Lean to sleep better. Many websites and advisors can help you learn how to sleep better. Start monitoring today with a sleep monitor (often found as an accessory in a wristwatch-style step-counter)

Your mind matters
Do not suffer in silence. Speak to your GP and/or pursue these options. Your GP and the internet will be able to put you in touch with local emergency lines – just in case

Age uk helpline
Offers support for depression, isolation, bereavement, anxiety, and memory problems. Lines are open 8am-7pm, 365 days a year
0800 678 1602

Counselling and therapy
MIND UK can provide sources of local services including talking therapy, crisis helplines, advocacy, employment and training schemes, counselling and befriending services mind.org.uk/information-support/local-minds

Emergency
The NHS offers local urgent mental health help lines – dial 911, go to nhs.uk or ask your GP

Samaritans
Telephone 116 123, or Text SHOUT to 85258
Samaritans.org

4 Book a health MOT (Chapter 3)

Your GP should offer you regular health checks, as a matter of course. Your pharmacist may also offer rudimentary tests such as for blood pressure and weight. At a minimum anyone between 40 and 74 should receive a health check every five years. If you have any type of long-term condition, you are likely to be invited to receive annual blood tests. Look out for free screenings. As you get older you often fall off the list, so if you've been screened in the past, check when you next visit the GP that you are still eligible.

Most private health providers will offer an MOT for between £200 to £1000, though I notice few take blood tests, which are a good non-invasive method of finding out what's going on inside.

A medical laboratory can offer a screening system, which includes a series of blood, urine and stool tests. For example, the one I use in central London, the Doctors Laboratory, with clinics in London and Manchester, offer a series of tests, grouped for different genders and ages, priced at about £400
tdlpathology.com

Remember that any niggling problems can be discussed with a trusted pharmacist, or your GP. Always try for a face-to-face consultation if available.

US Preventative Services Task Force offer advice on best practice in prevention services – better than anything I can find in the UK! *uspreventiveservicestaskforce.org*

5 Make change (Chapter 9)

Take up a cause

Demonstrate your commitment to the world by getting involved with something you strongly believe in. It could be joining a political party, a pressure group, or a charity

Start writing, podcasting or streaming

Attend rallies and talks

Further reading

Ashton Applewhite, *This Chair Rocks: A Manifesto Against Ageism. 2016.* Now published by Macmillan, 2019

Alastair Campbell, 2023, *But What can I Do?* Published 2003 by Penguin Books.

6 Reduce your carbon footprint (Chapter 9)

Consider the planet as well as the benefits to your body. Deciding to live a more sustainable lifestyle doesn't mean spending oodles of money, or joining a radical protest group; it simply means living a different type of life. It is part of your future and will be your legacy.

The One Planet Living movement is an international initiative, which may have a local network in your community *bioregional.com/one-planet-living*

Extinction rebellion

XR, as they call themselves, have over 1,000 local groups in 88 countries *rebellion.global*

Tree huggers

This is a website, not an activity. I've found it to be a useful and reliable source of information. In a post in 2018 they did a roundup of the various sustainability organisations that were available on FACEBOOK and have updated the list since.

treehugger.com/the-environmental-groups-that-dominate-facebook-4868636

Further reading

Schumacher EF, 1973, *Small is beautiful: A study of economics as if people mattered.* First published by Blond and Briggs Ltd Great Britain

Carl Honore, 2005, *In Praise of Slow: How a Worldwide Movement is Challenging the Cult of Speed,* Orion; Paperback Edition, 4 Aug 2005

7 Enjoy life (Chapter 11)

Last, but by no means least, give up things you don't enjoy and concentrate on things you do enjoy. If there are tasks that you hate, that you simply must do, try and find different ways of doing them to make them quicker, less frequent, or different.

Further reading

Martin EP Seligman, 2011, *Flourish: A Visionary New Understanding of Happiness and Well-Being,* Paperback edition, published 7 February, 2012, Atria, Simon and Schuster Inc., New York

Chapter 11's bibliography also contains a series of very readable and interesting books covering positivity, optimism and the meaning of life.

Coda

We are used to walking out of a room and letting the door close behind us, perhaps leaving a hint of perfume, or the echo of parting words. After I replace a book on the shelf, there remains just a memory of the story. Footsteps on the sand survive long after we have plunged into the waves and sometimes reappear as fossils thousands of years later. By living our life, we all leave our mark. Ideas still resonate; kindnesses are still remembered; omissions forgiven. Think on this as you come to the end of this book and close the covers. And say to yourself, that's all death ever is - just the last full stop.

The End

Acknowledgements

This book would never have been written without the tolerance and support of my husband Mike, who has read and commented on every word and every draft. But the professional confidence to write this came from the poet and writer Stephanie Norgate, my MA tutor at Chichester University and to my tutors at University College London, where I did my MSc in Clinical Nutrition. I am grateful for the insight and challenge provided by Professor Nathan Davies, Dr Adrian Slee, Dr Paul Robinson and Emeritus Professor of Medicine George Grimble, as well as a fantastic cohort of lecturers and fellow students.

I have been lucky enough to be able to call on many other experts during the course of my writing. In particular I would like to thank Dr Kellyn Lee, Sir Michael Marmot, and Professor Werner Khuehlbrandt, each of whom took time out from their busy lives to comment on sections of the book.

I have also been hugely influenced by the research I have read, by the articles and books I have pored over and the online and in-person lectures and conferences I have attended. One luminary from the world of gerontology stands out in this august group. It was hearing Professor Tom Kirkwood's Reith Lectures in 2001 entitled, *The End of Age* that commenced my thinking about what ageing actually was and how much better our lived experience of getting older could be. I once went to a conference where Tom Kirkwood was speaking, but so overawed was I by his presence that I could not summon the courage to talk to him. Perhaps this acknowledgement will go some way to redress than omission.

I started writing about the subject during the COVID-19 lockdowns of 2020, when the one thing we all had was time to think. Since we have been let out again, I have found friends and acquaintances alike keen to talk about the subject. Their observations have often made their way into this book. I was also fortunate to find an excellent group of readers who plodded through the first draft, especially Alex Lisle, whose thorough comments were extremely helpful. My editor Margaret Gaskin was able to transform the resulting text into a more ordered document and keep my writing positive, accurate and readable. Subsequently Maddy Fry went through it with a fine-tooth comb and asked different searching questions, which I hope the final manuscript has answered. More recently I have been able to work with a fantastic team of printers at Swallowtail Print, and the graphic designer Kaarin Wall at Wiz Graphics, who has turned a manuscript into a handsome book.

At first, vanity demanded that this book be hard bound and packed with illustrations. But the more I worked, the more I felt that an economical paperback would distribute the message more widely. I hope it is still something delightful to hold and read, but cheaper and thus more accessible. It is available at all good independent bookshops, online at bookshop.org or direct by post, from the publishers *SayTomato!*

Throughout the three years it has taken to research this book, I have held many interesting conversations with friends, clients and colleagues, who have each offered their own insights on the subject. These conversations give me hope that the book will find an appreciative audience. Sadly, my mother died at the age of 95, halfway through writing this book. She will never know how much the conversations we had together have influenced my thoughts. The book is dedicated to her – a remarkably intelligent and kind woman and a constantly loving and supportive mother.

My thanks to everyone involved are heartfelt. If there are still mistakes, they are mine and mine alone. If you have any thoughts or comments, or would like me to give a talk to your reading group, or local bookshop, I would love to hear from you.

wendy@wendyshillam.co.uk

List of illustrations

Chapter 1 Happy and healthy

Jeanne Calment on the day she became the World's oldest living person ©Eric CATARINA, Getty Image

Age-specific mortality μ(a), in two human populations with widely differing levels of mortality: from Sweden 1985, females (Keyfitz & Flieger 1990) and Gainj (highland New Guinea) 1970—77 males (Wood 1987), drawn by Wendy Shillam from Wood, JW. (2002) Mortality models for paleodemography. Paleodemography, Age Distributions from Skeletal Samples. Cambridge Studies in Biological and Evolutionary Anthropology 31. Ed Hoppa & Vaupel Cambridge University Press. 2002 p138

The survival curve for England and Wales 1851-2011 One world in data from ONS figures. Max Roser, Esteban Ortiz-Ospina and Hannah Ritchie (2013) "Life Expectancy". Published online at OurWorldInData.org. Retrieved April 2021 from: ourworldindata.org/life-expectancy. With thanks to Dr Max Roser, Oxford Martin School.

Chapter 2 The average and the exceptional

The exceptional Adolphe Quetelet, from a lithograph by Madou from the book, Adolphe Quetelet James Vandrunen, 1919.

The bell curve of normal distribution or Gaussian distribution. Source: Wiki Commons. Author D Wells.

Causes of death by age. Drawn by Wendy Shillam from data held in the UK Biobank cohort 2006 – 2023 UK Biobank *Death Summary Report from 2006 -* Published March 2023 biobank.ndph.ox.ac.uk/~bbdatan/DeathSummaryReport. html

Prevalence of long-term illness in the UK. Drawn by Wendy Shillam from ONS figures.

Chapter 3 The art and science of body maintenance

Ancel Keys Time Magazine – 1961, Wikki Commons

Chapter 4 The rhythm of life

Respiration and photosynthesis: the energy merry-go-round. Drawn by Wendy Shillam

Chapter 5 The gourmet

How our diet needs to change as we age. Drawn by Wendy Shillam

Comparison between UK and EU protein recommendations associated with different age groups. Note all UK ADULTS of whatever age and level of activity are advised to limit their protein intake to 0.75g/kg/day. Other figures taken from PROT-AGE study (cf). Drawn by Wendy Shillam

Australian dietary guidelines illustrating increased recommended dietary intakes (RDIs) per day with age. Here protein is measured in grams of pure protein. From Brownie S. et al. (2015) *The 2013 Australian dietary guidelines and recommendations for older Australians*. Australian Family Physician Volume 44, No.5, 2015 Pages 311-315

All-cause mortality compared to cause-specific mortality outcomes in a study population of 3,600,000 patients. HR=hazard ratio. Source: Krishnan B et al., (2018) Association of BMI with overall and cause-specific mortality: a population-based cohort study of 3·6 million adults in the UK. The Lancet, Volume 6, Issue 12, p944-953, December 01, 2018. Published: October 30, 2018 DOI:10.1016/S2213-8587(18)30288-2.

Chapter 6 The dancer

Dose response curve for exercise: World Health Organisation 2020. Creative Commons Attribution-NonCommercial-Share Alike 3.0 IGO licence (CC BY-NC-SA 3.0 IGO; https://creativecommons.org/licenses/by-nc-sa/3.0/igo). (https://www.ncbi.nlm.nih.gov/books/NBK566046/figure/ch4.fig1)

Agrippina Vaganova in 1910, from her book, Basic Principles of Classical Ballet, p.15, Courier Corporation. Photo taken by an unknown photographer of Agrippina Vaganova in "La Esmeralda". St. Petersburg, circa 1910. Photo comes from a private collection and was scanned by Mrlopez2681. 05:40, 9 September 2006 (UTC) Image: Public domain.

Chapter 7 The thinker

Eat! Move! Think! - important elements of a virtuous circle of health. Drawn by Wendy Shillam

Chapter 8 Drugs for healthy people

A late 19th/early 20th Century advertisement for the forerunner of Coca-Cola in the days when it contained cocaine. Source: Smithsonian Institute, Public Domain

Index – provisional

Chapter headings in CAPITALS
Names of scientists and specialist discussed in the text are in **Bold**
Illustrations and diagrams: page numbers in *italics*
Diagrams in *Italics*